THE COLLEGE PRESS NIV COMMENTARY

1 & 2 THESSALONIANS

THE COLLEGE PRESS NIV COMMENTARY

1 & 2 THESSALONIANS

JON A. WEATHERLY

New Testament Series Co-Editors:

Jack Cottrell, Ph.D.
Cincinnati Bible Seminary

Tony Ash, Ph.D.
Abilene Christian University

COLLEGE PRESS
PUBLISHING COMPANY
Joplin, Missouri

Copyright © 1996
College Press Publishing Company

All Scripture quotations, unless indicated, are taken from
THE HOLY BIBLE: NEW INTERNATIONAL VERSION®.
Copyright © 1973, 1978, 1984 by International Bible Society.
Used by permission of Zondervan Publishing House.
All rights reserved.

The "NIV" and "New International Version" trademarks are registered in the United States Patent and Trademark Office by International Bible Society. Use of either trademark requires the permission of International Bible Society.

Printed and Bound in the
United States of America
All Rights Reserved

Library of Congress Cataloging-in-Publication Data

Weatherly, Jon A.
   1 & 2 Thessalonians / Jon A. Weatherly.
     p.   cm. – (The College Press NIV commentary)
   Includes bibliographical references.
   ISBN 0-89900-636-1 (hardcover)
   1. Bible. N.T. Thessalonians—Commentaries. I. Bible. N.T. Thessalonians. English. 1996. II. Title. III. Series.
BS2725.3.W43 1996
227'.81077—dc20   96-35529
                                                                              CIP

A WORD FROM THE PUBLISHER

Years ago a movement was begun with the dream of uniting all Christians on the basis of a common purpose (world evangelism) under a common authority (The Word of God). The College Press NIV Commentary Series is a serious effort to join the scholarship of two branches of this unity movement so as to speak with one voice concerning the Word of God. Our desire is to provide a resource for your study of the New Testament that will benefit you whether you are preparing a Bible School lesson, a sermon, a college course or your own personal devotions. Today as we survey the wreckage of a broken world, we must turn again to the Lord and his Word, unite under his banner and communicate the life-giving message to those who are in desperate need. This is our purpose.

FOREWORD

This commentary has been produced through a full schedule of college and seminary teaching and church-based ministry. In the current climate of biblical studies, that schedule has necessitated some compromises. Journal articles, scholarly monographs and commentaries are today so numerous that the person who wants to keep current in the study of a biblical book must have the leisure to devote almost full time to the task. Therefore, I have not been able to consider all the issues as thoroughly as I might have liked. For most readers, however, this is probably a relief. I have tried to discuss only those matters which significantly affect our understanding of the text and have sufficient supporting evidence to warrant a hearing. So to those who find that an issue has been ignored, too briefly summarized, or too fully discussed, I offer my apologies. It is my hope that the setting in which I have written the book, having taught and preached on it in churches and a church-based college and seminary, will ensure a greater degree of relevance than might be found in some scholarly works and a greater degree of accuracy than in some popular ones.

Thanks for assistance with this project go to several people. I am grateful to the publishers and editors of the series for their invaluable help in bringing this work to publication. To my former professor and present colleague Dr. Jack Cottrell, who first offered the invitation, and to Mr. John Hunter of College Press, who graciously worked with me for its completion, I give special thanks. Another former professor and present colleague, Mr. Tom Friskney, first stimulated my study of the Thessalonian letters. His influence is felt on every page, but he should not be blamed for my mistakes. In particular I thank my family — my wife, Tammie, and our children, Cale and Allison — for their patience with me as I spent too many evenings, weekends and vacation times working on this project.

My parents, Chet and Millie Weatherly, more than anyone have provided the example for me of the integrity, love, discipline, hard work, generosity, endurance and expectancy which these letters teach. I dedicate this book to them with heartfelt gratitude.

ABBREVIATIONS

ABD	*Anchor Bible Dictionary*, ed. by David Noel Freedman
ASNU	*Acta seminarii neotestamentici upsaliensis*
ASV	*American Standard Version*
AV	*Authorized (King James) Version*
BAGD	*Bauer-Arndt-Gingrich-Danker Greek Lexicon, 1979*
BDF	*Blass-Debrunner-Funk Greek Grammar*
BETL	*Bibliotheca ephemeridum theologicarum lovaniensium*
Bib	*Biblica*
BNTC	*Black's New Testament Commentary*
CBQ	*Catholic Biblical Quarterly*
DPL	*Dictionary of Paul and His Letters*, ed. by Gerald F. Hawthorne, Ralph P. Martin and Daniel G. Reid
EDNT	*Exegetical Dictionary of the New Testament*, ed. by Horst Balz and Gerhard Schneider
ET	*English Translation*
ExpTim	*Expository Times*
FFNT	*Foundations and Facets: New Testament*
GELNTBSD	*Greek-English Lexicon of the New Testament Based on Semantic Domains (2nd ed.)*, ed. by Johannes P. Louw, Eugene A. Nida, Rondal B. Smith and Karen A. Munson
HCNT	*Hellenistic Commentary to the New Testament*, ed. by M. Eugene Boring, Klaus Berger and Carsten Colpe
HTR	*Harvard Theological Review*
HUT	*Hermeneutische Untersuchungen zur Theologie*
ICC	*International Critical Commentary*
JBL	*Journal of Biblical Literature*
JETS	*Journal of the Evangelical Theological Society*
JSNT	*Journal for the Study of the New Testament*
JSNTSup	*Journal for the Study of the New Testament Supplement Series*

LSJ	*Liddell-Scott-Jones-McKenzie Greek Lexicon (9th ed.)*
MHT	*Moulton-Howard-Turner Grammar of New Testament Greek*
MM	*Moulton-Milligan Vocabulary of the Greek Testament*
NASB	*New American Standard Bible*
NCB	*New Century Bible Commentary*
NIDNTT	*New International Dictionary of New Testament Theology*, ed. by Colin Brown
NICNT	*New International Commentary on the New Testament*
NIGTC	*New International Greek Testament Commentary*
NIV	*New International Version*
NovT	*Novum Testamentum*
NRSV	*New Revised Standard Version*
NTS	*New Testament Studies*
RSV	*Revised Standard Version*
TDNT	*Theological Dictionary of the New Testament*, ed. by Gerhard Kittel and Gerhard Friedrich
TEV	*Today's English Version*
TynBul	*Tyndale Bulletin*
UBS	*United Bible Societies*
UBSGNT	*United Bible Societies Greek New Testament*
WBC	*Word Biblical Commentary*
ZPEB	*Zondervan Pictorial Encyclopedia of the Bible*, ed. by Merrill Tenney
ZTK	*Zeitschrift für Theologie und Kirche*

THE BOOK OF
1 THESSALONIANS

INTRODUCTION

Though it is a relatively brief letter, 1 Thessalonians provides the modern Christian with a challenging glimpse into the life and thought of the first generation of Christianity. Its presentation of the ministry of Paul, the trials of the persecuted church, the ethical demands of the new life in Christ, and especially of the vivid expectation of Christ's return provides some of the foundational elements for genuine Christian experience in every era.

Major critical problems with 1 Thessalonians are fewer than with some other Pauline letters; the bulk of modern scholarship is largely agreed about the general circumstances under which the letter was written. But knowing those circumstances provides a necessary touchstone for the interpretation of the letter, so they will be briefly summarized below.

THE CITY OF THESSALONICA[1]

Founded by Cassander, a general of Alexander the Great, around 315 B.C., Thessalonica was a city of size and influence. Located at the head of the Thermatic Gulf, now called the Gulf of Salonika, a natural harbor on the Aegean coast of Macedonia, the northern part of the Greece, it was an important port city, providing a gateway to the Macedonian interi-

---

[1]For a summary of the current state of knowledge on the city of Thessalonica and its effect on Paul's mission and letters see Robert Jewett, *The Thessalonian Correspondence: Pauline Rhetoric and Millenarian Piety* (FFNT; Philadelphia: Fortress, 1986), pp. 113-132.

or. Its prominence as a transportation center was augmented when the Romans constructed the Via Egnatia or Egnatian Way, a highway crossing the Greek peninsula from east to west and ultimately connecting Asia in the east with Italy and Rome in the west. Inland from Thessalonica lay a fertile plain, which provided abundant agricultural resources for the city and the region.

It is little wonder, then, that in 146 B.C. the Romans designated Thessalonica as the capital of the province of Macedonia. The city itself had an independent government with magistrates known as "politarchs" (Acts 17:6, 8), providing a degree of autonomy from the imperial government and its taxes. The religious climate was dominated by paganism; the cults of Dionysus and the Cabirus appear to have been especially prominent. According to Acts 17:1 there was also a colony of Jews large enough to constitute at least one synagogue.

Altogether, then, Thessalonica appears to us as a busy, prosperous, cosmopolitan city, a place where the gospel could readily take root but also meet significant resistance. That image is confirmed to us by the description of Paul's mission in Acts and the corresponding elements of 1 Thessalonians.

PAUL'S MINISTRY IN THESSALONICA AND THE WRITING OF 1 THESSALONIANS

According to Acts, Paul visited Thessalonica with Timothy and Silas on what we call his second missionary journey (17:1). Having left Philippi after being jailed overnight, Paul traveled to the neighboring city on the Egnatian Way, perhaps pursuing a strategy of planting churches in cities on major transportation arteries so that the gospel could spread out from those centers. There, as was his custom, Paul preached in the synagogue as long as he was able (17:2-3). Acts indicates that his converts included Jews, God-fearers

(Gentiles who acknowledged the God of Israel but had not converted fully to Judaism), and some of the principal women (17:4). According to Acts these conversions prompted a jealous response from non-Christian Jews, presumably synagogue leaders, who incited a mob against the Christians (17:5-7). The magistrates appear to have recognized that the mob's anger was not prompted by any offense against the civil order and required only that Jason, apparently a prominent Christian convert, post a bond pledging no further trouble (17:8-9). The violence did, however, prompt Paul to leave the city, perhaps sooner than he had planned (17:10).

From Thessalonica Paul went to Berea. But the fervor of his Thessalonian opponents was intense, for they followed him there and incited similar opposition (17:13). Paul then went on alone to Athens, leaving Silas and Timothy behind (17:14-15). After Paul had preached in Athens with mixed results (17:16-34), he went on to Corinth (18:1). There Silas and Timothy rejoined him (18:5).

The text of 1 Thessalonians confirms and supplements this outline. Though Paul focuses on the conversion of Gentiles in 1:9 (see comments below), says little about the conversion of Jews, and does not quote the Old Testament, themes from the Jewish Scriptures and Judaism appear throughout the letter (cf. 1:4, 6, 10; 2:4, 10, 12, 15-16, 18; 3:3, 5; 4:3, 5-8, 16; 5:3, 5, 8-9, 23-24), implying an audience familiar with them. The letter acknowledges the opposition to Paul (2:2) and the ongoing problem of persecution in Thessalonica (1:6; 2:14; 3:3-4), elements entirely consistent with the anti-Christian violence which Acts depicts. It indicates that Paul left the city prematurely and under duress (2:17) and was prevented from returning (2:18). In particular it makes clear that from Athens Paul sent Timothy back to Thessalonica as a substitute for his own presence (3:1-3; see comments below) to strengthen the church and report about its progress to Paul. Timothy's return and report are recounted also (3:6).

It appears, then, that Timothy's report prompts the writing of this first letter. We can infer from the letter's contents that the report was mostly positive but did note some areas of serious concern. The letter serves to reassure the readers about their status as Christians (1:3-10; 3:11-13) and about Paul's concern for them despite his absence (2:1-12; 2:17-3:10), to strengthen them in the persecution which they endure (2:13-16; 3:4-5), and to reiterate instruction which they had already received about the standards by which they are to live as people in Christ surrounded by an immoral pagan culture (4:1-12). In particular Paul is concerned about their misunderstanding of the significance of Christ's return, especially regarding the status of those who have died as Christians (4:13-18), but also more generally (5:1-11). He also expresses specific concern about the need for Christians to support themselves responsibly (4:11-12; 5:14; cf. 2:6b-9), and to have proper respect for leaders (5:12) and for the spiritual gift of prophecy (5:19-22). In essence, then, this letter is a substitute for Paul's actual presence, containing the teaching which he would have delivered had it been possible for him to return to Thessalonica immediately. While a couple of specific problems had arisen, Paul's primary concern is to strengthen the young church in its commitment and the consistency of its practice.

DATE

If the reconstruction above is correct, then 1 Thessalonians was written during Paul's stay in Corinth on his second missionary journey.[2] It is conceivable that Paul could have written this letter on his third journey after his second visit to Thessalonica, but since the letter itself refers to only one visit, the obvious explanation is that Paul had made only one. Some have denied the accuracy of the sequence of events in Acts altogether, but the numerous points of confir-

---

[2]For full discussion of the evidence on the date of 1 Thessalonians, see Bruce, pp. xxxiv-xxxv.

mation between 1 Thessalonians and Acts as noted above make such a denial highly questionable.

Paul's stay in Corinth can be dated with an exceptional degree of precision. According to Acts 18:12-17, Gallio served as proconsul of Achaia during Paul's Corinthian mission. An inscription at Delphi puts Gallio as proconsul during the twelfth year of Claudius' imperial power, after the Roman senate's twenty-sixth proclamation of Claudius as emperor. Since the twenty-seventh proclamation was made in August of A.D. 52 and proconsuls took office usually in midsummer, Gallio can be assumed to have taken office in the summer of A.D. 50 or 51. The Acts account makes it appear that Paul was brought before Gallio not long after he took office and near the end of Paul's eighteen-month sojourn in the city. Therefore, a date of 50-51 is likely for this letter.

Relative to Paul's other letters, 1 Thessalonians is very early. Unless Galatians was written earlier, as is plausible, between the first and second missionary journeys, or 2 Thessalonians was written first (see the introduction to 2 Thessalonians below), this letter is Paul's earliest. If so, it is also likely to be the earliest book of the New Testament, unless, as we have no way to confirm, one of the Gospels or the letter of James was penned sometime in the forties of the first century. For students of Paul and of early Christianity generally, then, this letter has special import.

AUTHORSHIP

Few critical scholars have doubted that Paul composed this letter himself. The internal claim of the letter is clear and unequivocal, including not only the salutation (1:1), but the repeated personal references in the middle section of the letter (2:1-3:10). Likewise, the external evidence is clear. The letter was quoted in some of the earliest Christian literature outside the New Testament (Ign. Eph. 10:1; Ign. Rom. 2:1; Did. 16:6-7), attributed to Paul as early as Marcion (c. A.D. 140), and never questioned in the early centuries of Christianity.

Those who have contended that 1 Thessalonians is not an authentic letter of Paul have largely based their arguments on alleged discrepancies with Acts.[3] As implied above, it has been argued that this letter indicates that Paul's Thessalonian converts were pagans (1:9; 4:1-5) while Acts asserts that they were Jews and God-fearers (17:4). However, as noted in the comments below, Paul may have a particular reason for emphasizing converts from paganism, and Acts certainly emphasizes Jewish converts in Thessalonica as a part of a larger theme in Paul's ministry. Neither book, however, should be understood to be deliberately specifying the precise composition of the Thessalonian church.

Likewise, it has been argued that the movements of Timothy and Silas in 1 Thessalonians do not match those in Acts. In particular, Acts 18:5 shows them rejoining Paul in Corinth, whereas 1 Thessalonians 3:1-6 may show Timothy rejoining Paul in Athens. Several reconstructions of their specific movements can be offered which account for the material in both books. Paul may have initially left Timothy and Silas behind in Macedonia, and they may have returned to him briefly in Athens only to be sent back to Macedonia a second time. Alternately, Paul may have sent his associates back to Thessalonica after arriving in Athens, and Acts may simply condense their movements, giving the result that they were "left behind" while focusing attention on Paul. But most important is the observation that the use of "Athens" instead of "here" in 1 Thess 3:1 indicates that Paul probably wrote from a place other than Athens and so was reunited with Timothy at that place. Corinth clearly fits the details here, precisely in accord with the description in Acts.

A third argument based on alleged tensions with Acts concerns the length of Paul's stay. It is argued that Acts 17:2

---

[3]For a more detailed discussion of this argument see Donald Guthrie, *New Testament Introduction* (4th ed.; Downers Grove, IL: InterVarsity, 1990), pp. 589-591.

indicates a stay of three weeks, whereas this letter presumes a longer stay with its discussion of Paul's self-support and preaching. However, all that Acts 17:2 asserts is that Paul preached in the synagogue for three sabbaths, not that those three weeks comprised his entire stay. And if only three weeks were involved, Paul still could have preached, taught and worked with his hands.

Another challenge to authorship is found in hypotheses which argue that the letter is a compilation of several authentic or pseudepigraphical letters, edited together by a later follower of Paul.[4] Elaborate arguments for compilation are entirely conjectural and have found little support. Some have argued that 5:1-11 is a later, non-Pauline interpolation based on its vocabulary and content. The differences with the rest of Paul's letters are in fact few, however, and so this hypothesis has little support either.[5] More prominent has been the hypothesis that 2:13-16 are a later interpolation of non-Pauline material. Specific discussion of this issue can be found in the comments on the passage below.

ORGANIZATION

Most of Paul's letters follow a rather set pattern of salutation, thanksgiving, letter body, and closing greetings. This pattern is apparent in a wide variety of letters from the Greco-Roman world, indicating that Paul adapted the standard letter form for his own purposes.

1 Thessalonians follows this pattern approximately, as the outline below indicates. One variation comes at 2:13-16, where Paul appears to offer a second thanksgiving. Such

---

[4]For a summary and significant sources see R.F. Collins, "Apropos the Integrity of 1 Thess," *Studies on the First Letter to the Thessalonians* (BETL 66; Leuven: Leuven University Press, 1984), pp. 96-135.

[5]Cf. Joseph Plevnik, "1 Thess 5, 1-11: Its Authenticity, Intention and Message," *Bib* 60 (1979) 71-90.

formal irregularities are not surprising, however, if Paul felt free to adapt standard forms as the occasion demanded.

Recently Paul's letters have been analyzed according to the patterns of Greek rhetoric. Several recent works have employed this approach in understanding 1 Thessalonians, with the beneficial result of stressing that the letter is a unified composition with a specific purpose of communication.[6] Opinions vary, however, on where the precise rhetorical divisions lie, probably because Paul did not compose his letters strictly according to the canons of rhetoric, though he was probably influenced by them. In this commentary, therefore, no direct attention will be given to specifying the precise rhetorical contours of the letter.

THEOLOGICAL VALUE

As a small, young church in big, pagan city, the Thessalonian Christians faced challenges to their faith at every turn. Persecution, social pressure, temptations of the old lifestyle, conflict with new brothers and sisters in Christ, and surrender to despair were constant threats. Whatever the confidence with which they began their Christian pilgrimage, these believers were now faced with the daily ordeals of life in Christ in hostile surroundings.

Paul's answers to these problems are varied and significant. He confirms the truth of the gospel in the face of the doubts and struggles which they face, reminding them of the change which the gospel has brought to their lives and of the warnings which they had already received about the difficulties to come. He reminds them of his own manner of life with them, itself a confirmation of the truth of his message and an example of the self-sacrificial love and Christ-glorifying

---

[6]Among the major rhetorical analyses of 1 Thessalonians are Jewett, *Thessalonian Correspondence*, pp. 61-88; and Wanamaker, pp. 45-52 and *passim*.

integrity which comprise the core of the Christian lifestyle. That love expressed to one another will in turn draw the church together to stand up to the pressure of the hostile culture which surrounds it. Perhaps most importantly, Paul reminds the readers repeatedly that the work of God begun in them in Christ will not be complete until Christ returns. They can therefore look forward to his return with great expectancy, remembering that even death itself will then be utterly defeated, and living each moment in faithfulness as they await the fulfillment of their relationship with Christ.

The situation for Christians near the beginning of the third millennium is not much different from the one that Paul addressed. And so his reminders remain timely. The truth and power of the gospel, the love and integrity which characterize Christ's people, and the living hope of Christ's return are especially relevant to a people confronted with the contemporary diseases of relativism, hatred, selfishness, and despair. The conviction that this universe will end with God's eternal triumph is as foreign to modern thinking as is the idea that it began by God's command. But apart from such a conviction, which stands at the center of 1 Thessalonians, can humanity find meaning in what seems to be chaos? Without it, can humanity find a basis for moral decisions? Faced with such questions, today's reader will not have to read far in 1 Thessalonians to find both blessing and challenge.

OUTLINE

I. GREETING — 1:1

II. THANKSGIVING — 1:2-10

  A. The Initial Thanksgiving — 1:2-5

    1. Paul's Constant Prayers for the Readers — 1:2

    2. Their Exercise of Faith, Love and Hope — 1:3

    3. Their Election — 1:4

    4. The Power of the Gospel in Thessalonica — 1:5

  B. Reiteration and Further Specification — 1:6-10

    1. The Readers' Imitation of Paul and His Associates — 1:6a

    2. Their Endurance of Suffering — 1:6b

    3. Their Example to Other Churches — 1:7-8

    4. Reports of Their Conversion — 1:9-10

      a. Forsaking Idols to Serve the Living God — 1:9

      b. Awaiting the Return of Jesus — 1:10

III. PAUL'S RELATIONSHIP TO THE THESSALONIAN CHURCH — 2:1-3:13

  A. Paul's Behavior in Thessalonica — 2:1-12

    1. Paul's Motives — 2:1-6a

    2. Paul's Activity — 2:6b-12

  B. The Thessalonians' Endurance of Persecution — 2:13-16

    1. Their Genuine Reception of the Word — 2:13

    2. Their Imitation of the Judean Christians — 2:14

    3. The Continuity of Persecution Age to Age — 2:15-16

C. **Paul's Continuing Concern for the Church** — 2:17-3:10
1. His Desire to See the Thessalonians — 2:17-20
2. Timothy's Visit on Paul's Behalf — 3:1-5
3. Timothy's Report and Paul's Response — 3:6-10

D. **Paul's Prayer for the Thessalonians** — 3:11-13
1. That He Might Return to Them — 3:11
2. That They Might Abound in Love, and Be Blameless at the Lord's Return — 3:12-13

IV. EXHORTATION — 4:1-5:22
A. **Exhortation Concerning Christian Living** — 4:1-12
1. To Continue in Current Behavior — 4:1-2
2. To Remain Sexually Pure — 4:3-8
3. To Exercise Brotherly Love — 4:9-10
4. To Lead a Quiet, Honest Life — 4:11-12

B. **Exhortation Concerning the Lord's Return** — 4:13-5:11
1. The Dead in Christ and the Lord's Return — 4:13-18
2. The Suddenness of the Lord's Return — 5:1-11

C. **General Exhortations** — 5:12-22
1. Behavior in the Christian Community — 5:12-15
   a. Respect for Christian Leaders — 5:12-13
   b. Service and Forgiveness — 5:14-15
2. Constants of Christian Behavior — 5:16-18
3. Responding to Christian Prophecy — 5:19-22
   a. Yielding to the Spirit's Work — 5:19-20
   b. Testing Prophecy — 5:21-22

V. CONCLUSION — 5:23-28
A. **Benediction** — 5:23-24
B. **Final Words** — 5:25-28

BIBLIOGRAPHY
1 & 2 THESSALONIANS

COMMENTARIES

Commentaries are cited in the notes by author's last name alone.

Bruce, F.F. *1 & 2 Thessalonians*. WBC 45. Waco, TX: Word, 1982.

Best, Ernest. *The First and Second Epistles to the Thessalonians*. BNTC. 1972. Reprint, Peabody, MA: Hendrickson, 1986.

Frame, James Everett. *A Critical and Exegetical Commentary on the Epistles of St. Paul to the Thessalonians*. ICC. Edinburgh: T. & T. Clark, 1979 (reprint).

Marshall, I. Howard. *1 and 2 Thessalonians*. NCB. Grand Rapids: Eerdmans, 1983.

Morris, Leon. *The First and Second Epistles to the Thessalonians*. NICNT. Rev. ed. Grand Rapids: Eerdmans, 1991.

Wanamaker, Charles A. *The Epistles to the Thessalonians*. NIGTC. Grand Rapids: Eerdmans, 1990.

OTHER WORKS

Allison, Dale C. "The Pauline Epistles and the Synoptic Gospels: the Pattern of the Parallels," *NTS* 28 (1982) 1-31.

Aus, Roger D. "God's Plan and God's Power: Isaiah 66 and the Restraining Factors of 2 Thess 2:6-7," *JBL* 96 (1977) 537-553.

_____. "The Liturgical Background of the Necessity and Propriety of Giving Thanks According to 2 Thes 1:3," *JBL* 92 (1973) 432-438.

Bammel, Ernst. "Preparation for the Perils of the Last Days: 1 Thessalonians 3:3." In *Suffering and Martyrdom in the New Testament: Studies Presented to G. M. Styler by the Cambridge New Testament Seminar.* Ed. William Horbury and Brian McNeil. New York: Cambridge University Press, 1981.

Bassler, Jouette M. "The Enigmatic Sign: 2 Thessalonians 1:5," *CBQ* 46 (1984) 498-510.

Boers, Hendrikus. "The Form Critical Study of Paul's Letters. I Thessalonians as a Case Study," *NTS* 22 (1976) 140-158.

Collins, R.F. *Studies on the First Letter to the Thessalonians.* BETL 66. Leuven: Leuven University Press, 1984.

Cottrell, Jack. *What the Bible Says About God the Ruler.* Joplin, MO: College Press, 1984.

Donfried, Karl P. *The Theology of the Shorter Pauline Letters.* New York: Cambridge University Press, 1993.

Ellis, E. Earle. *Prophecy and Hermeneutic in Early Christianity.* Grand Rapids: Eerdmans, 1978.

Ferguson, Everett. *Backgrounds of Early Christianity.* 2nd ed. Grand Rapids: Eerdmans, 1993.

Friskney, Tom. *Thirteen Lessons on First and Second Thessalonians.* Joplin, MO: College Press, 1982.

Funk, Robert W. *Parables and Presence: Forms of the New Testament Tradition.* Philadelphia: Fortress, 1982.

Guthrie, Donald. *New Testament Introduction.* 4th ed. Downers Grove, IL: InterVarsity, 1990.

Harris, Murray J. *Raised Immortal: Resurrection and Immortality in the New Testament.* Grand Rapids: Eerdmans, 1983.

Hengel, Martin. *The Pre-Christian Paul.* Philadelphia: Trinity Press International, 1991.

Hewett, James A. "1 Thessalonians 3:11," *ExpTim* 87 (1975-76) 54-55.

Hock, Ronald F. *The Social Context of Paul's Ministry: Tentmaking and Apostleship.* Minneapolis: Fortress, 1980.

Holland, Glenn S. *The Tradition that You Received from Us: 2 Thessalonians in the Pauline Tradition.* HUT 24. Tübingen: Mohr, 1988.

Jewett, Robert. *The Thessalonian Correspondence: Pauline Rhetoric and Millenarian Piety.* FFNT. Philadelphia: Fortress, 1986.

Johnson, Luke T. "The New Testament's Anti-Jewish Slander and the Conventions of Ancient Polemic," *JBL* 108 (1989) 419-441.

Klijn, A.F.J. "1 Thessalonians 4.13-18 and Its Background in Apocalyptic Literature." In *Paul and Paulinism: Essays in Honour of C. K. Barrett.* Ed. M.D. Hooker and S.G. Wilson. London: SPCK, 1982, pp. 67-73.

Ladd, G.E. *A Theology of the New Testament.* Grand Rapids: Eerdmans, 1974.

Lightfoot, J.B. *Notes on Epistles of St. Paul.* 1885. Reprint, Grand Rapids: Baker, 1980.

Malherbe, Abraham J. "Exhortations in First Thessalonians," *NovT* 25 (1983) 238-256.

_____. "'Gentle as a Nurse': The Stoic Background to 1 Thess. II," *NovT* 12 (1970) 203-217.

_____. *Moral Exhortation, A Greco-Roman Sourcebook.* Library of Early Christianity. Philadelphia: Westminster, 1986.

_____. *Paul and the Thessalonians: The Philosophic Tradition of Pastoral Care.* Philadelphia: Fortress, 1987.

Marshall, I. Howard. "Pauline Theology in the Thessalonian Correspondence." In *Paul and Paulinism: Essays in Honour of C.K. Barrett*. Ed. M.D. Hooker and S.G. Wilson. London: SPCK, 1982, pp. 173-183.

Meeks, Wayne A. *The First Urban Christians: The Social World of the Apostle Paul*. New Haven, CT: Yale University Press, 1983.

Morris, Leon. *The Apostolic Preaching of the Cross*. 3rd ed. Grand Rapids: Eerdmans, 1965.

Moule, C.F.D. *The Origin of Christology*. New York: Cambridge University Press, 1977.

Pauline Theology, Volume I: Thessalonians, Philippians, Galatians, Philemon. Ed. Jouette M. Bassler. Minneapolis: Fortress, 1991.

Pate, C. Marvin. *The End of the Age Has Come: The Theology of Paul*. Grand Rapids: Zondervan, 1995.

Pearson, Birger A. "I Thessalonians 2:13-16: A Deutero-Pauline Interpolation," *HTR* 64 (1971) 79-94.

Plevnik, Joseph. "1 Thess 5,1-11: Its Authenticity, Intention and Message," *Bib* 60 (1979) 71-90.

_____. "The Taking Up of the Faithful and the Resurrection of the Dead in 1 Thessalonians 4:13-18," *CBQ* 46 (1984) 274-283.

Poythress, Vern S. "2 Thessalonians 1 Supports Amillennialism," *JETS* 37 (1994) 529-538.

Russell, R. "The Idle in 2 Thess 3.6-12: An Eschatological or a Social Problem," *NTS* 34 (1988) 105-119.

Schlueter, Carol J. *Filling Up the Measure: Polemical Hyperbole in 1 Thessalonians 2.14-16*. JSNTSup 98. Sheffield: Sheffield Academic Press, 1994.

Schmidt, Daryl. "1 Thess 2:13-16: Linguistic Evidence for an Interpolation," *JBL* 102 (1983) 269-279.

Schmithals, Walter. *Paul and the Gnostics*. Trans. J.E. Steely. Nashville: Abingdon, 1972.

Stowers, Stanley K. "Social Status, Public Speaking and Private Teaching: The Circumstances of Paul's Preaching Activity," *NovT* 26 (1984) 68-82.

The Thessalonian Correspondence. Raymond F. Collins, ed. BETL 87. Leuven: Leuven University Press, 1990.

Walton, Steve "What Has Aristotle to Do with Paul? Rhetorical Criticism and 1 Thessalonians," *TynBul* 46 (1995) 229-249.

Warfield, B.B. "The Prophecies of St. Paul." In *Biblical and Theological Studies*. 1886. Ed. Samuel G. Craig. Reprint, Philadelphia: Presbyterian & Reformed, 1952, pp. 463-475.

Weatherly, Jon A. "The Authenticity of 1 Thessalonians 2.13-16: Additional Evidence," *JSNT* 42 (1991) 79-98.

_____. *Jewish Responsibility for the Death of Jesus in Luke-Acts*. JSNTSup 106. Sheffield: Sheffield Academic Press, 1994.

Wenham, David. *Gospel Perspectives 4: The Rediscovery of Jesus' Eschatological Discourse*. Sheffield: JSOT, 1984.

_____. *Paul: Follower of Jesus or Founder of Christianity?* Grand Rapids: Eerdmans, 1995.

Winter, Bruce W. "The Entries and Ethics of Orators and Paul (1 Thessalonians 2:1-12)," *TynBul* 44 (1993) 55-74.

Witton, J. "A Neglected Meaning for *Skeuos* in 1 Thessalonians 4.4," *NTS* 28 (1982) 142-143.

Wright, N.T. *The Climax of the Covenant*. Minneapolis: Fortress, 1992.

1 THESSALONIANS 1

I. GREETING (1:1)

¹**Paul, Silas[a] and Timothy,**
To the church of the Thessalonians in God the Father and the Lord Jesus Christ:
Grace and peace to you.[b]

[a]*1* Greek *Silvanus*, a variant of *Silas*   [b]*1* Some early manuscripts *you from God our Father and the Lord Jesus Christ*

Letters in the first century normally began with a brief greeting identifying the writer and the recipients and offering some wish for the well-being of the recipients. Paul followed this convention in his letters but adapted even this most mundane of epistolary elements to express ideas central to the Christian gospel.

1:1 Paul, Silas and Timothy,
Paul first of all identifies himself by name as the writer of the letter. Though in other, later epistles he identifies himself as "an apostle" (Rom 1:1; 1 Cor 1:1; 2 Cor 1:1; Gal 1:1; Eph 1:1; Col 1:1; 1 Tim 1:1; 2 Tim 1:1; Titus 1:1), here he does not, perhaps because his authority is not at issue with the Thessalonian church. Along with Paul, Silas and Timothy are mentioned as well. It is possible that these two had some hand in composing the letter. However, the emphasis in chs. 2-3 on Paul's absence from Thessalonica and his concern despite the visit by Silas and Timothy indicates that this letter primarily is Paul's personal expression of care for the Thessalonian church. Paul perhaps includes Silas and

Timothy in the salutation to show that his associates, who have actually spent more time with the Thessalonian church than has Paul, stand with him in affirming this message.

Silas (as he is called in Acts) or Silvanus (as Paul refers to him in his letters) accompanied Paul on his second missionary journey, assuming a role similar to that of Barnabas on Paul's first journey. Since he was sent to Antioch to deliver the message from the council of Acts 15, we can conclude that he was a Jewish Christian from the Jerusalem church (Acts 15:22). The fact that Acts associates him with Paul only on this one journey (Acts 15-18) is corroborated by the fact that he is mentioned in Paul's letters only here, in 2 Thess 1:1 and 2 Cor 1:19, all at points in which Paul reflects on the activity of his second missionary journey. He is also mentioned in 1 Pet 5:12, where Peter indicates that Silas has had some role in composing that letter.

Timothy is among Paul's associates whom he mentions most frequently. Acts indicates that he joins Paul on his second missionary journey (16:1) and is with him on the third as well (19:22; 20:4). Paul mentions him with Silas in the salutation of 2 Thessalonians; in 2 Corinthians, Philippians and Colossians he is the only person mentioned with Paul at the opening of the letter. His role in Paul's letters is generally like his role in 1 Thessalonians: he serves as Paul's representative to bring messages and carry out instructions in places where Paul cannot be present personally.

To the church of the Thessalonians in God the Father and the Lord Jesus Christ:

The letter is addressed to "the church of the Thessalonians." The Greek word translated "church," ἐκκλησία (*ekklēsia*), has been widely analyzed according to its etymology to signify "the called-out ones."[1] But however true it may be

---

[1] Karl P. Donfried is one who continues this somewhat misleading tradition (*The Theology of the Shorter Pauline Letters* [New York: Cambridge University Press, 1993], p. 59).

that the church is composed of those whom God has called out from the world, the word *ekklēsia* would not have suggested this idea to Paul's readers.[2] The term was widely used in the Hellenistic world for assemblies of various kinds, including the assembly of citizens in Greek city-states, pagan religious conclaves, and various other secular assemblies. Significantly, though, the term was frequently used in the LXX to translate the Hebrew קהל (*qahal*), which often is used to refer to the assembly of Israel as the people of God. During the intertestamental period, the community that produced the Dead Sea Scrolls referred to themselves in Aramaic as the קהל אל (*qehal 'el*) ("assembly of God"; 1QM 4:10; 1QS^a 2:4), reflecting their belief that they were the people of God of the end times. The early Christians' use of this term probably reflects this background. It expresses their conviction that they belong to the assembly of God's people in the age of fulfillment. As is usually the case, Paul uses the word here to refer to what we would call a "local church," the assembly of God's people in a particular place, though he uses it in some contexts for the universal church.

The phrase "in God the Father and the Lord Jesus Christ" identifies the *ekklēsia* as one that is different from all other assemblies of people in Thessalonica: they are the ones who "turned to God from idols to serve the living and true God, and to wait for his Son from heaven, whom he raised from the dead" (vv. 9-10). The expression "in Christ" and variants like the one here are among the most frequent in Paul's letters — and certainly among the most discussed by scholars. Here, though the expression serves primarily to differentiate the church from others, it also expresses Paul's conviction that Christians are united with Christ and so experience both his death and his resurrected life in their own lives. That reality will become significant in this epistle as Paul discusses the Thessalonians' experience of persecution and their hope of

---

[2]Cf. the famous discussion of this topic in James Barr, *The Semantics of Biblical Language* (London: SCM, 1983 [reprint, 1961]), pp. 119-129.

the resurrection at the Lord's coming. Both, he will state, are consequences of their status "in Christ."

The fact that Paul so easily identifies the church as "in God" and "in Christ" reflects his conviction that Christ is indeed fully divine. As a Jew with rabbinic training, Paul would never have related something to God and to another unless that other one was himself God. Certainly Paul's conviction that Christ was deity began with Christ's appearance to Paul on the road to Damascus: Paul's question of the voice from heaven, "Who are you, *Lord*?" is answered, "I am Jesus . . . ." This conviction was reinforced as well by what Paul learned by revelation from the Lord and what he was taught by other Christians.

Grace and peace to you.

The salutation closes with Paul's characteristic "grace and peace." The term "grace" (χάρις, *charis*) is, of course, absolutely central to Paul's theology. Paul insists that salvation is to be found not in keeping the Mosaic law so as to gain merit before God, a task made impossible by human sinfulness, but by receiving God's free, unmerited gift of his favor through faith in Jesus Christ. As a word of greeting Paul may have used *charis* as a play on the similar-sounding χαίρειν (*chairein*), the ordinary greeting among Hellenistic peoples (cf. James 1:1; 2 John 10-11).[3] With this he combines "peace," the Greek εἰρήνη (*eirēnē*), probably as a translation of the Hebrew and Aramaic greeting שלום (*šalôm*). In OT usage this term signified not just the absence of hostility but positive well-being and fullness of life, the consequence of God's benevolent rule over his people. As Paul uses the expression in tandem with grace, it thus indicates that Christians have received the fulfillment of God's promised peace through the gospel (cf. Matt 10:13//Luke 10:6). Especially striking in this letter is the fact

---

[3]Bruce expresses doubt that *charis* in Paul's salutations is a play on *chairein*, offering instead that it is a variant on "mercy and peace" used as a greeting in some Jewish circles (*2 Apoc. Bar.* 78:2; Bruce, p. 8). In either case, however, Paul's emphasis on grace is deliberate and obvious.

that Paul stresses the peace which God gives (cf. 5:23) while at the same time recounting the suffering which the readers have experienced (1:6; 2:14; 3:3). Precisely because such peace persists in suffering, throughout the letter Paul stresses the comfort and encouragement that come from the gospel (2:3, 12; 3:2, 7; 4:1, 10, 18; 5:11, 14).

The combination of a play on the common Hellenistic greeting with a translation of the common Jewish greeting has been regarded by some as an indication of Paul's concern for the unity of Gentiles and Jews in the church. This conclusion may press the evidence too far, however. Grace is no less an OT concept than peace, and Jews living in a Hellenistic culture were accustomed to using the common Greek salutation (cf. 2 Macc 1:1; *2 Apoc. Bar.* 78:2).

In all of Paul's other epistles the phrase "grace and peace" is followed by the phrase "from God the Father and the Lord Jesus Christ" or some near variant of it. Though some manuscripts of 1 Thessalonians include that phrase here, it is omitted in others. Because it is more likely that a scribe inserted the phrase in order to bring this letter into conformity with the others than that anyone omitted it, it is probably not an original part of the letter and so was consigned to a footnote in the NIV.

II. THANKSGIVING (1:2-10)

A. THE INITIAL THANKSGIVING (1:2-5)

²We always thank God for all of you, mentioning you in our prayers. ³We continually remember before our God and Father your work produced by faith, your labor prompted by love, and your endurance inspired by hope in our Lord Jesus Christ.

⁴For we know, brothers loved by God, that he has chosen you, ⁵because our gospel came to you not simply with words, but also with power, with the Holy Spirit and with

deep conviction. You know how we lived among you for your sake.

Another characteristic of letters in the Greco-Roman world was that the salutation was often followed by a statement of thanksgiving to the deity worshiped by the writer. Though in many letters this thanksgiving was a mere formality, Paul uses such thanksgivings in all of his letters except Galatians to articulate some of the important themes on which he will elaborate.[4] As he does here, Paul's usual thanksgiving was offered for the faith and other Christian virtues that the readers have demonstrated by the way they have lived their lives in Paul's absence.

This section is a single sentence in the Greek text, with the main clause at the beginning of v. 1 ("We always thank God for all of you . . ."). The NIV has rendered it as four separate sentences for ease of understanding in English.

1. Paul's Constant Prayers for the Readers (1:2)

1:2 We always thank God for all of you, mentioning you in our prayers.

At several points in this statement, Paul stresses that his thanksgiving for the Thessalonian Christians is constant. The verb εὐχαριστοῦμεν (*eucharistoumen*, "thank") and the participle ποιούμενοι (*poioumenoi*, "making"; with μνείαν [*mneian*], "mention," the sense is "mentioning") are in the Greek present tense, indicating a continuing action. The adverb "always" (πάντοτε, *pantote*) further emphasizes that verbal aspect. Then the adjective "all" (πάντων, *pantōn*), alliterating with the adverb to provide further emphasis, stresses that Paul's thanksgiving includes everyone in the church. The plur-

---

[4]Because of the repeated thanksgivings in 2:13 and 3:9-10 the extent and purpose of the thanksgiving in 1 Thessalonians is a subject of ongoing debate among scholars. For a review of the issues, including the application of rhetorical criticism to resolve the problem, see Wanamaker, pp. 72-73.

al "prayers" also indicates a repeated practice. Overall the statement vividly emphasizes the regularity and persistence of Paul's prayers for the readers. The plural "prayers" may also indicate that Paul continued the rabbinic practice of praying regularly at particular times of the day. However, glimpses of his prayer life found in Acts and elsewhere in his letters show that it was not governed or restricted by ritualistic tradition.

2. Their Exercise of Faith, Love and Hope (1:3)

1:3 We continually remember before our God and Father

Again Paul stresses that his thanksgiving is continual. "Remember" translates the Greek μνημονεύοντες (*mnēmoneuontes*), again a present participle indicating continuing action, and the adverb ἀδιαλείπτως (*adialeiptōs*, literally, "without interruption") adds stress to this idea.[5] Here the example is established for the instruction on prayer which Paul gives in 5:17, where "continually" in the NIV represents the same Greek term. To "remember" the Thessalonians before God refers to the same kind of action as "mentioning" them in v. 2, but here the reason for the thanksgiving is specified.[6]

your work produced by faith,

Paul specifies the reason for his thanksgiving with a trio of terms — faith, love and hope — which appear together several

---

[5]The NIV translators, the UBS Greek text, and many commentators take ἀδιαλείπτως with the following phrase ("we . . . remember"). But because it occurs between the two participles ποιούμενοι and μνημονεύοντες, it could be taken with either. Wanamaker argues that it should be taken with the preceding to preserve the rhythm of the sentence (p. 74). In either case, however, the sense of the sentence is not significantly affected.

[6]The phrase "before our God and Father" actually occurs after "endurance inspired by hope in our Lord Jesus Christ" at the end of the verse. The NIV translators have placed it here because the balance of the sentence indicates that the phrase modifies "remember" (μνημονεύοντες). Dividing the verb from its modifier in this way serves to tie the entire verse together more closely.

times in Paul's letters (Rom 5:1-5; 1 Cor 13:13; Gal 5:5-6; Eph 4:2-5; Col 1:4-5; 1 Thess 5:8) as well as in literature influenced by Paul (Heb 6:10-12; 10:22-24; 1 Pet 1:3-8, 21-22).[7] Though the order most familiar to students of the Bible is probably "faith, hope and love" because of its occurrence in the well-known text 1 Cor 13:13, the order found in this text occurs everywhere else. Here each of the terms is connected to a particular response produced by it. Literally the text reads, "your work of faith, your labor of love and your steadfastness of hope"; the NIV translators have inserted the words "produced . . . prompted . . . inspired" to make clear the sense of the text, not to imply any difference among the three. With each of the three phrases in this context, Paul seems to refer not to some specific action which the church has taken so much as the general tenor of their lives as Christians since he left them.

"Faith," the response of assent to and trust in God and his message of salvation, stands at the head of the list because of its priority in the Christian life: all aspects of Christian living stem from our response of faith to the initiative God has taken for us in Christ. Paul sharply distinguishes "faith" from "works" as ways of salvation: he insists that no one can earn God's favor by keeping the Mosaic law (cf. Gal 2:16; Rom 3:28). But Paul always understands that genuine faith expresses itself in action. So here his thanksgiving is for the Thessalonians' "work produced by faith," that is, deeds that they have done as the natural and necessary result of their belief in the gospel of Jesus Christ.

your labor prompted by love,
"Love" is the Greek ἀγάπη (*agapē*), which in the New Testament is most frequently used to refer to the love of God for humanity despite their unworthiness and to the same kind of love which his people show to others. Here it is grounded

---

[7]Cf. the discussion of the three terms in Donfried, *Shorter Pauline Letters*, pp. 53-58.

on faith in the God who demonstrates his love to us in Christ, though as Paul indicates in 1 Cor 13:13, it shall supersede even faith as faith yields to sight while love endures. Like faith, love motivates action. The word translated "labor," κόπος (*kopos*), is often used to refer to especially difficult or tiresome work. In this context, however, Paul probably does not intend for it to indicate something more difficult than the "work produced by faith"; the different term simply avoids repetition. So the point of both expressions is very similar: genuine love, like genuine faith, produces action.

and your endurance inspired by hope in our Lord Jesus Christ.

"Hope" characteristically comes at the end of the list because of its orientation to the future. As used in the New Testament, the Greek term ἐλπίς (*elpis*) suggests a confident expectation about the future. Such confidence is grounded in God's own faithfulness to carry out the work which he has initiated in Christ, as Paul expresses in Phil 1:6. Hence, their hope is "in our Lord Jesus Christ" not just because they look forward confidently to his return (cf. 1:9-10; 4:13-5:11) but because they are already through their relationship with Christ experiencing the blessings of God that will be fully realized in the future. What stands in the way of the full realization of those blessings in the present is the ongoing struggle with evil, a struggle made more acute by the opposition which their new faith generates. But the confident expectation that God will indeed fulfill his promises to the final degree gives believers the assurance that they need to endure the persecution and other sufferings that come their way in the present age. Thus, endurance is the practical outgrowth of their hope.

These three phrases describing the Thessalonian Christians serve several purposes in the letter. As Paul offers thanksgiving, they show that his primary cause for thanksgiving is the Christian lifestyle of the readers. Mentioning their lifestyle at the beginning of the letter also serves as encouragement and reinforcement for continuing in that lifestyle. This also provides a basis for the moral exhortation that Paul gives implicitly in 2:1-12 and explicitly in 4:1-5:22. There Paul will call the readers to ongoing faithfulness in the manner of life that they already follow. The mention of hope at the climax of the list introduces the theme of 4:13-5:11, namely, the return of Christ.

3. Their Election (1:4)

1:4 For we know, brothers loved by God,
The response of the Thessalonians to the gospel message described in v. 3 is just that — a response to God's initiative in bringing salvation to them. So Paul continues the thanksgiving by focusing on God's work. The term "brothers," Paul's favorite form of address for his readers, was used by Jews to refer to other Jews (cf. Deut 15:3, 12). As Paul applies it to Christians, it stresses the new relationship which has been created among the readers because of what God the Father has done. The barriers and divisions which otherwise would have existed among them have been broken down by the new unity created by their common life in Christ.[8]

This brotherhood has been forged by the actions of God in making the Thessalonian believers his people. They are "loved by God": they are the objects of God's unmerited favor. Hence, they have been "chosen" by God. These two terms indicate that the readers' relationship with God is like Israel's (Deut 7:7; 14:2; Ps 33:12; Acts 13:17). As God chose Israel as his covenant people, so now he has chosen the Christians, but for even greater blessings (cf. Isa 14:1). Because Paul particularly focuses on converts from paganism

---

[8]It was customary in first-century Greek to refer to a group consisting of both men and women with a term of masculine gender. Hence, the NRSV's rendering of "brothers" as "brothers and sisters" is a legitimate equivalent for modern English readers sensitive to issues of gender inclusion, since the Greek expression was used to refer to both men and women.

in this chapter (v. 9), his use of language associated with Israel to refer to Christian believers is especially striking. They do not merely belong to a distinct group of people; they are part of the community of God's people that has received the blessings promised for the end time. In the rest of the chapter Paul will indicate that the Thessalonians' genuine faith and its consequences indicate this new relationship to God is genuine.

that he has chosen you

The idea of God's "choosing" or election has been a controversial one in Christian theology. Under the influence of Augustine and later of John Calvin, many have understood that Christians are only able to come to faith because God has first chosen them and so has irresistibly caused them to believe. In fact, Paul's use of the language of election indicates a different emphasis altogether.

By stressing that God has chosen the Christians, Paul acknowledges that God is sovereign, that he has supreme authority and determines who will belong to him. But the terminology focuses primarily on the relationship that results from God's choosing, not on the act of choosing itself. Paul emphasizes that through the initiative which God has taken in Christ, Christians are in a relationship with God which is secure both in the difficulties of this life (Rom 8:28-30) and in the final judgment (Rom 8:33) because it is based on the choice of the all-sovereign God.

Furthermore, Paul indicates that God's choice is conditional: that is, that God chooses believers on the basis of their faith, not that he first chooses them and so later causes them to believe. This is explicit in Rom 8:29 ("For those God foreknew he also predestined to be conformed to the likeness of his Son, that he might be the firstborn among many brethren"), a text similar in language to 1 Thess 1:4. It is also consistent with the fact that in Paul's letters the result of God's predestination or choice is never faith as such but the results of salvation conditioned on faith, including such things as conformity to the image of Christ (Rom 8:29), holiness and blamelessness (Eph 1:4; cf. Col 3:6), adoption into God's family (Eph 1:5), and ultimately the glorification of God himself (Eph 1:11-12).

If Paul's use of the language of election reflected a belief that God had chosen individuals before creation and so later *caused* them to believe, we might expect words like "chosen" to be used sometimes to refer to those who are elect but have not yet come to faith. This use, however, is nowhere in evidence in Paul or the rest of the New Testament. Instead, as I.H. Marshall has pointed out, the term always refers to those who have already responded to God's call.[9]

Most importantly, understanding the concept of election had genuine benefit for early Christians. In Paul's letters it gave believers the assurance that they were receiving the full advantage of all of God's saving activity in history. They are at the climax of what God had done; they are the beneficiaries of the plan of God from before creation. Whatever difficulties they may face in this age, they have the assurance of their standing with God in his eternal plan.[10]

4. The Power of the Gospel in Thessalonica (1:5)

1:5 because our gospel came to you not simply with words,
Paul will now demonstrate the reality of the Thessalonians' relationship with God by stressing the genuineness of the gospel which they received.[11] The terms "the gospel" and "the word," meaning the word of God, occur frequently in

---

[9]I. Howard Marshall, "Election and Calling to Salvation in 1 and 2 Thessalonians," *The Thessalonian Correspondence* (Raymond F. Collins, ed.; BETL 87; Leuven: Leuven University Press, 1990), pp. 259-266.

[10]For a full discussion of the theological issues of election and predestination, see Jack Cottrell, *What the Bible Says About God the Ruler* (Joplin, MO: College Press, 1984), pp. 331-352.

[11]The ὅτι at the beginning of v. 5 is best understood as causal, as the NIV translates it. For a discussion see Wanamaker, p. 78.

1 Thessalonians, along with other terms, especially "you know," which remind the readers of the message that they have already received. The frequency of these terms point to one aspect of Paul's purpose: he writes to remind the readers of the message that they have already received, encouraging them to remain firm and pointing out specifically how that message applies to the difficult circumstances they have faced.[12]

Here Paul stresses the genuineness of the gospel by recounting how the Thessalonians first heard and received it. He knows that they are God's chosen because they have received the genuine message of salvation, and that genuineness is demonstrated first of all by the sincerity of the people who brought it. The ancient world, no less than our own, had a generous share of unscrupulous purveyors of philosophical and religious ideas. Speaking an appealing message that they themselves did not believe, such preachers did not demonstrate by their lives their own belief in their words, and neither did their message produce what they claimed. Paul, however, draws a contrast with the readers' experience of the gospel. Paul's use of the term "gospel" (εὐαγγέλιον, *euangelion*) sharpens the focus on these ideas. In Isaiah the related verb εὐαγγελίζω (*euangelizō*) is used to refer to the proclamation of the good news of God's salvation (Isa 40:9; 52:7; 60:6; 61:1). Jesus used this language to refer to his ministry (Luke 4:17-20), especially as the announcement of the imminent coming of God's kingdom (Matt 4:29; 9:35; 24:14). As used by Paul the term usually refers to the content of the message preached, though sometimes it can refer to the act of preaching itself.[13] Here the two points of reference stand close together. The genuineness of the gospel message insures that the Thessalonian Christians are indeed God's people, but the fact that the message is genuine is demonstrated in part by the way in which it was preached.

---

[12]Donfried, *Shorter Pauline Letters*, pp. 23-24.
[13]Georg Strecker, "εὐαγγέλιον," *EDNT*, 2:72.

but also with power, with the Holy Spirit, and with deep conviction.

These three characteristics distinguish the gospel from other messages which the readers may have encountered. "Power" here refers to the power of God, as implied by the focus on God's actions in the previous verse. Paul probably has in mind his demonstration of God's power through miracles (cf. Rom 15:18-19), though the expression here is perhaps not confined to miracles alone. For Paul, as for New Testament writers generally, miracles served as tokens of the greater salvation which was available through the gospel. So having seen the power of God demonstrated in miraculous actions, the Thessalonian Christians also recognized that God's power was at work in them as they put their faith in Christ.

Paul indicates the source of that power in the following phrase. The Holy Spirit both empowers the apostle to do miraculous deeds and, more importantly, empowers the new Christians to bring their lives into conformity with the gospel which they have received. Because the Old Testament views the pouring out of the Spirit of God on all flesh as a part of God's end-time work of salvation (Joel 2:28-32; Isa 44:3-5; 32:15; Ezek 36:27; 37:14), this reminder of the Spirit's connection to the gospel stresses as did v. 4 that the Thessalonian Christians have received the fulfillment of God's Old Testament promises.

The phrase "deep conviction" is emphatic in the Greek text, underscoring the absolute sincerity of the one who believes the gospel. Though it could refer to the profound belief of the readers at their conversion, the fact that the following clause refers to Paul's own manner of life suggests that the term refers to Paul's sincerity as a messenger. The profound personal commitment of Paul and his associates to the gospel stands is sharp contrast to an insincere message that comes "simply with words."

The previous phrase, "with words" may well have prompted Paul's readers to expect him to draw a contrast with his deeds, as many philosophers of the time did. Paul's contrast, however, is on the message of the gospel and God's power in Paul's preaching of it.[14] This shift helps the readers to focus on the real significance of what they have received from Paul.

You know how we lived among you for your sake.

Paul and his associates demonstrated their own sincere belief in the gospel by the way that they lived among the Thessalonians. Paul does not offer specific characteristics which they demonstrated, at this point relying instead on the Thessalonians' own memory to supply the details. But the fact that they lived such lives "for your sake" indicates their unselfish, generous concern for others demonstrated in their actions. Later in 2:1-12 Paul will elaborate on this brief description.

B. REITERATION AND FURTHER SPECIFICATION OF THE THANKSGIVING (1:6-10)

⁶You became imitators of us and of the Lord; in spite of severe suffering, you welcomed the message with the joy given by the Holy Spirit. ⁷And so you became a model to all the believers in Macedonia and Achaia. ⁸The Lord's message rang out from you not only in Macedonia and Achaia – your faith in God has become known everywhere. Therefore we do not need to say anything about it, ⁹for they themselves report what kind of reception you gave us. They tell how you turned to God from idols to serve the living and true God, ¹⁰and to wait for his Son from heaven, whom he raised from the dead – Jesus, who rescues us from the coming wrath.

---

[14]Abraham J. Malherbe, "Exhortations in First Thessalonians," *NovT* 25 (1983) 247-248.

1. The Readers' Imitation of Paul and His Associates (1:6a)

1:6 You became imitators of us and of the Lord;

The sincere belief of Paul, Silas and Timothy was reproduced in the readers, indicating further their genuine status as God's people.[15] Like others who offered moral or religious instruction in the ancient world, Paul often admonished his convert to imitate him (1 Thess 2:14; 2 Thess 3:7-9; 1 Cor 4:16; 11:1; Eph 5:1; Phil 3:17).[16] In such instructions, Paul indicates either directly or indirectly that in imitating him his readers ultimately are imitating the Lord. Paul offers a variety of specific behaviors which are or ought to be imitated in these passages; he never suggests that his converts should be like him in absolutely every respect. But in offering himself as a model, he provides a concrete example for the abstract, verbal instruction which they have received. The next statement indicates that he particularly has in mind the Thessalonians' following him in steadfast faith despite suffering (cf. 2:2, 14).[17] By implication, as they imitate Paul's suffering, they also

---

[15]The "you" at the beginning of the verse is emphatic in the Greek text, prompting Morris to suggest that Paul emphasizes the subject to stress his certainty that the Thessalonians are among the elect (p. 47). However, the emphasis probably stems primarily from the shift in focus from the missionaries (v. 5) to the converts (v. 6).

[16]*HCNT*, § 812, cites Plutarch (*Moralia*, "How a Man May Become Aware of His Progress in Virtue," 14) as an example of the imitation of human examples in Hellenistic moral teaching: "We must therefore believe we are making but little progress so long as the admiration which we feel for successful men remains inert within us and does not of its own self stir us to imitation."

[17]The NIV here represents the ambiguity of the Greek text well. "You welcomed" is a Greek circumstantial participle (δεξάμενοι, *dexamenoi*), which could be taken either in an instrumental sense ("by receiving . . .") or a temporal sense ("when you received . . ."). Though commentators have attempted to decide between these two (cf. the contrasting positions of Marshall [pp. 54-55] and Wanamaker [pp. 80-81]), insisting on one hard-and-fast category is probably unnecessary. Paul does not insist here that all genuine conversions are accompanied by persecution at the time of conversion. Rather, he assumes that opposition to conversion is consistent with the constant opposition to which the Lord and his followers are subject.

imitate Christ's (cf. 2:15; Phil 3:10; Col 1:24). In reminding his readers of their initial steadfastness in suffering, Paul builds a foundation to encourage them to further steadfastness (4:1-5:22).

2. Their Endurance of Suffering (1:6b)

in spite of severe suffering,

The Thessalonian Christians suffered undoubtedly because of the tension that arose with family and neighbors because of their conversion.[18] Abandoning pagan worship (v. 9) separated them from the practices which had formerly bound them together with other members of their community (cf. Acts 19:23-41 for an example of the consequences of such dislocation). And though such conflict in their social relationships is probably sufficient to explain Paul's references to their suffering, the Thessalonians may have also suffered persecution from more official sources, such as local or imperial rulers, to whom the gospel might have appeared subversive.[19] Leaving the old life for the gospel was for them a costly transaction. In 2:14-16 Paul will remind the readers that other Christians have shared a similar cost.

you welcomed the message with the joy given by the Holy Spirit.

But ironically, this very suffering is indicative of the power of the gospel (v. 5), since that power has its origin in Christ's self-sacrificial suffering on the cross. But because the gospel

---

[18]Abraham J. Malherbe unnecessarily limits the suffering to an inner conflict caused by the Thessalonians' break with the past (*Paul and the Thessalonians: The Philosophic Tradition of Pastoral Care* [Philadelphia: Fortress, 1987], p. 48). The comparison with the Lord's suffering, the example provided to others (v. 7), and the further elaboration on the theme later in the book (2:14-16; 3:3) point to outward persecution. Cf. the comments on 1 Thess 3:3 below.

[19]Donfried argues for such persecution, which may even have led to martyrdom in Thessalonica (*Shorter Pauline Letters*, pp. 19-23).

message is not just about Christ's death but also about his resurrection and exaltation, sharing in Christ's suffering is a source of joy. Joy is not what one would expect to find in suffering; it does not arise naturally in the circumstances Paul describes. So Paul reminds the readers that this joy has a supernatural source: it is the "joy of the Holy Spirit," joy present with them because God's Spirit is present with them (Gal 5:22; Rom 14:17), given by the exalted Christ, bringing to his people the blessing and power of God that will be fully realized when Christ returns (cf. 1 Thess 4:18; 5:11; Phil 3:1, 20-21). Thus, the fact that the Thessalonians had joy despite suffering shows again that they were genuine people of God (cf. Mark 4:16): they had the joy that comes from God's authentic salvation which transcends present, outward circumstances (cf. Matt 5:10-12; Acts 4:31; 5:40-42; Rom 5:3-5; 2 Cor 1:5-7; 4:7-18; Col 1:24; James 1:2; 1 Pet 1:6-8; 4:13-14).[20]

3. Their Example to Other Churches (1:7-8a)

1:7 And so you became a model to all the believers in Macedonia and Achaia.

The idea of imitation introduced in v. 6 is now carried a step further in v. 7. By imitating Paul, and ultimately the Lord, in steadfast suffering, the Thessalonian Christians have provided a model for others who believe the same gospel. Paul indicates that the sphere of their influence includes their own region, Macedonia (the northern portion of the Greek peninsula) as well as the region to the south, Achaia (including Athens and Corinth, from which Paul writes). The word translated "model" is τύπος (*typos*). Originally this word referred to a mark or impression made by striking something, like the image on a coin. Figuratively it was used to refer to a model or pattern, especially for ethical conduct. This account

---

[20]Cf. Klaus Berger, "χαρά," *EDNT*, 3:454-455; William G. Morrice, "Joy," *DPL*, pp. 511-512.

and others like it in Paul's letters (Rom 1:8; Eph 1:15; Col 1:4-5) indicates that early Christians received and circulated reports about their brothers and sisters in other places and took encouragement from them. Not only did the first generation of Christians repeat the gospel story of Jesus' life, death and resurrection; they also regularly shared the experiences of other Christians. All this serves to make concrete what they were taught about Christian living.

1:8 The Lord's message rang out from you not only in Macedonia and Achaia —

The expression "the Lord's message" (literally "the word of the Lord") refers here not to the gospel story but to what Paul has been discussing in v. 7: the story of the Thessalonians' steadfastness. This is made clear by the fact that the latter part of the verse refers to this message as "your faith." The fact that Paul can refer to an account of response to the gospel as "the word of the Lord" indicates its supreme value. Such material was integral to God's word for his people because it recounted what God had done among his people. Thus, Luke's writing of Acts as a companion volume to his Gospel has its roots in this oral sharing of information about the churches.[21]

your faith in God has become known everywhere.

Paul widens the Thessalonians' scope of influence from the immediate regions to "everywhere." Though this expression obviously does not mean that literally all the world — or even all the Roman empire — had heard the report, it does stress that the gospel in all its aspects was shared without borders. Paul uses similar expressions elsewhere (Rom 1:8; 1 Cor 1:2; 2 Cor 2:14; Col 1:6, 23; 1 Tim 2:8), stressing that the Christian gospel is the message of salvation for all people.

---

[21]Cf. Jacob Jervell, *Luke and the People of God. A New Look at Luke-Acts* (Minneapolis: Augsburg, 1972), pp. 23-36.

The fact that Paul refers to their faith as "faith in God" rather than "in Christ" is consistent with his stress on their conversion to Christian faith from paganism. Had Paul intended to address Jewish Christians, faith in God would not have distinguished them from other Jews (see comments on v. 9). This emphasis may indicate that pressure from the readers' pagan families and neighbors was the primary source of their persecution.

4. Reports of Their Conversion (1:8b-10)

Therefore we do not need to say anything about it, 1:9 for they themselves report what kind of reception you gave us.
The point of this statement is that the Thessalonians' faith is well known among all the churches in which Paul has been ministering.[22] Again, we see how important such accounts were to the life of the early Christians. The focus of the report is still on the Thessalonians' initial acceptance of the gospel despite opposition. Now, though, the specific focus is on the success of the missionaries' visit to Thessalonica. A prepositional phrase περὶ ἡμῶν (*peri hēmōn*, "concerning us") appears in v. 9 and is left untranslated by the NIV. It places stress on Paul and his associates as the subjects of the report in circulation. The word εἴσοδος (*eisodos*), translated here as "reception" in the NIV, literally means "entrance" and refers

---

[22]Because here Paul says that he had no need to tell others about the Thessalonians, while in 2 Thess 1:4 he says that he boasts about them, Wanamaker argues that 2 Thessalonians was written first: Paul had told the story of the Thessalonians to others, wrote 2 Thessalonians and reported as much, and then wrote 1 Thessalonians, at which point other Christians already knew the story of the Thessalonians' faith (pp. 83-84). This explanation strains Paul's rhetoric in this passage: to say that he has no need to tell anyone about the Thessalonians is merely to say that their faith is well known, not that absolutely everyone has heard of it or that the story might not be repeated. Further, this context indicates that the story is well known not because Paul has told it but because it has spread through many sources.

to Paul's entire visit to Thessalonica. The clause literally reads, "For concerning us they themselves report what kind of entrance we had with you." It stresses less the Thessalonians' reception of Paul, as the NIV has it, than the success of Paul's visit, though obviously one implies the other. Paul will elaborate on this idea as he repeats *eisodos* in 2:1 (there translated as "visit" in the NIV) and discusses his experience with the Thessalonians at length in ch. 2-3.

Forsaking Idols to Serve the Living God (1:9b)

They tell how you turned to God from idols

That the messenger and his message cannot be separated is once more clear from the fact that Paul focuses again on the response to his preaching. The NIV accurately represents the redundancy of the Greek text which stresses that it is to God that the Thessalonians have turned. Here Paul draws upon Old Testament language (cf. Jer 10:1-10) to describe their conversion from paganism.[23] The term "idols" stresses that the Thessalonians' worship had centered on images of multiple deities. In contrast, the God of Israel is one God (Deut 6:4), supreme and transcendent over all, and can never be represented as or reduced to an image (Deut 5:8-10).

---

[23]This text is widely assumed to incorporate a pre-Pauline traditional formulation to describe conversion from paganism to Christianity. But the fact that the language has its roots in the Old Testament urges caution about drawing such conclusions, though it would be surprising if Paul were the first to describe the conversion of pagans to Christianity in Old Testament terms. Furthermore, if it was indeed a widely circulated formula, Paul or one of his associates may well have composed it, since they were among the most active missionaries to Gentiles (cf. E. Earle Ellis, "Traditions in 1 Corinthians," *NTS* 32 [1986] 495-496). On the other hand, Paul in some cases explicitly identifies traditional formulations which he learned from others and adapted for his purposes (e.g., 1 Cor 15:3-8). Wanamaker offers a full discussion of the issues (pp. 85-89). Note also the similarity between this language and Luke's accounts of Paul's speeches in Lystra (Acts 14:15) and, more broadly, Athens (Acts 17:22-31).

Other so-called "gods" are no gods at all; they are the imaginary creations of the people who worship them. Hence, the God of Israel is "living," in contrast to the lifeless pagan deities, and "true" or "genuine," in contrast to the false pagan gods.

to serve the living and true God,

As the only true God, the God of Israel possesses absolute authority; consequently, the only right response to him is "to serve." The Greek infinitive translated "to serve," δουλεύειν (*douleuein*), refers to the service of a slave to a master, stressing the obligation of the relationship, and is in the present tense, emphasizing that the service is continuing. For Paul such service is what makes a person truly free, for the alternative is slavery to sin, which yields death (Rom 6:15-23). Thus, Paul can comfortably describe Christians as God's children as well as his slaves (e.g., Rom 8:16). The virtues mentioned in v. 3 are obvious examples of the new service to the one true God.

In this contrast between the true God and idols lies the heart of the gospel's universal claim. The objects of pagan worship were generally conceived to have authority over a specific, limited realm, often thought to be tied to a particular place or people. The God of Israel, on the other hand, is Creator and Lord of all. Hence, his message of salvation is a message for all people, and so Paul seeks to proclaim that message to all.

The conversion of the Gentiles to faith in the one true God is viewed by the Old Testament as a significant part of God's great act of salvation in the last days (Isa 2:2-4; 25:6-8; 42:6; 49:6; Micah 4:1-3; Zech 8:20-23). Having been called especially to preach to the Gentiles, Paul saw his own ministry as a part of this great event. In this text, he offers the Thessalonians' conversion from paganism as further evidence that the gospel is genuine, for through the gospel God's promise to bring the nations to faith in him is being fulfilled.

This factor probably best explains Paul's emphasis in this

passage on Gentile converts in the Thessalonian church. Many scholars have drawn attention to the fact that in Acts 17:1-9, Luke indicates that the Thessalonian church consisted of both Jews and Gentiles. Some have speculated that Paul writes 1 Thessalonians specifically to the Gentile segment of the Thessalonian church. This idea, however, would appear to be inconsistent with Paul's stress on the unity of Jew and Gentile in the church. Others have argued that Luke has overemphasized the Jewish element of the Thessalonian church because of his own theological interests. But resorting to this conclusion is unnecessary when Paul's purpose in 1 Thessalonians 1 is recognized.

At this point Paul continues to recount the experience of the Thessalonian Christians in order to remind them of the authenticity of the message that they have received. Since conversion of the Gentiles is, according to the Old Testament prophets, a result of God's end-time act of salvation, such conversions are another indication that the Thessalonians have put their faith in the true message of God. Paul thus neither denies that there are Jewish Christians in the Thessalonian church nor ignores them in this letter. Instead, he focuses here on Gentile converts as further evidence that the gospel of Jesus Christ is much more than mere words (v. 5).[24]

Awaiting the Return of Jesus (1:10)

1:10 and to wait for his Son from heaven, whom he raised

---

[24]Traugott Holtz has noted that the use of the "wrath" in 1 Thess 1:10 without an expressed subject and in a futuristic sense is not comprehensible without an understanding of its usage in the LXX and Hellenistic Judaism; hence, he concludes that Paul's missionary preaching must have been similarly influenced by Hellenistic Jewish terminology, and that the synagogue was the likely locale for his preaching, as Acts describes ("Traditionen im 1. Thessalonischerbrief," *Die Mitte des Neuen Testaments. Einheit und Vielfalt neutestamentlicher Theologie. Festschrift für Eduard Schweizer zum siebzigsten Geburtstag* (Ulrich Luz and Heder Weder, eds.; Göttingen: Vandenhoeck & Ruprecht, 1983), pp. 56-57.

from the dead —

This verse further specifies the object of the Thessalonians' faith. Verse 9 by itself could describe the conversion of a pagan to Judaism, and some have suggested that Paul is using language drawn from Jewish sources there. But here the content of the Thessalonians' faith is explicitly Christian: they believe not only in the true God but more specifically in Jesus Christ, who was raised from the dead by God and now reigns with him from heaven, the place of universal authority. In this specific conviction the Thessalonian Christians, both Gentiles and Jews, would be distinct from all other people. The genuine gospel message assumes that there is one true God, but it focuses on what he has done in Jesus Christ, whom he raised from the dead and who will return for his people.

Jesus, who rescues us from the coming wrath.

But this verse serves to do more than distinguish the Thessalonians' faith from other groups'. It also explicates further the basis for the Thessalonians' steadfastness in suffering. Regardless of what happens to them, they have the assurance that they belong to the God who raised Jesus from the dead. Thus, God's power to overcome their own difficulties, including death itself, is guaranteed. Because Christ is presently in heaven, they have the assurance of his absolute and supreme power at work in their lives, even when outward circumstances would seem to indicate otherwise.[25] Indeed, in times of persecution it may seem that the unbelievers have the best of it. But God's wrath is about to bring punishment on those who have rebelled against God's authority. The readers' own lives as pagans (v. 9) would make them objects of that same wrath, but through Jesus they have the assurance that they have been removed from the sphere of God's wrath and are instead numbered among his beloved people (v. 4).

---

[25]*HCNT*, § 813, cites *Sib. Or.* 3.555-62 as an example of the different perspective of non-Christian Judaism: both Christians and Jews expected a judgment, but while the writer of the oracles could only hope and pray for deliverance, Christians had certainty of their deliverance because of Jesus.

The word translated "deliver," ῥύομαι (*rhyomai*) is not as common as σῴζω (*sōzō*, "save") in Paul's letters, but when it does occur it emphasizes salvation *from* something – here, from God's wrath.[26] The full realization of both the wrath of God and the deliverance from that wrath will occur when God's Son comes returns from heaven. So as they experience persecution in the present, the Thessalonian Christians can focus on that full realization in the future: they "wait" with confidence that God will finish the work which he began with Christ's resurrection and continues in them. As they wait for that consummation, the power that raised Jesus from the dead is continuing at work in them.

The concept of God's wrath is sometimes difficult to hold together with his love. Some mistakenly equate the concept of God's wrath with capricious human anger prompted by selfishness and pride. The biblical concept, however, is grounded in God's holiness and the consequent necessity that he punish sin. Wrath is thus God's consistent, just and holy response in bringing punishment for sin (cf. Rom 2:5,8; 3:5-6; 2 Thess 1:5-10). It is therefore necessarily God's wrath directly and personally, not some impersonal consequence of disaster that inevitably follows evil, as some have argued. Likewise, wrath is perfectly consistent with God's supreme desire to forgive sinners. Indeed, God's desire to bring forgiveness and the holy necessity that sin be punished are what make the cross necessary (Rom 3:25-26).[27]

Paul saves the personal name "Jesus" for a point of emphasis in the sentence. In so doing he identifies unambiguously the one of whom he speaks. The Son of God raised from the dead and coming to rescue his people is Jesus of Nazareth, a figure of history known personally by Paul's contemporaries. That the gospel message is grounded in history is assumed by Paul at every point.

The connection between the Gentiles' conversion and

---

[26]Wanamaker, p. 88.
[27]See Leon Morris, *The Apostolic Preaching of the Cross* (3rd ed.; Grand Rapids: Eerdmans, 1965), pp. 144-213.

Jesus' return is significant here. Jesus told his disciples that God's purpose of bringing the gospel to the Gentiles would be fulfilled prior to his return (Matt 24:14; Mark 13:10). From the Old Testament perspective, this preaching is an event of the end-time; from the post-Easter perspective, the end-time climaxes with Jesus' return.

This verse also announces a theme which will occupy an important portion of the letter. In 4:13-5:11 Paul will discuss further the significance of the Lord's coming, reminding the readers of teaching which they had already received and correcting their misunderstanding of certain points. Here, as in that later elaboration, we see that Paul's teaching on Christ's return is not a matter of esoteric doctrinal details; rather, it has an immediate and profound impact on the way that a believer responds to the difficulties of the present life.

1 THESSALONIANS 2

III. PAUL'S RELATIONSHIP TO THE THESSALONIAN CHURCH (2:1-3:13)

A. PAUL'S BEHAVIOR IN THESSALONICA (2:1-12)

Still focusing on the truth of the gospel which the readers had received, Paul now shifts his discussion to the way that he and his associates brought that gospel to Thessalonica.[1] The purity of their motives and actions is consistent with the divine message that they proclaim. So just as the Thessalonians' reception of the gospel demonstrates that it is truly God's message, so now the behavior of the missionaries does the same. Unlike many traveling religious teachers and philosophers, these missionaries were motivated by their desire to please God, not by pride or greed.[2] And their work was characterized by an urgency and love consistent with their message.

It is difficult to know whether Paul is responding in this section to a specific problem in the church. Some have suggested that, as in Galatians or the Corinthian epistles, Paul was defending his apostleship against opponents who claimed that he did not have genuine apostolic authority.[3] But the

---

[1] For a discussion of the place of this section in the rhetorical structure of the letter, see Wanamaker, pp. 90-91.

[2] On the contrast between Paul's behavior as described here and the typical behavior of professional orators of his day, see Bruce W. Winter, "The Entries and Ethics of Orators and Paul (1 Thessalonians 2:1-12)," *TynBul* 44 (1993) 55-74.

[3] E.g., Morris, p. 57. Cf. the summary of major opinions and research on

emphasis of this passage is less on the authority of Paul than on the significance of his behavior; he mentions his apostolic authority in a way that assumes the readers' acceptance of it (v. 6). If he has any anxiety about their attitude toward him, it would appear to be that they would mistake his absence from them as a lack of concern (cf. 2:17-20). Therefore, he focuses on his consistent love and care for them while he was in Thessalonica founding the church. This discussion then prepares for the emphasis of 2:17-3:10: Paul's absence from the Thessalonians should not be interpreted as a consequence of his indifference toward them, for he has demonstrated his deep concern in many ways.

But this section has a wider connection to the rest of 1 Thessalonians as well. By showing that his life is consistent with the message that he preaches, Paul demonstrates how one who believes the gospel is to put it into practice. With this emphasis, this discussion will provide the basis for Paul's later exhortations to please God (4:1), love others (4:9), and work for one's own support (4:11-12).[4]

1. Paul's Motives (2:1-6)

¹You know, brothers, that our visit to you was not a failure. ²We had previously suffered and been insulted in Philippi, as you know, but with the help of our God we dared to tell you his gospel in spite of strong opposition. ³For the appeal we make does not spring from error or impure motives, nor are we trying to trick you. ⁴On the contrary, we speak as men approved by God to be entrusted

---

the issue in Abraham J. Malherbe, "'Gentle as a Nurse': The Stoic Background to 1 Thess. II," *NovT* 12 (1970) 203-204; and the more recent discussion in Steve Walton, "What Has Aristotle to Do with Paul? Rhetorical Criticism and 1 Thessalonians," *TynBul* 46 (1995) 229-249.

[4]Cf. the discussion of the moral example provided in this passage in Wanamaker, p. 91.

with the gospel. We are not trying to please men but God, who tests our hearts. ⁵You know we never used flattery, nor did we put on a mask to cover up greed –God is our witness. ⁶We were not looking for praise from men, not from you or anyone else.

As apostles of Christ we could have been a burden to you,

2:1 You know, brothers, that our visit to you

Here Paul picks up two aspects of 1:5 ("our gospel came to you not simply with words . . . . You know how we lived among you for your sake") for elaboration. For "you" he uses an emphatic Greek pronoun, αὐτοί (*autoi*), to draw attention to the fact that the Thessalonians' personal experience confirms what he is about to say. The effect might be paraphrased, "You of all people know . . . ." The term translated "visit" (εἴσοδος, *eisodos*) is the same term translated "reception" in 1:9. The difference in translation reflects the different focus of each text: in the earlier case Paul was focusing especially on the response to his work in Thessalonica, while here he focuses on his own behavior. But the repetition of the Greek term helps to tie the two sections together smoothly. Furthermore, because as the context will develop, Paul will contrast his "visit" with the typical behavior of professional orators of his time, it is likely that he uses *eisodos* as "quasi-technical term" for his professional conduct.[5]

was not a failure.

"Failure" translates the Greek term κενός (*kenos*), which indicates something empty of importance or significance. The point that Paul makes is not so much that his work was a success in terms of making converts or establishing a church, though such was in fact the case. Instead, he will emphasize that his manner of life demonstrated an authentic devotion to

---

[5]Winter, "Entries and Ethics," pp. 67-68.

God. Therefore, the gospel that he proclaimed was not like other, here-today-and-gone-tomorrow religious or philosophical messages; it reflected genuine approval from God, a message not with words alone but also with power (1:5). Because that approval will yield the result described in 1:10 — deliverance from God's wrath at Christ's coming — Paul's work is not vain but full of the most weighty significance for eternity (cf. 3:5).[6] This significance is stressed with the perfect-tense verb γέγονεν (*gegonen*, "was"), which points to the ongoing effect of Paul's work.

2:2 We had previously suffered and been insulted in Philippi, as you know,

The experiences that Paul recounts from Philippi, the site of his preaching just before his arrival in Thessalonica, are reflected in Acts 16:11-40. The two terms προπάσχω (*propaschō*, "suffer previously") and ὑβρίζω (*hybrizō*, "insult") summarize aptly Luke's account of those experiences, which involved not only beating and imprisonment (Acts 16:22-23) but also ethnic insults (Acts 16:20) and affronts to Paul's status as a Roman citizen (Acts 16:37).[7]

but with the help of our God we dared to tell you his gospel

---

[6]Wanamaker suggests that οὐ κενή (*ou kenē*, "not a failure") here must mean "either that his mission to the Thessalonians was characterized by power or that it produced good results" and opts for the latter since it is more consistent with Paul's other uses of the expression (p. 92; cf. 1 Cor 15:10, 58; 2 Cor 6:1; Gal 2:2; Phil 2:16; 1 Thess 3:5). Those passages, however, demonstrate an eschatological focus in Paul's use of the phrase. In each case Paul's work or the readers' reception of the gospel is "vain" or "a failure" if by receiving an incorrect gospel or abandoning faith in the true gospel, those to whom Paul preached should be lost for eternity. It should be stressed, then, that the focus is less on the number of converts than on what will happen to them eternally.

[7]"Opposition" at the end of v. 2 in the NIV translates ἀγών (*agōn*), literally "struggle." But the NIV rendering is sound, since the term most easily refers to the persecutions mentioned in the earlier part of the verse (cf. Wanamaker, p. 93).

in spite of strong opposition.

These experiences help to make Paul's point in two ways. Implicitly his willingness to suffer for the message that he preaches demonstrates his sincerity. Explicitly his boldness in continuing to preach in the face of similar opposition in Thessalonica (Acts 17:5-9) demonstrates God's power at work in him to proclaim God's genuine good news. Paul emphasizes that God was active in his Thessalonian ministry: the phrase "with the help of our God we dared" translates a Greek phrase that could more literally be rendered "we were made bold by God," and "his gospel" is literally "the gospel of God." Ironically, then, the opposition that Paul faced served to underline the genuinely divine power of his message all the more.[8]

2:3 For the appeal that we make

Insincerity would not endure the kind of treatment that Paul received in Philippi and Thessalonica. The readers can therefore be reminded of what they have believed from the beginning — that Paul's message comes from pure motives. The term translated "appeal," παράκλησις (*paraklēsis*), suggests a message that will make demands on the lives of the audience; it was used in the first century to refer to both religious messages and secular ones.[9] This term fits nicely with Paul's point: in contrast to others who might have made demands on the Thessalonians for their own gain, the demands of his message spring from the truth.

does not spring from error or impure motives, nor are we trying to trick you.

Paul combines three terms to emphasize this contrast, expressing the range of falsehood which many of the readers

---

[8]Malherbe has shown a difference here between Paul and Cynic philosophers of his day: the latter used persecution as a reason for their boldness in condemning their persecutors, while Paul showed that his boldness came from God in spite of his persecution ("Exhortations in First Thessalonians," pp. 248-249).

[9]Cf. Johannes Thomas, "παρακαλέω, παράκλησις," *EDNT*, 3:23-27.

might have experienced from others who claimed to have a message for them. "Error" translates the Greek πλάνη (*planē*), which implies the misleading of people. Originally derived from a verb which had the literal meaning "to cause to wander from the path," the metaphor in this word was long forgotten in Paul's time, the metaphorical sense having become the ordinary sense of the word.[10] "Impure motives" translates ἀκαθαρσία (*akatharsia*), literally "uncleanness," here reflecting the unclean heart of the preacher or teacher who seeks to deceive. Though this term often refers to sexual immorality, the context here suggests a broader reference. "Trickery" renders δόλος nicely: this term implies the deliberate use of deceptive methods.[11] What is significant about the terms, however, is not so much their individual meanings as the fact that Paul uses all of them to indicate that his behavior was free of dishonesty of any kind. This contrast shows that Paul is different from other, less honest religious and philosophical teachers and provides an example of the kind of life which his converts should lead.

2:4 On the contrary, we speak as men approved by God to be entrusted with the gospel.

The conjunction ἀλλά (*alla*), here translated "on the contrary," marks a distinct contrast with what has preceded. Emphasizing that God has initiated his ministry, Paul begins the first sentence here with the statement of God's endorsement, literally, "As we have been approved by God to be entrusted with the gospel, so we speak." The dramatic appearance of the Lord Jesus to Paul on the Damascus road and the events that immediately followed it, including Paul's call as an apostle (cf. Acts 9:15; 22:15, 21; 26:16-19), are what established for him his confidence that God had indeed entrusted him with the gospel. He is therefore compelled to the highest level of integrity in his ministry.

---

[10]Cf. *GELNTBSD*, § 31.8.
[11]Cf. *GELNTBSD*, § 88.154.

We are not trying to please men but God, who tests our hearts.
Having been called by God, he seeks to please him alone, unlike others who may seek the approval of their human audience for their own gain. Certainly the kind of opposition that Paul faced in Thessalonica would demonstrate that he did not seek to please people! And knowing that what is hidden to other people is not hidden to God, Paul purges his heart of the kind of deception catalogued in v. 3. If he had tried to deceive others, he would show by his actions that he did not truly believe that God could really know his true, inner self.

Paul uses a word play to underline the connection between his call and his behavior, using the same verb twice in this verse. The verb δοκιμάζω (*dokimazō*) can mean either to test in order to determine whether something is genuine or to accept something as having passed the test, that is, to approve. Paul uses the second sense to say that God has "approved" of him in his apostolic ministry (δεδοκιμάσμεθα, *dedokimasmetha*), and then the first meaning to indicate that God "tests" his heart (δοκιμάζοντι, *dokimazonti*). The first instance is in the Greek perfect tense, suggesting that God's approval is an action completed with a continuing effect, clearly referring to Paul's apostolic call noted above. The second is in the present tense, indicating a continuing action — God's ongoing examination of Paul's motives. Thus, Paul's confidence that God has "approved" of him as an apostle does not place him beyond scrutiny; instead, because of his call he is deeply conscious that God continually "proves" the content of his inner being. But this is not a perspective that belongs to apostles only; in 4:1 Paul will remind the readers that every Christian's objective is to please God continually.

2:5 You know we never used flattery,
"Flattery" as a persuasive method was well established[12]

---
[12]For examples of texts illustrating the practice of flattery among Greek rhetoricians, see the entry for κολακία [*sic*] in MM, p. 352; Malherbe, "'Gentle as a Nurse,'" pp. 206-207, 216.

among those who were trained in Greek rhetoric and might have been expected from an itinerant preacher like Paul. But because Paul sought to please God rather than other people, he refused to use praise to appeal to others' vanity. His confidence in his integrity on this point is sufficient that he appeals directly to the readers' knowledge of his behavior.

nor did we put on a mask to cover up greed — God is our witness.

Likewise, Paul did not misrepresent himself for material gain, a point which he will underline later in the letter as he recounts his labor to support himself (2:9). "Greed" here is πλεονεξία (*pleonexia*), literally a desire for more — either more than one needs or more than others have. The NIV's "put on a mask" renders the Greek πρόφασις (*prophasis*), actually a less metaphorical expression meaning either or "pretext" or "motive." The latter meaning is probably more consistent with this context; in this case the sense would be "nor did we act with a motive of greed."[13] The point in either case is clear, however: Paul's actions in Thessalonica were not a way to disguise his grasping for material gain.[14] And so, confident in God's ability to know the heart as in v. 4, Paul appeals to God's witness to corroborate what he says.

2:6 We were not looking for praise from men, not from you or anyone else.

Though the language shifts here somewhat from v. 4, the point of that verse is largely repeated here. Seeking either to be praised by humans or to please humans both reflect the same perspective which Paul rejects. As his ministry has

---

[13]Cf. the discussion of this term in Wanamaker, p. 97.

[14]*HCNT*, § 814, cites Aelius Aristides' (*Discourses*, 4) description of a hypocritical Cynic philosopher's greed: "For these are the men who believe . . . that to take is to be generous. They have achieved such wisdom, that they do not exact money, but they know how to take gifts which are the equivalent of money. And if ever someone appears to have sent too little, they always remain firm in their resolve."

begun with God's call and continues under God's scrutiny, he does not seek the human praise which might motivate others. Though that praise might still come from his converts or from others who would be impressed by Paul's manner or the success of his efforts, it is not what he pursues. Paul's indifference toward human praise also lies behind his later discussion in 1 Cor 1:18-2:5, where he indicates that he refuses to follow the standards of "wisdom" expected by Greek culture so that the gospel will not be obscured. Probably because he is not at this time under the attack which he later experienced from some in Corinth, in this passage Paul's stance is less defensive than in 1 Corinthians: he appeals simply and directly to his selfless behavior as the Thessalonians will remember it.

As apostles of Christ we could have been a burden to you,

There is some difference of opinion as to whether this clause should be taken as the conclusion of the sentence beginning in v. 5 (KJV, RV, ASV, RSV, NASB, TEV, NRSV, *UBSGNT*) or as the introduction to the sentence of v. 7 (NIV).[15] In favor of linking it to the earlier material is the fact that it is a circumstantial participial phrase parallel to the one in the first part of v. 6, where the conjunction οὔτε (*oute*, "neither") anticipates another item in the series. In addition, the fact that the next clause ("but we were gentle with you") begins with the conjunction ἀλλά (*alla*, "but, however") favors the rendering that begins a new sentence at that point. In this case the sense is concessive: "We were not looking for praise from men, not from you or anyone else, although as apostles of Christ we could have been a burden." The NIV has opted to see the conjunction as indicating a contrast between the main clause beginning in v. 7 and the participle in v. 6, an unusual though not entirely impossible construction. Though there is probably more to favor the rendering of the other

---

[15]Most editions of the Greek NT as well as the NRSV number verse 7 at this point also.

versions, the larger point is not significantly changed with the punctuation of the NIV.

And that larger point is a further elaboration of Paul's integrity. His status as an apostle was derived from the status of the Christ who called him. The Greek ἀπόστολος (*apostolos*) indicates a messenger or spokesman who derives authority from the one who sends him with the message. On the basis of that authority, Paul could have expected a variety of benefits from those to whom he preached — the praise of those to whom he preached, as mentioned previously, but especially the right to be supported financially, as he elaborated in 1 Cor 9.[16] Most itinerant philosophers and religious teachers in Paul's time supported themselves either through fees which they charged or through the patronage of wealthy people. This practice, however, created the appearance, if not the reality, that the teacher's obligation to those who supported him would compel him to compromise the truth.

The point that Paul makes in 1 Cor 9 is that he willingly surrenders his rights for the sake of winning converts to the gospel. Implicitly he makes the same point here: to avoid any suggestion of greed or other self-seeking, he voluntarily relinquished his rights to money or prominence in order to benefit those to whom he preached. But explicitly he stresses another aspect of this situation: he did not want his financial support to be a "burden," literally a heavy weight (βάρος, *baros*), to the Thessalonians (cf. 2 Cor 11:9). Perhaps reflected here is the general poverty of the Macedonian Christians which Paul recounts in 2 Cor 8:2, though Paul also refused to

---

[16]Paul's discussion in Phil 4:10-20 of the monetary gift received from the Philippian church illustrates that he made it a practice to accept financial support from churches already established though he refused it from the people to whom he was currently preaching. In this regard it is important to note that in Acts 18:1-5 Paul supported himself in Corinth by tentmaking until the arrival of Silas and Timothy from Macedonia, presumably bearing an earlier gift from Philippi (2 Cor 11:9; Phil 4:10, 15). Cf. the discussion in Janet M. Everts, "Financial Support," *DPL*, pp. 295-300.

take money from those to whom he was preaching in other cities (cf. 2 Cor 12:14-18).

The plural "apostles" in this verse has caused some discussion as to whether Paul included Silvanus and Timothy as apostles. Clearly the plural could naturally refer to them. Could Paul have used the word apostle to refer to them? In its less restrictive sense, the term could be used to refer to someone sent out as a missionary with a divine commission; such may be the case here. Paul does occasionally use the term "apostle" to refer to persons other than "the twelve" and himself (1 Cor 15:7; 2 Cor 8:23; Rom 16:7; Phil 2:25; cf. Acts 14:4, 14). But more commonly in the New Testament "apostle" was used as a technical term to refer to the twelve apostles appointed by Jesus, perhaps to others who saw the risen Lord and were commissioned by him (including Barnabas and Silvanus?), and to Paul, the "one abnormally born" (1 Cor 15:8). Because Paul habitually uses the first person plural "we" throughout 1 Thessalonians to refer primarily to himself, it is likely that he uses the plural here for consistency, referring only to himself as an apostle. But regardless of the specific sense and reference here, the larger issue of apostolic authority and uniqueness in Paul's letters is clear. The fact that Paul goes to great lengths elsewhere to insist on his own distinct authority as an apostle, to equate his authority with that of others like Peter, and to distinguish that authority from the claims of rivals demonstrates that the term cannot be reduced to mean merely "missionary" or "church planter" when it is used in the narrow, technical sense. Significantly, Paul referred to himself as the one to whom the Lord appeared "last of all" (1 Cor 15:8). Hence, as the last to have "seen the Lord" (1 Cor 9:1), he had apostolic authority which none who came later could claim.[17]

---

[17]Cf. Bruce, p. 31; Paul W. Barnett, "Apostle," *DPL*, pp. 45-51.

2. Paul's Activity (2:7-12)

⁷but we were gentle among you, like a mother caring for her little children. ⁸We loved you so much that we were delighted to share with you not only the gospel of God but our lives as well, because you had become so dear to us. ⁹Surely you remember, brothers, our toil and hardship; we worked night and day in order not to be a burden to anyone while we preached the gospel of God to you.

¹⁰You are witnesses, and so is God, of how holy, righteous and blameless we were among you who believed. ¹¹For you know that we dealt with each of you as a father deals with his own children, ¹²encouraging, comforting and urging you to live lives worthy of God, who calls you into his kingdom and glory.

2:7 but we were gentle among you,

A difficult textual variant occurs in this verse. The word translated "gentle" (ἤπιοι, *ēpioi*) appears in a number of early manuscripts as "infants" (νήπιοι, *nēpioi*). Deciding which reading is more likely the original is difficult for several reasons. Because the preceding word ends with the Greek letter *nu*, a copyist with the original *nēpioi* could have inadvertently left out the second *nu*, especially since in early manuscripts no spaces were left between words. However, the *nu* could also have been inadvertently doubled to alter an original *ēpioi*. Clearly, "gentle" makes for a more consistent sense in context, and because it was widely used to describe an ideal philosopher, Paul may have deliberately chosen the term here.[18] But the jarring mixed metaphor produced by "infants" is just the kind of thing that one finds elsewhere in Paul's letters (e.g., Gal 4:19, where both Paul and the Galatians are figuratively giving birth).

Since it is usually assumed that scribes corrected the text

---

[18] Cf. Malherbe, "'Gentle as a Nurse,'" p. 211.

to make it easier rather than harder to understand, textual scholarship usually favors the more difficult reading, in this case "infants." And the best manuscripts tend to favor this reading also.[19] On the other hand, many regard "infants" as simply too difficult to be likely here, noting especially that "gentle" contrasts nicely with the arrogance mentioned in v. 6. Nevertheless, since in the preceding phrase Paul has mentioned ἀπόστολοι (*apostoloi*, "apostles"), the contrast in sense with *nēpioi* may have provided the motivation for this otherwise difficult word. If this reading is indeed correct, then Paul's contrast is sharp: instead of behaving as important apostles, he and his associates were like tiny infants.

The general sense of Paul's expression is the same no matter which reading is the original. Paul's humble behavior as a missionary is a reflection of the grace that he preaches. As an apostle, Paul could demand the honor due his office. But because he has standing as an apostle only because of God's grace, humility — either like an infant's (cf. Mark 10:15) or expressed in gentleness — is the rule for him. In fact, the entire gospel message, based on Christ's love (2 Cor 5:14) and self-sacrificial humility (Phil 2:6-11), compels such behavior.[20]

like a mother caring for her little children.

Therefore, instead of seeking his own benefit, Paul sought to nurture and protect his converts. He compares himself to a τροφός (*trophos*), a term which could be used either for a nursemaid who substituted for a mother or for the mother

---

[19] In favor of νήπιοι are the third-century papyrus fragment 𝔓[65], the original hand of Codex Sinaiticus, Codex Vaticanus, and the original hand of Codex Bezae. For a full discussion see Bruce M. Metzger, *A Textual Commentary on the Greek New Testament*, (corrected ed.; New York: United Bible Societies, 1975), pp. 629-630.

[20] Malherbe notes that Cynic philosophers taught that a speaker must be gentle with an audience in order to be bold with them ("'Gentle as a Nurse,'" p. 211). The powerful theological basis for Paul's behavior — certainly more important for him than the practices of the Cynics, helpful as they might be — must not be missed, however.

herself.²¹ "Caring for" translates θάλπω (*thalpō*), a term which literally meant "to warm" but was used as a figure of speech to indicate sustaining, watchful care (cf. Eph 5:29). Such love will later in the letter be the model for the readers' own behavior toward each other (1 Thess 3:12), motivated as it is by the same gospel.

2:8 We loved you so much that we were delighted to share with you not only the gospel of God but our lives as well, because you had become so dear to us.

Because the gospel is the message of God's love, Paul is compelled to give to his hearers much more than just the message itself, for to do less would put the messenger's behavior at odds with the message. Paul begins this statement by describing his feeling toward the Thessalonians ("loved") with the verb ὁμείρομαι (*homeiromai*). This word is unusual, found only here in the New Testament. There is evidence that it belonged to the dialect of Cilicia, Paul's home region.²² If so, then it probably indicates Paul's deep feeling for the Thessalonians, feelings grounded in the relationship they shared as Christians. Another alternative is that the word is related to the cult of Dionysus in Thessalonica, in which case Paul borrows it to imply that genuine affection of this kind is found only through the gospel.²³ The Thessalonians became "dear" or "beloved" (ἀγαπητός, *agapētos*) to Paul because as Christians they were "beloved" of God (1:4). Thus, the shar-

---

²¹Cf. BAGD, pp. 827-828; *GELNTBSD*, § 35.52; Günter Haufe, "τροφός," *EDNT*, 3:371. Bruce notes that the emphatic possessive ἑαυτῆς (*heautēs*) favors a mother who nurtures "her own" children (p. 31), but Donfried suggests that "nurse" may be the sense because of a potential allusion to the cult of Dionysus, popular in Thessalonica, in which female attendants called "nurses" by Homer played a role (*Shorter Pauline Letters*, pp. 13-14). Wanamaker calls attention to the fact that Paul here reflects the generally positive view of women, especially in a maternal role, held in his time (p. 101).

²²Norbert Baumert, "Ὁμείρομεμοι in 1Thess 2,8," *Bib* 68 (1987) 552-563.

²³Donfried, *Shorter Pauline Letters*, p. 14.

ing of his life is not merely a necessity of the gospel but something pleasing to Paul, motivated by the bond between him and his brothers and sisters in Christ. The message of God's love in the gospel is so much a part of his life that sharing his life comes naturally.

2:9 Surely you remember, brothers, our toil and hardship;
The sharing of his life which Paul mentions in the previous verse is no mere abstraction. It took shape as he gave his time and energy. Here Paul alludes to his practice of supporting himself so that he could preach without placing financial demands on his audience. As he explained later in 1 Corinthians 9:1-18, he willingly surrendered his right to such support because receiving money for preaching had the potential to hinder the gospel. His work, of course, was making tents, evidently something that he did not only in Corinth, as Acts 18:1-3 relates, but in many other cities where he preached, including Thessalonica.[24] Though certainly an honest occupation, as manual labor tentmaking was not socially prominent in the Hellenistic world.[25] As a religious teacher, therefore, Paul took a voluntary step down the social ladder by engaging in such work.

The extent of Paul's labor is evident here in the terms he uses. The two terms for work, κόπος (*kopos*) and μόχθος (*mochthos*), are paired together also in 2 Thess 3:8 and 2 Cor 11:27, in each case recounting Paul's own work in connection

---

[24]Ronald F. Hock notes that Paul's trade may have included leatherworking of various kinds (*The Social Context of Paul's Ministry: Tentmaking and Apostleship* [Minneapolis: Fortress, 1980], pp. 20-21).

[25]Malherbe, *Paul and the Thessalonians*, pp. 55-56. Martin Hengel has argued that Paul's Roman citizenship and family traditions (Rom 11:1; Phil 3:5) indicates some social standing (*The Pre-Christian Paul* [Philadelphia: Trinity Press International, 1991], pp. 15-17). But this observation probably underlines all the more Paul's social self-demotion to support himself as a craftsman. Stanley K. Stowers notes the complications which Paul's lack of social status could have created for his preaching ("Social Status, Public Speaking and Private Teaching: The Circumstances of Paul's Preaching Activity," *NovT* 26 [1984], 68-82).

with the gospel. Both terms imply demanding, tiring work, and the combination emphasizes the idea.

we worked night and day in order not to be a burden to anyone while we preached the gospel of God to you.
Both here and in 2 Thess 3:8 Paul speaks of such labor "night and day"; similarly in 2 Cor 11:27 he speaks of going without sleep. We can probably conclude that Paul worked at his trade during the day and perhaps before sunrise or after sunset as well, undoubtedly sharing the gospel with those who did business with him, and spent other daylight and evening hours preaching and teaching (cf. 1:3).[26] As in v. 6b, Paul's motive for this exertion is his relationship to the Thessalonian Christians: he wanted to relieve them of any burden they might take on to support him.

This labor is connected directly to the preaching of the gospel, which is grammatically the most prominent idea in the verse. The verb translated "preached" here is κηρύσσω (*kērussō*), a term borrowed from the secular sphere where it was used for the proclamation of an official message from a ruler or other person of power. Because of that association, the term implies some dignity for the person doing the proclaiming. Thus, the term stands in contrast with Paul's description of his labor, since one with so important a role as a herald of the gospel of God would probably not be expected to support himself by manual labor, especially since artisans like tentmakers often earned barely enough to survive and were regarded as little better than slaves among many in the higher social classes.[27] However, in light of what that

---

[26]Hock has shown that artisans like tentmakers often had to work from dawn to dusk to support themselves at a subsistence level (*Social Context*, pp. 31-37).

[27]Bruce is among many who observe that rabbinic literature indicated that one who studied Torah should also have a secular occupation (*Pirke Aboth* 2.2; Bruce, p. 34). However, because these statements come from the second century A.D., it is not certain that they reflect the views of Paul's contemporaries (so Hock, *Social Context*, pp. 22-23; but see Hengel, *Pre-Christian Paul*, pp. 15-16).

gospel is, Paul's self-support is perfectly logical; it embodied the humble self-sacrifice of Christ and removed an obstacle to the acceptance of the gospel. The good news of what God has done in Christ had transformed the entire network of society and its expectations for Paul.

This reminder of Paul's manner of life among the Thessalonians further reinforces his own sincerity, which in turn will strengthen the Thessalonians' confidence in the gospel which Paul preached. In addition, it serves as an example of the kind of life which they themselves will be exhorted to lead (4:11; 2 Thess 3:8). Paul is not the only one whose life is to be transformed by the gospel!

2:10 You are witnesses, and so is God,

Repeatedly since v. 1 Paul has appealed directly to the Thessalonians' knowledge of his behavior: "you know" recurs almost like a refrain in this section (vv. 1, 2, 5, 11), and in v. 9 Paul calls on the readers to "remember." Here we see the climax of that reiterated appeal, as Paul calls on the readers to serve as witnesses. The concept that two or three witnesses were needed to establish the truth of a charge (Deut 17:6; 19:15; cf. 2 Cor 13:1; 1 Tim 5:19) probably has influenced Paul's rhetoric here. He appeals to the readers and to God himself (cf. Rom 1:9) as multiple, reliable witnesses that everything he has said to this about his behavior is true. The punctuation of the NIV in this verse reflects the Greek sentence structure. First Paul declares that the readers are witnesses; then, emphasizing again that he lives as he does to please God, he adds God's testimony to theirs. This appeal brings to a rousing close Paul's description of his behavior, emphasizing that its truthfulness cannot be doubted.

of how holy, righteous and blameless we were

As he has elsewhere, Paul lists off several terms to summarize his behavior.[28] "Holy" is ὁσίως (*hosiōs*), which would

---

[28]The terms are adverbs, instead of the adjective forms which would

suggest a proper respect for the deity. "Righteous" is δικαίως (*dikaiōs*), indicating adherence to the requirements of the law and justice; following "holy" it probably indicates adherence to human law.[29] "Blameless" is ἀμέμπτως (*amemptōs*), a word which occurs in the New Testament only twice, both in 1 Thessalonians (cf. 5:23); the related form ἄμεμπτος (*amemptos*) occurs once in 1 Thessalonians (cf. 3:13) and four times in other books. While the term would not for Paul imply absolute moral perfection in his behavior in Thessalonica (cf. Rom 3:10, 23; 7:14-25), it does indicate a serious assertion that his conduct would cause him no shame before either human or divine witnesses. Taken together, these three terms underscore Paul's unimpeachable integrity in all aspects of his life. Such is the same integrity which Paul prays will belong to the Thessalonians through God's power (2:12; 3:13; 5:23).

among you who believed.

"You who believed" could be more awkwardly but accurately translated, "you who are believers," since the present participle πιστεύουσιν (*pisteuousin*) emphasizes continuing action. This expression suggests that Paul's "witnesses" are already giving their testimony about him through their continuing faith in Jesus Christ as a result of his preaching. It also provides the basis for the fatherly concern of v. 11 and for the encouragement to righteous living in v. 12 — both are consequences of genuine belief in Christ.

2:11 For you know that we dealt with each of you as a father deals with his own children,

Again Paul reminds the readers of what they "know," and again he uses the image of a nurturing parent (cf. v. 7) to

---

better fit the sentence structure. Wanamaker suggests that the adverbial forms stress the behavior of the missionaries as opposed to their persons (p. 105). However, this distinction may be overly subtle.

[29]Friedrich Hauck, ὅσιος, κτλ," *TDNT*, 5:490.

evoke his relationship with the readers.³⁰ And again, he uses emphatic terms to underline the concepts. As a father, Paul has not played favorites; his care has extended to "each one" of the Thessalonian Christians. The emphatic possessive ἑαυτοῦ (*heautou*, "his own") stresses further this precious bond between Paul and these believers, his genuine children because of their faith in Jesus Christ. In the Greek text this verse is grammatically subordinate to "how holy, righteous and blameless we were" in v. 10; thus, this verse continues and elaborates on the description there.

2:12 encouraging, comforting and urging you

Paul's fatherly actions focus particularly on the transformation of his spiritual children's conduct, described here with another series of terms, again a grammatically subordinate continuation of v. 10. In v. 3 Paul had referred to the basis of his "appeal," (παράκλησις, *paraklēsis*); here he uses a related verb, παρακαλέω (*parakaleō*, "encourage") with a similar meaning. This term is frequent in Paul's letters, occurring over fifty times, including ten in 1 and 2 Thessalonians. Here it indicates encouragement toward a particular objective, namely godly living. "Appealing" "exhorting" or "urging" are fitting alternate translations in this context. "Comforting" is from παραμυθέομαι (*paramytheomai*), a word similar in meaning to *parakaleō* but stressing more particularly the friendly and consoling nature of Paul's encouragement. "Urging" translates μαρτύρομαι (*martyromai*), a term which implies a strong emphasis or insistence.³¹ As a word related to "witnesses" (μάρτυρες, *martyres*) in v. 10, this term provides a fitting stylistic touch to round out a statement that began with a cognate expression.

---

³⁰Bruce notes that as early as Chrysostom and Pelagius it was noted that, consistent with the ancient view of gender roles in parenting, Paul compares himself to a mother when referring to cherishing his converts and to a father when referring to instructing them (cf. 1 Cor 4:14-15; Bruce, p. 36).

³¹*GELNTBSD*, § 33.319.

to live lives worthy of God,

The goal of this exhortation is a life lived in consistent response to God's initiative in salvation. "To live" is from περιπατέω (*peripateō*), literally meaning "to walk," a common way in Greek influenced by Hebrew to express the manner of one's life or one's behavior. Paul speaks of walking "in a manner worthy" elsewhere (Eph 4:1; Phil 1:27; Col 1:10), in each case calling the readers to put into practice the reality of what Christ has done in their lives. In this way the expression for Paul never suggests an attempt to earn salvation by proving to be "good enough" for it. The stress is the opposite: the worthiness consists entirely in responding to salvation already received by practicing outwardly the blessings which one has received inwardly.

who calls you into his kingdom and glory.

Normally Paul speaks of the "call" of God in the aorist tense, referring to the initial call of God issued in the preaching of the gospel. Here, however, the verb is in the present tense, implying continuing action. The most likely sense of the term here, then, is God's ongoing call of his people to their final objective at the return of Christ. So Paul's emphasis is on his exhortation that their behavior in the present is to be conformed to what they will receive in the future.

This future Paul refers to as God's "kingdom and glory." "Kingdom" is an especially important term in the theology of the New Testament. Prominent in the preaching of John the Baptist and especially of Jesus, the Kingdom of God refers to the extension of God's reign or rule over all humanity. In essence, it is the fulfillment of God's promise in the Old Testament to reverse the effects of human sin by bringing salvation and judgment and restoring the world to its original, ideal state. In Jesus' teaching the kingdom was both a present or nearly present reality (e.g., Luke 11:25) but something that was also yet to come in the future (e.g., Matt 6:10). In other words, God's promise was already fulfilled as Jesus appeared and especially as he arose from the dead, but the completion and fullness of that promise awaits Christ's return.[32] This is precisely Paul's usage of the term as well. For Christians the kingdom of God is already a reality that affects their behavior (Rom 14:17; 1 Cor 4:20). On the other hand, it is also, as in this passage, something yet to be experienced: God is still in the process of calling believers into it (cf. 2 Thess 1:5; 1 Cor 6:9-10; 15:50; Gal 5:21; Eph 5:5; Col 3:24).[33] Likewise, glory — the manifestation of God's grandeur, majesty and power as he is active in creation and his people — is for Paul something that is already a part of the present experience of Christians as in Christ God has fulfilled the promise of the old covenant to reveal his glory to all the world (2 Cor 3:6-18; Hab 2:14). Yet that glory is also yet to be revealed in its fullness at Christ's return (cf. Col 1:27; 3:4).[34] By using these terms as the future objectives of God's ongoing call here, Paul concludes this section, as he did in 1:10, with a reference to the return of Christ, preparing again for the crucial discussion of eschatology in 4:13-5:11.

B. THE THESSALONIANS' ENDURANCE OF PERSECUTION (2:13-16)

Having recounted his own actions in Thessalonica, Paul returns his focus to the lives of the Thessalonian Christians themselves. The genuineness of his own life, as demonstrated by his behavior in preaching the gospel in Thessalonica, can now be seen in the lives of his converts, the readers of the epistle. Having previously offered thanksgiving for the Thessalonians' faithful labor for the Lord (1:2ff), Paul now offers specific thanksgiving for their endurance of persecu-

---

[32]Cf. Chrys C. Caragounis, "Kingdom of God/Heaven," *DJG*, pp. 417-430; G. E. Ladd, *A Theology of the New Testament* (Grand Rapids: Eerdmans, 1974) pp. 57-119.

[33]Cf. Larry J. Kreitzer, "Kingdom of God/Christ," *DPL*, pp. 524-526.

[34]Cf. Richard Gaffin, "Glory, Glorification," *DPL*, pp. 348-350.

tion, coupled with a vigorous condemnation of the persecutors.

These verses have generated considerable controversy in critical scholarship because of what they have been taken to indicate about the relationship between Christians and Jews. Along with certain other texts in the New Testament, this text has been understood by many Christians to condemn the Jewish nation as a whole for the crucifixion of Jesus. The consequent notion that the Jewish people are a "deicide race" has been used at several points in history to justify all kinds of repression and violence against Jews living in predominantly Christian areas. Some modern scholars, finding such antisemitism to be morally repugnant, have sought to marginalize the significance of these verses for Christians. Some have gone so far as to assert that this text and others like it should be altered or excluded from modern Bibles to eliminate the offense of antisemitism.[35]

Others have noted that this text is difficult to square with Paul's remarks about Israel in Rom 11:25-27 and that it contains certain linguistic peculiarities. Arguing that because of these factors this text could not have been composed by Paul, these scholars propose that the text is a post-Pauline scribal insertion and not an authentic part of the epistle.[36] Thus, the antisemitism of the text is a reflection of the views of a later scribe, not of Paul himself.

Several observations about these controversial points need to be made here. The first concerns the real object of condemnation in these verses. If, as many have assumed, these

---

[35]E.g., Norman A. Beck, *Mature Christianity in the 21st Century: The Recognition and Repudiation of the Anti-Jewish Polemic of the New Testament* (rev. ed.; New York: Crossroad, 1994), pp. 81-84.

[36]The arguments against the authenticity of the section are set forth in the following: Birger A. Pearson, "I Thessalonians 2:13-16: A Deutero-Pauline Interpolation," *HTR* 64 (1971) 79-94; Hendrikus Boers, "The Form Critical Study of Paul's Letters. I Thessalonians as a Case Study," *NTS* 22 (1976) 140-158; Daryl Schmidt, "1 Thess 2:13-16: Linguistic Evidence for an Interpolation," *JBL* 102 (1983) 269-279.

verses sentence all Jews to eternal punishment for the crucifixion of Jesus, then something which can fairly be termed antisemitism is probably to be found here. But several factors, discussed in the comments below, indicate that the word "Jews" in v. 14 refers not to the Jewish people as a whole but to the specific residents of Judea who instigated the death of Jesus and the persecution of Christians in Jerusalem. What the text affirms, then, is not the condemnation of all Jews but of those who have opposed the saving actions of God by crucifying Jesus and persecuting his followers. This perspective is thus entirely consistent with Paul's statement about the salvation of "all Israel" in Rom 11:25-27, a salvation which is based on repentance and faith in Jesus.

Secondly, the flow of the context is entirely coherent when these verses are included. After discussing his previous contact with the readers (2:1-12), Paul then reflects on their recent circumstances (vv. 13-16) to explain the basis for his desire to revisit Thessalonica (vv. 17-20). Indeed, the emphatic first-person pronoun "we also" (ἡμεῖς, *hēmeis*) in v. 17 is best explained if Paul is here resuming a discussion of his experiences after having shifted briefly to the experiences of the readers in vv. 13-16.

Thirdly, although the complex linguistic issues in these verses cannot be taken up in detail, some observations are in order.[37] Careful analysis of the language of this text indicates that though the entire text is consistent with Paul's style elsewhere, vv. 15-16 nevertheless contain several features unusual for Paul. These are best explained if, as Paul appears to have done elsewhere, he has here inserted into his letter a quotation of an early Christian hymn or traditional saying (cf. Rom 1:1-4; Phil 2:6-11). The frequency with which early Christians met persecution certainly makes it likely that they composed and repeated hymns or proverbs in response to their suffering, as

---

[37]A full discussion of the linguistic issues regarding the authenticity of this text can be found in my article "The Authenticity of 1 Thessalonians 2.13-16: Additional Evidence," *JSNT* 42 (1991) 79-98.

did the Hebrew Psalmists (e.g., Ps 137), in which they expressed their confidence in God's final punishment of their persecutors.

Formally the text constitutes a renewed thanksgiving similar to the one which begins the epistle (1:2ff). As he did earlier, Paul uses the thanksgiving section, common to letters in his era, as a means of announcing the letter's major themes. This renewal of the thanksgiving gives opportunity to expand upon earlier themes in a more specific way.

Previously (1:2-10), Paul had given thanks for the Thessalonians' genuine reception of the gospel as displayed in their behavior. The same themes are sounded here, but the focus on their behavior is narrowed to their endurance of persecution. This, Paul says, indicates the genuineness of their faith, since their experience of suffering is the same as that of the very first Christians in Jerusalem, the Old Testament prophets, Paul, and even the Lord Jesus himself. By aligning the experience of the Thessalonians with that of God's people in the present and the past, Paul counters any fears that the Thessalonians might have had concerning the meaning of their suffering. For those who mistakenly understood that becoming a Christian meant that suffering would vanish and the end-time blessings of God would be experienced immediately in their fullness, Paul insists that until the Lord's return, Christians will be persecuted for their faith. Indeed, such an experience does not indicate that the promises of the gospel are untrue or that the sufferer does not actually belong to the Lord. Rather, persecution is a sign of the genuineness of one's faith, for it is the common experience of God's people at all times, including the Lord Jesus himself. Hence, Paul can offer thanks for the Thessalonians' suffering because it is another sign that they have truly received the genuine word of God.

But Paul's point is not that the suffering of Christians will never end. This section closes with a solemn pronouncement that the persecutors will be judged for their stubborn opposition to the gospel. As he did at the close of the first thanksgiving (1:10) and of the section preceding this one (2:12), so here Paul concludes this section with a statement about the consummation of God's work at Christ's return. Having spoken before of the Christians' deliverance from God's wrath, Paul here reminds the readers that God's wrath is imminent for those who oppose his gospel and his people. For the Thessalonian Christians that statement serves as a reminder that they can look forward not only to the end of their suffering but also to their vindication before their enemies when the Lord returns.

1. Their Genuine Reception of the Word (2:13)

¹³And we also thank God continually because, when you received the word of God, which you heard from us, you accepted it not as the word of men, but as it actually is, the word of God, which is at work in you who believe.

2:13 And we also thank God continually

The Greek text of the verse begins with the expression καὶ διὰ τοῦτο (*kai dia touto*; "and because of this"). For the sake of clarity the NIV translators omitted this phrase, understanding it simply as a duplicate of the clause at the end of the verse ("because, when you received . . ."). But the preposition διά (*dia*) in this phrase is unlikely to have precisely the same force as the conjunction ὅτι (*hoti*, "because") at the end of the verse. The preposition is used to indicate not so much what Paul gave thanks for, namely the Thessalonians' genuine reception of the gospel mentioned later, but the reason or stimulus which impels Paul's giving of thanks.[38] This reason is to be found in the preceding context, where Paul sets forth the purity of his own motives and actions in declaring the true word of God. So here Paul indicates that he offers thanks for

---

[38] The specific linguistic arguments can be found in Weatherly, "Authenticity," pp. 81-82.

the Thessalonians' faith in Jesus because, as he indicated earlier, to produce such faith is the focus of his life and ministry.

As in 1:2-3 Paul stresses that his thanksgiving for the Thessalonians is continual. By repeating here a statement of thanksgiving, Paul underlines his concern for the Thessalonian church despite his untimely absence. Though forced to leave and unable to return, Paul wants to assure the congregation of his ongoing commitment to their progress as Christians. Paul uses the emphatic pronoun ἡμεῖς (*hēmeis*) in the subject of this clause, which probably serves to stress this point further: we ourselves [though not with you] give thanks [for your faith]. The Thessalonians should therefore ignore any doubts about Paul, such as that his absence indicated indifference to the their welfare.

because, when you received the word of God, which you heard from us, you accepted it not as the word of men, but as it actually is, the word of God, which is at work in you who believe.

The term translated as "received," παραλαμβάνω (*paralambanō*), is one that Paul uses elsewhere in the Thessalonian epistles (1 Thess 4:1; 2 Thess 3:6) as well as in his other epistles (1 Cor 11:23; 15:1, 3; Gal 1:9; Phil 4:9; Col 2:6) for the reception of Christian oral teaching. This verb, often coupled with the complementary term παραδίδωμι (*paradidōmi*; "deliver"), was commonly used for the transmission of a stable body of oral teaching, such as the legal traditions of Jewish rabbis. Paul used this nomenclature to refer to his own preaching and teaching, thereby stressing that his message came from an authoritative source — apostles, like himself, chosen by the Lord and witnesses of his resurrection — and was consistent, the same teaching delivered in all places and by all the apostles. It is the original gospel message, without adulteration; consequently it can indeed be regarded, as he indicates here, as the word of God, not merely a message with human origin (cf. 1:5; Gal 1:12).

The Thessalonian Christians were not mistaken, then, in

accepting (δέχομαι [*dechomai*], signifying beyond *paralambanō* their receiving of the gospel with faith) the gospel as God's word, for, Paul asserts, that is what it actually is. Paul emphasizes this point by repetition: the two occurrences of the phrase "the word of God" in the NIV represent a repeated phrase in the Greek text. That it is the divine word is further indicated by what it does: it is continually at work in those who are believing, producing the qualities and behaviors which Paul mentioned in the first thanksgiving section (1:3), especially the "endurance inspired by hope" in the face of the persecution described in the following verse.

In Galatians Paul deals at length with those who argued that his message was merely his own and not God's (Gal 1:10-2:21), and similar issues arise in the Corinthian epistles as well (1 Cor 1:18-2:16; 2 Cor 11:1-12:21). Here his insistence on his faithful transmission of the gospel and on its divine origin seem not so much to answer the objections of critics as to reassure the readers whose suffering has caused them to doubt the truth of their belief. Lest they conclude that their suffering means that their faith is false, Paul reminds them of their initial response of faith to the gospel and of what the gospel has produced in their lives since.[39] This provides the basis for his reflection on their persecution in the verses following.

2. Their Imitation of the Judean Christians (2:14)

[14]For you, brothers, became imitators of God's churches in Judea, which are in Christ Jesus: You suffered from your own countrymen the same things those churches suffered from the Jews,

---

[39]The contrast between "word of men" and "word of God" certainly does not here imply that apart from some distinct work of God's Spirit the gospel can be experienced merely as a human word; cf. Marshall, "Election and Calling," p. 266.

2:14 For you, brothers, became imitators of God's churches in Judea, which are in Christ Jesus:
Once again Paul uses the emphatic personal pronoun, this time to refer to the Thessalonians (ὑμεῖς, *humeis*, "you"). Here the emphasis serves to shift the focus from Paul to the Thessalonian Christians. The effect of the gospel can be seen in their endurance of persecution, an experience which they share with the original churches in Judea. The reference to the Thessalonians as "imitators" of the Judean churches parallels the earlier remark in 1:6, where Paul himself was the one imitated. There the imitation was direct: in receiving the gospel the Thessalonians did indeed follow the example they saw in Paul. Here the expression may be used more loosely, simply indicating the common experience of both groups of Christians. However, the fact that Paul refers so briefly to the persecution of Christians in Judea could indicate that the Thessalonians had heard accounts of the Judean churches from Paul and his associates and so could be said to "imitate" consciously their example in suffering. Apparently something much like the early chapters of Acts formed part of Paul's instruction of his converts — and may have provided source material for Luke's later composition of those chapters.

The basis of the Thessalonians' "imitation" of their Judean brothers and sisters is their common identity "in Christ Jesus." This common and important Pauline phrase is the last in the string of words which identifies the "churches" and so has a position of importance for what follows. It is the fact that both the Judean and the Thessalonian Christians are "in Christ" that explains their persecution. Their unity in Christ means that they will suffer as did the Lord to whom they belong (v. 15). Consequently, far from causing them to doubt the gospel, persecution should affirm for the readers that they truly belong to the Lord.

You suffered from your own countrymen the same things those churches suffered from the Jews,
It has been widely assumed that Paul compares the

Thessalonians' persecution to the earlier Judean persecution because in both cases the Christians were persecuted by Jews. However, the phrase "in Judea," a geographical expression rather than an ethnic one, indicates that the point of comparison is not that both are persecuted by Jews but that both are persecuted by the people in their own regions. Thus, "countrymen" refers to others living in Thessalonica, whether Jews or Gentiles; in fact, the term would be most unusual if in fact it referred to Jews alone as "countrymen" of a church that included many Gentiles (see comments on 1:9 above). The expression is therefore consistent with the portrayal in Acts of one phase of the Thessalonian persecution, where Jewish opponents enlist a mob of rabble from the marketplace to riot against the Christians (Acts 17:5). The same observation applies to the word translated "the Jews" ('Ιουδαῖοι, *Ioudaioi*). Though "Jews" in a modern context refers most commonly to the people of a particular religious and ethnic group, the Greek term in the first century indicated first of all the people from a particular place, namely Judeans.[40] Since that geographical orientation is primary in the context, it should be understood as Paul's intention for the term here. Thus, it signifies not all "Jews" everywhere but those in Judea in particular who are said to have persecuted Christians.

Furthermore, it is important to note that both the persecutors and those persecuted in Judea were ethnic Jews. Paul in no way ignores that point; instead, he uses the general expression "the Jews/Judeans" as such terms were commonly used by Greek writers to refer to a specific group of such people understood from the context. Josephus, for example, employs the word to designate specifically those Jews who fought against Rome in the rebellion of AD 66-70, even in contexts where they are distinguished from other Jews who had no part in the uprising (e.g., *Jewish Wars* 2.466; 5.109-10; 6.71-79,

---

[40]Cf. Malcolm Lowe, "Who Were the ΙΟΥΔΑΙΟΙ?" *NovT* 18 (1976) 101-130.

251-53).⁴¹ The implication of all this is that in these verses Paul does not condemn Jews generally but those who have opposed the saving work of God by rejecting Jesus and the prophets, persecuting Christians, and hindering the gospel. For Paul, as for the other New Testament writers, salvation for the Jew as well as for the Gentile is based on the response of faith to the gospel of Jesus (Rom 1:16).

3. The Continuity of Persecution Age to Age (2:15-16)

¹⁵**who killed the Lord Jesus and the prophets and also drove us out. They displease God and are hostile to all men ¹⁶in their effort to keep us from speaking to the Gentiles so that they may be saved. In this way they always heap up their sins to the limit. The wrath of God has come upon them at last.ᵃ**

ᵃ*16 Or them fully*

2:15 who killed the Lord Jesus and the prophets and also drove us out.

The series of statements in vv. 15-16 contain a number of unusual features: the language is rhythmic, the structure is parallel, certain expressions are similar to ones found in the synoptic Gospels (Matt 23:29-38; 24:2b; Luke 11:49-50), and other expressions are not typical of Paul ("killed the Lord Jesus," "drove out"). Taken together, these may indicate that Paul has here incorporated a well known Christian hymn or some other poetic tradition in circulation among the churches.⁴² If this is indeed the case, then the quotation would serve to remind the readers that the proper perspective on their persecution could be found in teachings which they had already "received" (v. 13).

---

⁴¹Cf. my *Jewish Responsibility for the Death of Jesus in Luke-Acts* (JSNTSup 106; Sheffield: Sheffield Academic Press, 1994), pp. 109-113.

⁴²For a full discussion of the evidence see ibid., pp. 177-193.

The ascription here of responsibility for Jesus' death to Jews reflects the same perspective as the Gospels, all of which indicate that Jesus was crucified at the instigation of the Sanhedrin leadership and at the demand of a Jewish crowd before Pilate. It is nevertheless significant that none of the Gospels suggest that all Jews should be held responsible for Jesus' death. In Acts, the accusation is made directly ("this Jesus, whom *you* crucified," Acts 2:36; cf. 2:23; 3:13-15, 17; 4:10, 27; 5:30; 7:52; 10:39), but only to or about those Jews actually associated with Jerusalem at the time of Jesus' death (cf. Acts 13:27-29). Furthermore, just as Acts shows that the Sanhedrin leadership followed their actions against Jesus with persecution of Christians in Jerusalem, so here Paul equates the persecutors of the Judean churches with those "who killed the Lord Jesus."

But in this context the historical connection between Jesus' death and the Christians' persecution is less accented than the theological one. Because Christians belong to Christ, in their service for Christ they will suffer as he did, according to Paul (cf. Phil 1:29-30; Col 1:24). In the present age the blessings of being "in Christ" are always accompanied by the hardships.

A similar theological connection makes possible the link to the killing of the prophets, who lived generations before. Here Paul draws upon a well known Jewish motif to express the similarity between the present persecutors of the church and the enemies of God's spokesmen in the past. The Old Testament alludes occasionally to the killing of the prophets (e.g., 1 Kgs 18:4; 19:10-14), but the experience of persecution among the Jews in the centuries between the testaments led to an intense interest in the persecution of earlier generations. Thus, a variety of works were composed in that period which purported to narrate the execution of biblical prophets.[43] By Jesus' time, the killing of the prophets had become a watchword for the

---

[43]E.g. *The Martyrdom and Ascension of Isaiah* and *The Lives of the Prophets* in James H. Charlesworth, ed., *The Old Testament Pseudepigrapha* (2 vols.; Garden City, NY: Doubleday, 1985), 2:143-76, 379-400.

persecution of the faithful of Israel by the unfaithful. It is an idea that appears often in Jesus' teaching (Matt 5:12; 23:29-34, 37; Luke 4:24; 6:23; 11:47-50; 13:33-34), and Paul draws upon it here as well. The note serves to indicate that the persecution of Christians in the present is the common experience of God's people in every generation, affirming the truth that "all who want to live a godly life in Christ Jesus will be persecuted" (2 Tim 3:12).

The fourth link in this chain is Paul himself. The kind of people who killed Jesus and persecuted the prophets also have persecuted Paul. The verb ἐκδιώκω (*ekdiōkō*, a word not found elsewhere in Paul's letters), translated "drove out" in the NIV, could have the more general sense of "persecuted," or it could refer more specifically to compelling someone to flee or even to pursuing someone from place to place. If it has this latter sense, it corresponds closely to the description of Paul's experience in Thessalonica in Acts, where he is forced from Thessalonica by Jewish opponents who then followed him to Berea (Acts 17:5-9, 13-14). But Paul was familiar with such persecution from the other side as well, for it was he who intended to pursue Christians as far as Damascus to bring them back for arrest. Indeed, if this text is based on a tradition which circulated prior to Paul's writing of 1 Thessalonians, then it could have referred in its pre-Pauline context to something like the persecution which Paul himself inflicted on Judean Christians before his own conversion.

They displease God and are hostile to all men

The obvious consequence of the preceding list of offenses is that the actions of the persecutors are not pleasing to God. But Paul does not merely point out the obvious with this note. The Jewish persecutors of Christianity offered religious justification for their actions; like Paul prior to his conversion, they believed that Christians blasphemed God and his law and so must be punished. Paul's point is ironic: the action by which the persecutors seek to please God is the very action which will bring God's wrath.

Coupled to the statement that the persecutors do not please God is the assertion that they "are hostile to all men." Again, Paul's expression offers an ironic twist. In the Greco-Roman world misunderstanding and resentment against Jews was not uncommon. Observant Jews refused to participate in the religious practices of their pagan neighbors or to eat foods regarded as unclean in the Mosaic law. Because shared religious observances and common meals were often important events in community life, the refusal of Jews to share in such activities was often misunderstood as anti-social. Consequently, statements like this one are found at several points in Hellenistic literature where Jews are discussed (e.g., Josephus, *Against Apion* 2.121; Tacitus, *Histories* 5.5.2).[44] Paul's point, however, is not that Jews are anti-social because of their devotion to the one true God: Christians were similarly slandered for their refusal to engage in casual pagan worship (cf. Tacitus, *Annals* 15.44.5). Instead he locates the hostility in the particular opposition of non-Christian Jews to the gospel, which is the message of salvation for all people. As in other matters, for Paul the crucial issue here is faith in Jesus; the refusal of such faith, not a person's ethnicity, is what causes his heated response in this text.

2:16 in their effort to keep us from speaking to the Gentiles so that they may be saved.

The reference to efforts to prevent Paul's preaching to Gentiles certainly reflects the actions of his opponents in forcing him to flee from cities in Macedonia. Indeed, several times in Acts Paul's Jewish persecutors are motivated by his offer of salvation to Gentiles (Acts 13:45-50; 14:2, 19; 17:5-9, 13; 18:12; cf. 2 Cor 11:24). A similar problem arose for Paul from within Christian circles when certain Jewish Christians objected to the admission of Gentiles to the church without

---

[44] A comprehensive collection of such references can be found in Menahem Stern, ed., *Greek and Latin Authors on Jews and Judaism* (2 vols.; Jerusalem: Israel Academy of Sciences and Humanities, 1974, 1980).

circumcision. The issue is addressed in Acts 15 and in Galatians, but difficulties over this matter continued in Paul's later ministry (Acts 21:20-21).

It has been plausibly suggested that the rising forces of Jewish nationalism in Palestine lay behind both species of opposition: as Jewish nationalists pressured Jewish Christians to separate from Gentiles, some Jewish Christians capitulated to the point of demanding circumcision of Gentile converts (cf. Gal 6:12-13).[45] Those like Paul who were known not just to associate with Gentiles but to preach salvation to them would have been the particular objects of scorn. Paul presents this issue as a matter of urgency, for he sees that the requirement of circumcision not only distorts the message of salvation but also makes it less easily received by Gentiles. His opponents are thus seeking to thwart the salvation of "all men," and thereby the evil of their actions is manifested fully.

In this way they always heap up their sins to the limit.

The expression "heap up . . . to the limit" translates the Greek verb ἀναπληρόω (*anaplēroō*), which when used literally indicates the filling a vessel to its rim so that the contents are about to spill out. The same verb is used in the LXX at Gen 15:16, where the sins of the Amorites are said to be not yet full. The image of filling a measure of sin is found in Matt 23:32, where Jesus uses it in reference to his opponents among the Pharisees, who likewise are linked to those who killed the prophets (v. 31). In each of these cases the filling up of a vessel or measure of sins indicates that the time is ripe for judgment; the same is true here also. Paul adds that these opponents "always" heap up their sins, probably expressing again that this opposition to God's messengers stretches back continuously through biblical history. As in generations past the unfaithful heaped up their sins by opposing the prophets, so they do so now by opposing Christians and the gospel.

---

[45]Robert Jewett, "The Agitators and the Galatian Congregation," *NTS* 17 (1970-71) 204-206.

The wrath of God has come upon them at last.

The final sentence of this section serves as a solemn announcement of judgment. But whether that judgment is already realized or lies in the future is a matter of some dispute.[46] The verb translated "has come," ἔφθασεν (*ephthasen*), is in the aorist tense, which normally indicates a past action. If this is the meaning here, then Paul asserts that the judgment due for the sins of these Jewish opponents has already come. Paul could perhaps have understood this judgment as having come in some event of recent history. Suggestions have included the expulsion of Jews from Rome by Claudius or a great massacre of Jews in Jerusalem, both of which occurred around AD 49.[47] However, though Paul undoubtedly saw certain events of history as manifestations of God's wrath (e.g., Rom 1:17ff), it is unlikely that Paul would regard such an event as manifesting God's wrath finally ("at last," NIV) or "fully" (NIV margin). Particularly in light of the previous statement of 1:10 which referred to God's wrath as something yet to come, it is more likely that the verb *ephthasen* should be taken in the idiomatic sense attested in modern Greek, so that it signifies something on the verge of arrival.[48] Hence,

---

[46]A summary of the history of interpretation on this question can be found in Carol J. Schlueter, *Filling Up the Measure: Polemical Hyperbole in 1 Thessalonians 2.14-16* (JSNTSup 98; Sheffield: Sheffield Academic Press, 1994) pp. 16-32.

[47]Ernst Bammel, "Judenverfolgung und Naherwartung: Zur Eschatologie des Ersten Thessalonicherbriefs," *ZTK* 56 (1959) 295-301; Jewett, "Agitators," p. 205, n. 5. Those who have argued that this text is a post-Pauline interpolation insist that the reference must be to an event no less devastating than the destruction of Jerusalem in A.D. 70 (Pearson, "Interpolation," pp. 82-83).

[48]The idiomatic sense is discussed in Kenneth W. Clark, "Realised Eschatology," *JBL* 59 (1940) 967-983; Chrys C. Caragounis, "Kingdom of God, Son of Man and Jesus' Self-Understanding," *TynBul* 40 (1989) 20-23. *HCNT*, § 816, cites a parallel from 1QM 4.2, where the Qumran covenanters pronounced that God's wrath had come upon other Jews not in their community "to the uttermost." The Aramaic perfect tense is used in the scroll, a "prophetic perfect" referring to an action yet to come in the future. ἔφθασεν may be the equivalent to a prophetic perfect here, perhaps drawn from similar apocalyptic language.

Paul's meaning appears to be "The wrath of God is about to come upon them at last." This understanding is also consistent with the image of the filling up of sins as it is found elsewhere, indicating as it normally does the imminence of judgment. The statement thus serves to reassure the readers that God is ready to vindicate his people and punish their oppressors at the imminent final judgment (cf. 5:1-11).

The difficult question as to whether the Greek expression εἰς τέλος (*eis telos*) should be rendered "at last" (i.e., "at the end" as a part of God's final judgment) or "fully" (i.e., "completely" as a part of God's ultimate judgment) is reflected in the NIV's footnote. However, since both senses would almost certainly refer to the climax of God's judgment at Christ's return, it is probably unnecessary to make the distinction. Marshall's rendering, "fully and finally," probably captures Paul's sense here.[49]

Paul's words in this passage are obviously harsh. Compared to his sympathetic discussion of Jewish rejection of the gospel in Romans 9-11, his severity here has appeared to some to be contradictory. But in both cases Paul expresses his conviction that the gospel of Jesus Christ is the one and only message of salvation for all humanity, both Jews and Gentiles (cf. Rom 1:16). The condemnation here stems from the opponents' stubborn rejection of the salvation offered in Christ, and the hope Paul has in Romans 11 for the salvation of Israel in the future depends explicitly on the conversion of non-Christian Jews to faith in Jesus (Rom 11:23). Response to the gospel, not ethnicity, is what determines the outcome of divine judgment for all people according to Paul.

It can be fairly said that Paul's language here involves an element of hyperbole.[50] The stringent and absolute language in part reflects the rhetorical practices of Paul's time, in which opponents were often condemned in exaggerated

---

[49]Marshall, p. 81.
[50]Schlueter, *Filling Up the Measure*, pp. 111-185.

terms.⁵¹ We would be wrong to conclude from this text that Paul regarded every action of non-Christian Jews to be deliberately hostile to all people, for example. But the use of hyperbole does not make the statement any less a direct and sincere statement of Paul's perspective. Because Paul understood that God's purpose for all humanity was fulfilled only through Christ, opposition to the gospel was for him fairly and appropriately described as displeasing to God, hostile to all people, and so deserving of full and final condemnation. Such language, even if expressed here with an element of exaggeration, referred to genuine realities for Paul; it cannot be dismissed as merely an angry outburst.

The unfortunate fact remains, however, that in too many instances Christians have used this text and others like it in the New Testament as pretexts for the oppression of Jewish people. The fact that the Holocaust was perpetrated by a so-called Christian nation is a solemn reminder of the degree to which New Testament teaching can be misappropriated. Christians today would do well to remind themselves that Paul condemned not Jews but unbelievers, that he instructed Christians to live at peace with all people, and that he reserved the exercise of judgment to God himself (Rom 12:17-21). Christians can and must hold to their faith in Jesus as the only way of salvation without bigotry or vindictiveness. To do otherwise betrays the very gospel that they seek to uphold.

C. PAUL'S CONTINUING CONCERN FOR THE CHURCH (2:17-3:10)

1. His Desire to See the Thessalonians (2:17-20)

¹⁷But, brothers, when we were torn away from you for a short time (in person, not in thought), out of our intense

---

⁵¹Luke T. Johnson, "The New Testament's Anti-Jewish Slander and the Conventions of Ancient Polemic," *JBL* 108 (1989) 419-441.

longing we made every effort to see you. ¹⁸For we wanted to come to you — certainly I, Paul, did, again and again — but Satan stopped us. ¹⁹For what is our hope, our joy, or the crown in which we will glory in the presence of our Lord Jesus when he comes? Is it not you? ²⁰Indeed, you are our glory and joy.

Having recounted at length his conduct among the Thessalonians and having alluded to their recent experiences of persecution, Paul now brings his discussion to a crucial point. Apparently some in Thessalonica had misinterpreted Paul's absence during their persecution as an indication that he had no real devotion to them. So here Paul will stress that his love for the readers is no less real in his absence than it was while he was present. This he demonstrates by making several points about his behavior: he had made a sincere effort to visit them, he was prevented from visiting not by lack of desire but by Satan, he sent Timothy to the church both to strengthen them and to report to him, and he has rejoiced to hear that they stand firm in their faith.[52] Here especially we see that the apostle Paul was a man for whom the gospel was no mere abstraction but a matter of the deepest passion, producing human relationships of profound emotional intensity and commitment. The church for which Christ died was the church for which Paul lived.

In the course of these personal notes, Paul also emphasizes two crucial concepts: the focus of his labors as an apostle and his source of joy before the Lord are steadfast, faithful, mature converts;[53] and persecution, though it can be a dangerous test,

---

[52]Robert W. Funk has noted that several passages parallel to this one set forth Paul's desire to be present with his converts, letters and emissaries serving as indirect means by which his apostolic authority and power can be made present (cf. Rom 1:8-13; 15:14-33; 1 Cor 4:14-21; 16:11; 2 Cor 8:16-23; 9:1-5; Phil 2:19-24; Phlm 21-22; *Parables and Presence: Forms of the New Testament Tradition* [Philadelphia: Fortress, 1982], pp. 21-24).

[53]Wanamaker argues that Paul praises the Thessalonians for their faithfulness at the end of this section to lay the rhetorical groundwork for the

is the common and inevitable experience of every Christian. These ideas will come into play later in the letter as Paul discusses Christ's return (4:16-5:11). That event will bring an end to the suffering characteristic of this present age, for then even the effects of death itself will be reversed as the dead in Christ arise to be reunited with the living. But in the meantime the believers must maintain their steadfast watchfulness through their trials.

2:17 But, brothers, when we were torn away from you for a short time (in person, not in thought),

Because vv. 13-16 represent a shift in subject matter from Paul's conduct to the Thessalonians' persecution, Paul resumes the earlier focus with an emphatic pronoun, ἡμεῖς (hēmeis). The rest of the sentence is similarly emphatic, stressing repeatedly the depth of feeling which Paul has for the Thessalonians despite his absence. Again Paul turns to metaphors of family relationships (cf. 2:7, 11): "Torn away" translates ἀπορφανίζω (aporphanizō), which in its literal sense refers either to a parent's loss of a child or a child's being orphaned.[54] This anguished separation is qualified in several ways, however. Temporally it is short, a prospect which Paul can only anticipate at this point, since, as the subsequent discussion shows, he has not yet been reunited with the readers. "A short time" translates πρὸς καιρὸν ὥρας (pros kairon hōras), literally "for a time of an hour," a metaphor for a relatively short period. For Paul that period may be short not simply because he expects at some point to return to Thessalonica but because he is confident of eternal reunion at the Lord's return, as 4:13-18 will make clear (cf. 2 Cor 4:17). The enforced separation implies no lessening of the spiritual and emotional bond between Paul and his converts; though

---

epistle's later exhortation (pp. 119-120). Though such a practice was clearly a part of rhetorical methods in Paul's time, the absence of more than implied praise in 3:6-10 cautions against this conclusion.

[54]BAGD, p. 98; Wanamaker, p. 120.

absent "in person" (literally, "in presence," or "in face"), they remain very much present "in thought" (literally, "in heart"; cf. 1 Cor 5:3; Col 2:5). But that ongoing, intangible bond is not enough for Paul: he seeks to see, literally, "your face" (untranslated in the NIV) repeating the Greek expression πρόσωπον (*prosōpon*) earlier translated "in person."

out of our intense longing we made every effort to see you.

"Made every effort" translates σπουδάζω (*spoudazō*), a term used to indicate intense, focused exertion. It is modified by a comparative adverb, περισσοτέρως (*perissoterōs*), used for emphasis; it may suggest that because Paul's absence from the Thessalonians was forced by persecution (Acts 17:5-10), he was all the more eager to be reunited with them. At the end of the Greek sentence, a position of emphasis, another phrase appears to underline this idea, transposed and translated by the NIV as "out of our intense desire." The combined rhetorical force of these expressions drives home Paul's point with the greatest vigor. Only a power beyond his control could have prevented Paul from visiting the Thessalonians.

2:18 For we wanted to come to you — certainly I, Paul, did, again and again —

That great power is now named explicitly and at the end of the sentence, again a position of emphasis. First, though, Paul adds additional words to emphasize further his longing to see the Thessalonians. In keeping with the earlier style of the letter, Paul at first uses the first person plural. However, because Timothy, who might be construed as one of the "we" in Paul's statement, had in fact visited the Thessalonians recently, Paul shifts emphatically to the singular to make clear that he speaks particularly of himself.[55] "Again and again" translates

---

[55]This shift suggests that throughout the letter Paul uses the first person plural as a stylistic device to refer to himself — an "editorial plural" — with at most a secondary reference to his associates mentioned in the salutation of the letter (1:1; cf. 3:1).

the Greek ἅπαξ καὶ δίς (*hapax kai dis*), literally "once or twice," an idiom emphasizing repeated action.[56]

but Satan stopped us.

Satan's power has certainly prevented Paul from visiting his Thessalonian converts, though we can only guess exactly how Paul was prevented.[57] But in the verses that follow, Paul will show that Satan has not had the last word. Though somehow obstructed from returning to Thessalonica, Paul has been able to send his representative, Timothy, to the church — and to send this letter as well. Furthermore, the ultimate design of the devil, to turn the Thessalonian Christians from following Christ, has been frustrated by their ongoing faithfulness (3:5). In this way God has shown his power in Christ to be greater than that of the adversary, even though outwardly it may appear that the adversary has had the best of it. By noting this ironic twist of events, Paul implicitly calls on the readers to look beyond outward appearances to understand the reality of God's triumph already at work in the life of the church. Such instruction will become explicit in 5:4-11, where the exhortation to alertness and self-control in light of the Lord's imminent coming expresses this perspective in a different way.

2:19 For what is our hope, our joy, or the crown in which we will glory

Paul's earlier description of his labors for the Thessalonians and of his desire to see them again now receives their full explanation. Because of his call as an apostle (2:4), the focus of Paul's ministry is to present to the Lord a people who belong to him through the gospel. From this outlook Paul can use a series of terms which focus on the future to describe the Thessalonian converts. "Hope" (cf. 1:3 and the

---

[56]Morris, p. 88, n. 89.

[57]The persecution recounted in Acts 17:5-9 and Paul's "thorn in the flesh" (2 Cor 12:7) are the leading alternatives; cf. the discussion in Bruce, pp. 55-56.

comments there) has this focus unambiguously: part of Paul's confident expectation is that through him God will in part fulfill his eternal purpose to reconcile to himself a people from all nations (cf. Eph 1:1-14; 3:2-13; Phil 2:16). The other two terms, "joy" (cf. Phil 4:1) and "crown," take on this same eschatological perspective as they appear in this context, especially because of the specific reference to the Lord's return at the end of the sentence. Paul's converts are his joy not simply because of their relationship in the present but more particularly because their reconciliation to God will mean rejoicing at the end of the age. Likewise, they are Paul's crown — στέφανος (*stephanos*) here referring to the crown given to signify victory, honor or high office[58] — because when the Lord returns they will represent the triumphant fulfillment of both Paul's divine commission and the larger purpose of God. In these Paul says he will "glory"; literally these are things "of boasting" (καύχησις, *kauchēsis*), a term which Paul uses often, always with the acknowledgement that proper boasting, whether in this age or in the age to come, is not in oneself but in what Christ has done for and through the person (cf. Rom 3:21-27; 5:11; 1 Cor 1:31; 2 Cor 1:14; 7:4, 14; 8:24; 9:2).[59]

in the presence of our Lord Jesus when he comes?

The occasion of that reward is the Lord's "presence," the Greek παρουσία (*parousia*), a term which occurs six times in the Thessalonian epistles referring to Christ's return (1 Thess 2:19; 3:13; 4:15; 5:23; 2 Thess 2:1, 8; cf. v. 9), but only once with that reference elsewhere in Paul's letters (1 Cor 15:23; cf. Matt 24:3, 27, 37, 39; Jas 5:7, 8; 2 Pet 1:16; 3:4; 1 John 2:28). The primary meaning of the term is "presence" as translated in the NIV. But the use of the term in the New Testament to refer to Christ's second coming probably is related both to its use for official visits by the emperor or other high government officials and to its use for the manifestation of God to

---

[58]Cf. *GELNTBSD*, § 6.192.
[59]Cf. Josef Zmijewski, "καυχάομαι, κτλ," *EDNT*, 2:278-279.

Israel at key points in biblical history.[60] It is therefore a fitting term to use when the giving of final rewards and punishments is emphasized in the discussion, as it is here. Furthermore, as Wanamaker notes, the idea that the Lord's "presence" would specifically mean reward for Christian believers and punishment for those who oppress them, would be a source of strength and encouragement for a small band of believers whose opponents seemed to have the upper hand.[61]

Is it not you? 2:20 Indeed, you are our glory and joy.

Paul emphatically states that the Thessalonian Christians are all these things, interrupting what began as a simple question with one which anticipates a positive answer: the Greek clause translated, "Is it not you?" actually comes in the middle of the sentence which precedes it in the NIV, and "you" is emphasized with the adverbial καί (*kai*) which precedes it. The statement of v. 20 then serves as yet another emphatic statement to this effect. Paul here answers the question of v. 19, the answer to which is already obvious, using an emphatic personal pronoun, ὑμεῖς (*humeis*) and again using terms of triumph and reward.

The statement as a whole explains Paul's desire to be reunited with the Thessalonians. Because they represent the fulfillment of his divine commission for eternity, Paul longs to be with them, not only to strengthen them so that the remain faithful (3:2-5) but also because he yearns even now to be with those with whom he shares this eternal relationship. By implication he also exhorts them to remain faithful so that they will indeed prove to be all that he has described (cf. 3:5, 9-10, 13). Again Paul rounds out a section of his discussion by mentioning the Lord's coming, anticipating his focus on the collected and reunited people of God in 4:13-18.

---

[60]Cf. Walter Radl, "παρουσία," *EDNT*, 3:43-44. For a survey of the development of scholarly opinion on the parousia in general, see Colin Brown, "The Parousia and Eschatology in the NT," *NIDNTT*, 2:901-935.

[61]Wanamaker, p. 125.

1 THESSALONIANS 3

2. Timothy's Visit on Paul's Behalf (3:1-5)

¹So when we could stand it no longer, we thought it best to be left by ourselves in Athens. ²We sent Timothy, who is our brother and God's fellow worker[a] in spreading the gospel of Christ, to strengthen and encourage you in your faith, ³so that no one would be unsettled by these trials. You know quite well that we were destined for them. ⁴In fact, when we were with you, we kept telling you that we would be persecuted. And it turned out that way, as you well know. ⁵For this reason, when I could stand it no longer, I sent to find out about your faith. I was afraid that in some way the tempter might have tempted you and our efforts might have been useless.

[a]2 Some manuscripts *brother and fellow worker*; other manuscripts *brother and God's servant*

The break between chapters 2 and 3 interrupts the flow of Paul's argument. Here, as indicated by the NIV's thematic headings, Paul continues his account of his absence from the Thessalonian church during their persecution. The specific subject to which Paul returns is an explanation of Timothy's visit to the Thessalonians as a substitute for his own presence. This, he says, was intended to strengthen them to remain faithful in persecutions which they suffered as an essential part of their experience as Christians.

3:1 So when we could stand it no longer, we thought it best to be left by ourselves in Athens.

Paul's concern for the Thessalonians in his absence motivated him to take a specific and personally costly step. To be left alone in Athens would take a practical toll as Paul was left by himself to do his missionary work as well as the ordinary, day-to-day tasks which he shared with his colleagues. More important, however, is the toll of loneliness, undoubtedly a high one for a man like Paul who treasured his relationship with fellow Christians, especially as he has expressed their importance to him in this context. "Alone" is therefore emphasized in the Greek sentence structure, μόνοι (*monoi*) appearing last in the clause. Only a powerful catalyst, a concern for the Thessalonians so great that Paul could no longer bear his uncertainty, brought about this decision to send his colleague to Thessalonica.

Several incidental points are worth noting here. One is the fact that in this instance, Paul's use of the plural "we" is a stylistic device referring to Paul alone.[1] Secondly, the language here points toward what has been the traditional understanding of the place of writing of this letter. Since Paul refers to "Athens" rather than "here," we can assume that he has since moved on to another city, presumably Corinth, from which he writes.[2] Thirdly, Paul's point here and in v. 2 appears to be that he made the decision not to return to Thessalonica but instead to leave Timothy and Silas in Macedonia, specifically sending Timothy to Thessalonica, and to go by himself to Athens, where he would remain alone. In this respect the account here is very much in accord with the description of Paul's movements in Acts 17:14-15; Luke simply focuses on Paul and is less specific about his associates' journeys.[3]

---

[1]Wanamaker notes that while many commentators regard the plural here as referring also to Silvanus, the logic of the context, especially v. 5, indicates an epistolary plural referring to Paul alone (pp. 126-127). Bruce's insistence to the contrary is based on nothing except a general impression that other plurals in 1 Thessalonians refer to Paul and his associates (pp. 60-61). If Silvanus is included here, then Acts 17:14-18:5 is much more difficult to square with this text.

[2]Donfried, *Shorter Pauline Letters*, p. 8.

[3]Wanamaker notes the plausibility of the hypothesis that Silas remained

3:2 We sent Timothy, who is our brother and God's fellow worker

A difficult textual variation occurs in manuscripts at this verse. The reading followed in the main body of the NIV includes an unusual expression for Paul, who usually refers to his associates as his own fellow workers (συνεργός, *synergos*; cf. Rom 16:3, 9, 21; Phil 2:25; 4:3; Col 4:11; Phlm 1, 24), not as God's (1 Cor 3:9 is an important exception). This reading is represented only in a few, relatively late manuscripts. A few other manuscripts omit "God's" (τοῦ θεοῦ, *tou theou*), so that Timothy is referred to as Paul's fellow worker, consistent with Paul's normal usage.

Several manuscripts, some early and important, have "servant" (διάκονος, *diakonos*), in place of "fellow worker," producing a phrase which is also more consistent with Paul's language elsewhere. Still others, no doubt reflecting the variations in the copies on which they relied, combine the two, referring to Timothy as "our brother and God's servant and our fellow worker," or "our brother, God's servant and fellow worker." These last two can be dismissed easily because they are clearly the result of copyists combining variants which already existed; no plausible explanation can be offered for how these longer texts would have come to be shortened.

This leaves the choice between the readings found in the NIV's text and footnote. Here the decision depends on determining which reading, if original, would explain how the others arose. Because it is difficult to establish how a scribe would have mistakenly written the unusual expression "God's fellow worker" instead of one of the other texts, while it is much easier to account for an alteration to a more common expression, the NIV translators have with good reason followed this reading even though it is not found in what are generally regarded as the most reliable manuscripts. The

---

in Berea while Timothy returned to Thessalonica (p. 127). Though it is possible that Timothy was with Paul briefly in Athens before leaving Paul, the language here does not require it, as Morris presupposes (pp. 92-93).

principle that the more difficult reading is usually the original is decisive here.[4]

in spreading the gospel of Christ,

The strength of this expression appears, then, to have been deliberate on Paul's part. Stressing that despite his absence he did what was best for the Thessalonians, he describes Timothy in striking terms. He is not only "our brother," and so one to whom the Thessalonians were bound in Christ, but also "God's fellow worker in spreading the gospel of Christ," one dedicated to labor in the pivotal work of God himself, working with God and through his power.[5] In this respect, then, Timothy is as important a visitor as Paul himself. No one should mistake Timothy's visit, therefore, as a sign of Paul's neglect. And it was apparently an effective visit as well: later epistles show that Paul continued to send Timothy to churches as his representative in his absence (1 Cor 4:17; 16:10; Phil 2:19-24).

to strengthen and encourage you in your faith,

The purpose of Timothy's visit is indicated with two expressions. He comes to "strengthen" the Thessalonians; here Paul uses στηρίζω (*stērizō*), an expression which implies making the believers firm or unchanging in belief despite difficulty.[6] The second term, "to encourage," is παρακαλέω (*parakaleō*), the same expression which Paul used to describe

---

[4]For a full discussion of this variant illustrating the use of principles of textual criticism see Bruce M. Metzger, *The Text of the New Testament: Its Transmission, Corruption, and Restoration* (2nd ed; New York: Oxford University Press, 1968), pp. 240-242.

[5]E. Earle Ellis has argued that Paul sometimes uses "brother" as a technical term meaning "fellow worker," distinguishing his associates from other Christians (*Prophecy and Hermeneutic in Early Christianity* [Grand Rapids: Eerdmans, 1978], pp. 13-22). Marshall suggests that this conclusion runs past the evidence (p. 90). Certainly in this context it is enough to see the term as an indication of the vital bond between Timothy, Paul and the readers.

[6]*GELNTBSD*, § 74.19.

his own work "as a father with his own children" in 2:11-12 (see comments there). Here the encouragement is particularly on behalf of the Thessalonians' faith, specifically so that instead of abandoning their faith in persecution, they will grow stronger (cf. Rom 5:3-5). Paul has already indicated that the Thessalonians have proved their faith in persecution (1:6-8), but there the focus was on their initial conversion more than their ongoing faithfulness. Acutely aware of the difficulties faced by new converts in adopting and maintaining Christian belief and behavior in a hostile environment, Paul knows that a hard-won faith can be still be lost.[7] Therefore, this concern for strength and encouragement is always relevant, and so Paul will repeat these two verbs in 2 Thess 2:17 as his ongoing prayer for the Thessalonians.

3:3 so that no one would be unsettled by these trials.

The division of verses comes at an unfortunate point here, separating the statement of Timothy's mission from its purpose. The NIV's punctuation makes the connection clear, however. Timothy's mission was to prevent the persecution of the Thessalonian Christians from harming their faith. Such harm could come in several ways. One, of course, is the pressure to disavow one's faith and so avoid the persecution that comes because of it. More complex — and the issue which is perhaps more at hand as Paul discusses the problem — is the challenge that suffering creates for the very core of Christian faith. If one believes that Jesus Christ has established the rule of God among his people, that one is reconciled to God and receives the fullness of God's blessings in Christ, then persecution and suffering are difficult to understand. The suffering believer is tempted to conclude that God has abandoned him or her, or that the gospel was false from the start — that in fact it does nothing to change the basic human condition.

---

[7]Bruce does not take into account the focus on conversion in 1:8 when he assumes that Paul's statement there is based on the report that Paul has received from Timothy as recounted in 3:6 (p. 62).

Such doubts may have arisen in the Thessalonian church, prompting Paul's discussion here.[8]

You know quite well that we were destined for them.

Paul's approach to that question here is to assert what he says the readers already know from their previous instruction: suffering is the predictable lot of Christians in this age (the second "we" clearly includes the readers). In fact, Paul uses language here that implies that God has foreordained that his people should suffer. "Destined" in v. 3 translates κεῖμαι (*keimai*), a verb used occasionally in the New Testament to refer to God's "placing" of something for a particular purpose (cf. Phil 1:16; Luke 2:34).

3:4 In fact, when we were with you, we kept telling you that we would be persecuted. And it turned out that way, as you well know.

The phrase translated "we would be persecuted" is μέλλομεν θλίβεσθαι (*mellomen thlibesthai*). The verb μέλλω (*mellō*) is often used by Paul to indicate something that is about to happen because of God's action (cf. Gal 3:23);[9] the present infinitive *thlibesthai* indicates that the persecution is a continuing action, the common experience of believers at all times. The effect of this language is to assure the readers that God is still in control of their lives when they are persecuted; in fact, the persecution is part of his larger purpose for them.

The larger reasons that "everyone who wants to live a godly life in Christ Jesus will be persecuted" (2 Tim 3:12) are multifaceted but interrelated. One is the fact that suffering has been the experience of God's people in every age. This is the implication made earlier in 2:15, where Paul compared the suffering of the Judean Christians to that of the prophets (see comments there; cf. Matt 5:10-12). If the righteous of

---

[8]So Robert Jewett, *The Thessalonian Correspondence: Pauline Rhetoric and Millenarian Piety* (Philadelphia: Fortress, 1986), pp. 93-94.

[9]Cf. BAGD, p. 501.

ages past have suffered, those in the present should expect the same. In particular and most crucially, Jesus himself suffered, and so those who are "in Christ" should expect to share in his sufferings as well as in his blessings (Col 1:24; Mark 10:30; John 15:18-21; Rev 7:14). For this reason, as Paul will write later in 2 Thessalonians, suffering is a cause for rejoicing, not simply because it produces character (Rom 5:3-5), but because it is a sign that one truly belongs to the kingdom of the suffering Christ (2 Thess 1:4-5; cf. Acts 5:41).

Another reason that believers will inevitably suffer is the ongoing activity of Satan in the world. Paul has alluded to this fact in 2:18, and he will point out again in v. 5 that the Thessalonians' persecution is in one respect a temptation from Satan to depart from the faith. This perspective gives the readers a specific motivation to endure with faithfulness so that they do not succumb to the trials of the tempter.

Why, though, do Christians experience both blessing and suffering at the same time? Why is Satan still active if he has indeed been defeated by Christ? To answer this question, we must remember that the basic structure of Paul's gospel — indeed, of the theology of the entire New Testament — is that while God has by Christ's death and resurrection inaugurated the fulfillment of his promises of the end time, the climax of that fulfillment awaits Christ's return. This perspective has its roots, naturally enough, in the teaching of Jesus.

The theme is particularly clear in Jesus' warning to his disciples about the trials to come to them prior to his return. Matt 24:21 is an excellent example of this kind of teaching. There describing suffering associated with the coming destruction of Jerusalem but typical of what his followers will experience at all times after his death (cf. Matt 24:9), Jesus draws upon the imagery of Daniel 12:1-2, a text which associates great tribulation with the deliverance of God's people, the resurrection and the final judgment. The warning for the disciples is that they must expect to suffer because they will live in the age of fulfillment, when the final tribulation of the righteous and the judgment of the wicked have already begun.[10] Paul assumes this point as well: the suffering of God's people is a sign that the final act of God's great plan of salvation is underway (cf. 1 Pet 4:17). The final separation of the righteous and wicked (Matt 13:24-30, 36-43), the final revelation and destruction of the Evil One at the root of all persecution (2 Thess 2:8; see comments below), comes only when Christ returns in glory. Therefore, because they live in the age just before the Lord's return (1 Thess 5:1-11), believers should expect tribulation at any time, not merely in some special period which has not yet arrived. For all these reasons, the Thessalonians should be assured that persecution and suffering, far from being signs of the gospel's failure, are the expected and inevitable experience of God's people until Christ returns, but one in which they can stand firm with utter confidence (cf. John 16:33; Rom 8:17, 36-39; 2 Cor 4:7-18; Col 1:24; 2 Tim 2:11-13).

Several details of these verses underline these points. The verb translated in the NIV as "be unsettled," σαίνω (sainō) appears only here in the New Testament. Literally the word was used of the wagging of a dog's tail, but more commonly in the New Testament period it was used to mean "fawn upon" or "flatter." If it has that meaning here, the specific sense would be "to be deceived." However, ancient translations and Greek commentators took a different metaphorical sense from its literal meaning, the one followed in the NIV's

---

[10]Cf. Jacob Kremer, "θλῖψις, θλίβω," *EDNT*, 2:151-153; Heinrich Schlier, "θλίβω, θλῖψις," *TDNT*, 4:142-146. Dan 12:1 is the OT text verbally most similar to Matt 24:21, but it belongs to a larger species of texts which speak both of blessing and distress as a consequence of God's great eschatological "day" (e.g., Hab 3:16-19). The concept that God's people would be troubled as God's salvation was about to arrive was a common idea in intertestamental Jewish literature (*Jub.* 23:11-13; *2 Apoc. Bar.* 70:2-10; 2 Esdr 5:1-12; 13:29-33). Cf. the discussion of this text in connection with the concept of eschatological tribulation in E. Bammel, "Preparation for the Perils of the Last Days: 1 Thessalonians 3:3," *Suffering and Martyrdom in the New Testament: Studies Presented to G. M. Styler by the Cambridge New Testament Seminar* (ed. William Horbury and Brian McNeil; New York: Cambridge University Press, 1981), pp. 91-100.

translation, which uses the wagging action as an image of instability or wavering.[11]

This latter interpretation, which takes the verb in a sense attested in some ancient texts, appears to be more consistent with the context, since deception by flattery does not appear likely in a setting of persecution. The Thessalonians' prior instruction about suffering is emphasized variously. In v. 3 "quite well" is the dynamic equivalent of the emphatic subject αὐτοί (*autoi*); literally the clause reads, "you yourselves know." Paul's prior instruction of the Thessalonians is expressed in v. 4 with a verb in the imperfect tense, προελέγομεν (*proelegomen*), indicating a continuing or repeated part of Paul's instruction. The last sentence of v. 4 in the NIV translates a clause in which Paul emphasizes the correspondence between what has happened (εγένετο, *egeneto*) with what the readers know (οἴδατε, *oidate*) with a terse comparison in which καί (*kai*), used adverbially, emphasizes both verbs. Overall, the very repetitiveness of these verses is a method of emphasizing that the Thessalonians have been taught since their conversion to expect suffering (cf. Acts 14:22). Having been so instructed, they should therefore be confident that God's will is at work in their lives even in times of difficulty.

3:5 For this reason, when I could stand it no longer, I sent to find out about your faith.

Paul picks up the thread of v. 1, repeating the statement, this time in the singular, that he sent Timothy only when he could no longer stand the uncertainty about the Thessalonian Christians' condition. In particular he is concerned about their faith — whether because of the persecution they have abandoned their faith in Jesus. Here, as in many cases, the complementary concepts of faith as belief and as faithfulness are inseparable.

---

[11]BAGD, p. 740; Friedrich Lang, "σαίνω," *TDNT*, 8:54-56.

I was afraid that in some way the tempter might have tempted you

Paul's fear is that as Satan had successfully prevented Paul from visiting the Thessalonians, he may also have succeeded through the persecution ("for this reason") in tempting them to abandon their faith. The repetitive translation "the tempter might have tempted" captures the repetition of the Greek text, which emphasizes through that repetition Satan's malignant work in temptation. πειράζω (*peirazō*), "to tempt," can refer to tests and trials of all kinds, but here it is used specifically in the sense of a burden or challenge to one's faithfulness. Because this is a temptation for the Thessalonians to be unfaithful, it is somewhat parallel to Jesus' own temptation (Matt 4:1-11; Luke 4:1-11), which has as its object Jesus' abandonment of his true messianic mission of self-sacrifice. Such opposition to the saving work of God through Christ and the gospel — by blinding the world, dividing the church, drawing believers into immorality, or counterfeiting the gospel — is what Paul consistently sets forth as the work of Satan (cf. 1 Cor 7:5; 2 Cor 2:10-11; 4:4; 11:13-15; 2 Thess 2:9-12).

and our efforts might have been useless.

If such a temptation were successful, Paul's efforts would be κένος (*kenos*), "useless" or "a failure" as in 2:1 (see comments there). Here the parallel to Paul's remarks in 1 Cor 3:10-15 and Phil 2:14-16 is clear. In all these cases Paul's implicit challenge is for the readers to remain faithful to the gospel so that they do not lose what they have received in Christ and so leave Paul's labors without results.

3. Timothy's Report and Paul's Response (3:6-10)

⁶But Timothy has just now come to us from you and has brought good news about your faith and love. He has told us that you always have pleasant memories of us and that you long to see us, just as we also long to see you. ⁷Therefore,

brothers, in all our distress and persecution we were encouraged about you because of your faith. ⁸For now we really live, since you are standing firm in the Lord. ⁹How can we thank God enough for you in return for all the joy we have in the presence of our God because of you? ¹⁰Night and day we pray most earnestly that we may see you again and supply what is lacking in your faith.

Paul indicates in this section that his hopes rather than his fears for the Thessalonians were met when Timothy returned to recount their steadfastness. The language here is based on Paul's earlier statements: it focuses on the Thessalonians as his source of joy before the Lord because they represent the fulfillment of his divine commission. Implicitly Paul continues to drive home how important it is that they remain firm in their faith. This section also begins the transition to the later section of the letter. Up to this point, Paul has focused primarily on the past, but with the prayer of v. 10, the focus shifts to the future, where it will remain for the rest of the letter.

3:6 But Timothy has just now come to us from you and has brought good news about your faith and love. He has told us that you always have pleasant memories of us and that you long to see us, just as we also long to see you.

In the Greek text this verse is an extended genitive absolute, grammatically subordinate to the statement "we were encouraged" in v. 7. The structure makes Paul's statement in v. 7 the climax of the sentence, though the length and complexity of v. 6 give it a particular emphasis as well. "Just now" represents ἄρτι (*arti*), which, when used as it is here to refer to an event of the past, indicates the immediate past.[12] "Brought good news" translates the verb εὐαγγελίζομαι (*euangelizomai*), which Paul normally uses of the preaching of the gospel (Rom 1:15; 10:15; 15:20; 1 Cor 1:17; 9:16, 18; 15:1, 2; 2 Cor 10:16; 11:7; Gal 1:8, 9, 11, 16, 23; 4:13; Eph 2:17;

---

[12]Cf. *GELNTBSD*, §§ 67.38-39.

3:8). If the use of the verb here, the only one in the Thessalonian letters (the corresponding noun occurs in 1 Thess 1:5; 2:2, 4, 8, 9; 3:2; 2 Thess 1:8; 2:14), is a deliberate play on words on Paul's part, it implies that the reports about the faith of Christians constitute a part of the "gospel," a consequence of God's great act of salvation in Christ. In this case, Timothy's report amounts to a reciprocation of Paul's bringing the good news to the Thessalonians; in effect, news of their steadfast faith is an announcement of God's good news to Paul just as his preaching Jesus to them was the same. That reports of the faith of young churches were commonly circulated among early Christians is clear from this remark, as it is in 1:8 (see comments there).

The specific content of this good news is essentially twofold as the sentence is constructed. First is the Thessalonians' faith and love. These cardinal virtues are here repeated from 1:3 (see comments there), but the fact that they are so central to all Christian identity probably explains their presence here more than a deliberate allusion to that earlier statement. The second element is the Thessalonians' attitude toward Paul. They reciprocate his positive memories and desire to be reunited. This idea is emphasized not only by the fact that the statement parallels what Paul has said about himself in the preceding context but also by an emphatic statement of comparison, "just as we also . . . you." To "have pleasant memories" here implies more than mere nostalgia: because Paul has been their teacher in the gospel, remembering him well means that the Thessalonians follow his teaching. Paul's concerns about them — whether prompted by his hasty departure, their persecution or his enforced absence — have be assuaged.

3:7 Therefore, brothers, in all our distress and persecution we were encouraged about you because of your faith.

Though this verse in Greek constitutes the main clause for which v. 6 prepared, the length of the preliminary clauses led Paul to introduce διὰ τοῦτο (*dia touto*, "therefore"), a grammatically redundant element, to make clear that the report of the Thessalonians' faithfulness (the emphasis of πίστις [*pistis*], "faith," here) is his source of encouragement. Throughout this verse, as with the preceding one, Paul uses language which reverses the flow of the preceding discussion. Now he emphasizes that he himself has been "encouraged," repeating παρακαλέω (*parakaleō*) from v. 2. Likewise, he suffers as do all Christians (cf. vv. 3-4). In addition to θλίψις (*thlipsis*, "persecution"), which Paul used in v. 3, he refers to his experience as ἀνάγκη (*anankē*, "distress"), a general term for trouble.[13] So, as the Thessalonians needed the visit of Timothy for their encouragement in suffering, so now Paul receives the same encouragement in suffering as Timothy returns from them with a favorable report. Whether the suffering consisted of external factors or Paul's "concern for all the churches" (2 Cor 11:28) is a moot point, since all flows from his commitment to the gospel. Timothy's report, then, shows that Paul's labors, the source of his difficulties, have certainly not been "useless" (v. 5).

3:8 For now we really live, since you are standing firm in the Lord.

Introduced by ὅτι (*hoti*, "for" in the NIV), this verse further elaborates the cause of Paul's encouragement in v. 7.[14] The expression "we really live" may seem extreme unless we understand the concept of life and death from which Paul makes it. For Paul, to suffer in this present age means to be under the sentence of death, especially as the Christian suffers on behalf of the gospel.

---

[13]*GELNTBSD*, § 22.1. The conclusion, based on the usage in 1 Cor 7:26, 28, that together ἀνάκη and θλῖψις for Paul refer to troubles of the end time, though consistent with Paul's thought, should not be pressed from the language alone: the "present distress" of 1 Cor 7 may be some more mundane problem like a famine, and the terms are paired in the LXX (Job 15:24; Pss 24:17 [25:17]; 118:143 [119:143]) with no special eschatological focus (*contra* Wanamaker, p. 135).

[14]Cf. Bruce, p. 67.

All such suffering is ultimately a consequence of the universal presence of sin in the world (cf. Rom 5:12-19). But because of the resurrection, death is never the only tale to tell for the Christian; the life of the Lord is at work in the believer at the same time (2 Cor 1:9; 4:10-12, cf. vv. 13-18). And so it is here. The burden Paul felt for the Thessalonians is an aspect of the "death" principle at work, but the Lord has overcome this burden with "life" through the Thessalonians' steadfastness. In this respect the joy that Paul feels because of Timothy's report is a glimpse of the joy of eternity, when "life" in Christ reaches its fulfillment (cf. 2 Cor 4:17).

Thus, Paul writes often of the strength which he received from the steadfastness and growth of his converts (Rom 15:32; 1 Cor 16:18; 2 Cor 7:3, 13; Phlm 7, 20). Here Paul receives life because the Thessalonians "are standing firm"; the present-tense verb indicates their continuing action. The statement that their firmness is "in the Lord" appears to be deliberate, since "Lord" evokes Christ's authority over every aspect of their lives.[15] The Greek particle ἐάν (*ean*), here translated "since," does not in this case indicate anything less than full certainty about the clause which it introduces, as it could if the verb in its clause were in the subjunctive mood.[16] But while it does not cast doubt on the steadfastness of the readers, with the verb's emphasis on continuing action it probably does imply an exhortation that they be sure to remain firm.[17]

3:9 How can we thank God enough for you in return for all the joy we have

Here Paul launches a lengthy rhetorical question, expressing in characteristic Pauline fashion his inability to respond with any measure of adequacy to the blessings of God's grace.

---

[15]The general tendency of Paul to use "Lord" to refer to Christ when emphasizing submission to his authority has been observed by C. F. D. Moule, *The Origin of Christology* (New York: Cambridge University Press, 1977), pp. 58-60.

[16]BDF, § 372.1a.

[17]Walter Grundmann, "στήκω, ἵστημι," *TDNT*, 7:637.

"In return" reflects ἀνταποδίδωμι (*antapodidōmi*), literally "to pay back," the same verb that appears in Paul's quotation of Job 41:11 in Rom 11:35, an elaborate rhetorical question expressing the same concept as this text. For Paul all human effort is inadequate as a response to any of God's initiatives to save and bless his people, and so his joy over the Thessalonians' faith, though it might seem to others to be relatively insignificant, is for him another example of the overwhelming grace of the Almighty.

in the presence of our God because of you?

This joy is a species of the eschatological joy (cf. 2:20 and comments above). This idea is stressed here with the phrase emphasized at the end of the clause, "in the presence of our God," language that suggests the present reality of the end-time appearance of God's people before him. Though in one sense absent from the Lord in this age (2 Cor 5:6), Paul could nevertheless speak as he does here of being already in his presence as the blessings of the future are already a reality in part, particularly through the ministry of the Holy Spirit (Rom 8:1-27, especially vv. 15-17, 26-27). The intensity of this joy is emphasized not only with the adjective "all" but also with the use of the cognates χαρά (*chara*, "joy") and χαίρω (*chairō*, "rejoice"), literally, "all the joy with which I rejoiced."

3:10 Night and day we pray most earnestly

This sentence in the NIV translates what is actually another genitive absolute in the Greek text, an element grammatically subordinate to the rhetorical question of v. 9. This syntactical connection helps the reader see a crucial connection between these two verses. Though Paul has been blessed by the Thessalonians' steadfastness with joy that belongs to eternity, the final fulfillment of God's purpose for the Thessalonians has yet to be realized. Therefore, their growth and faithfulness must continue until God's work reaches its climax at Christ's return (v. 13).

"Night and day" connects this statement to Paul's earlier

one about his labor while he was with the Thessalonians (2:9). Both statements speak of actions taken on their behalf, in effect of time used for the sake of eternity. The terms in Greek are in the genitive, indicating prayer during both night and day, though not necessarily constantly. "Pray" translates δέομαι (*deomai*), a term which particularly emphasizes requests or petitions made with urgency on behalf of oneself or someone else.[18] Intensifying this term further, Paul uses the adverb ὑπερεκπερισσοῦ (*hyperekperissou*, "exceedingly"), a word whose length matches its sense; "most earnestly" is the NIV's contextually appropriate rendering.

that we may see you again and supply what is lacking in your faith.

The objects of Paul's prayer are a resumption of his earlier concerns. He wants to see the Thessalonians again personally (πρόσωπον, *prosōpon*, is untranslated in the NIV but carries this force as it did in 2:17), clearly not only for himself but also for their encouragement (cf. vv. 1-5). That encouragement is aimed at the second object of the prayer, provision for what is lacking in their faith. Having just spoken of the strength of their faith (v. 6), Paul apparently does not imply here that their faith is somehow defective. But strong as it has proved to be, it has not yet achieved the dimensions which God intends for them; in fact, faith cannot achieve its full dimensions in this present age (cf. 1 Cor 13:8-13).

To supply what is lacking in it, then, implies God's furnishing them with the ongoing instruction and encouragement that they need to endure to the end.[19] The verb translated as "supply" in the NIV, καταρτίζω (*katartizō*), particularly indicates completion, suggesting that the development of their faith is a process with a particular objective. This very process has been the purpose of Timothy's visit and of Paul's letter, especially of the direct ethical instruction of ch. 4-5; it is the

---

[18]Cf. *GELNTBSD*, § 33.170.
[19]Ulrich Wilckens, "ὕστερος, κτλ," *TDNT*, 8:599.

object of Paul's prayers for them (vv. 12-13); and it will also be the purpose of Paul's planned return to Thessalonica (v. 11).

D. PAUL'S PRAYER FOR THE THESSALONIANS (3:11-13)

¹¹Now may our God and Father himself and our Lord Jesus clear the way for us to come to you. ¹²May the Lord make your love increase and overflow for each other and for everyone else, just as ours does for you. ¹³May he strengthen your hearts so that you will be blameless and holy in the presence of our God and Father when our Lord Jesus comes with all his holy ones.

Closing this major section of the epistle is a summary of Paul's prayer for himself and the readers. Formally this section has been classified as a wish-prayer, in which God is referred to in the third person and the verbs appear in the Greek optative mood (as here) or the future indicative (cf. 1 Thess 5:23-24; 2 Thess 2:16-17; 3:5, 15; Gal 6:16; Rom 15:5-6, 13, 33; 16:20, 22; 1 Cor 1:8-9; 2 Cor 13:14; Phil 4:19; 2 Tim 1:16, 18; 2:25; 4:16b).[20] In terms of content Paul reiterates several themes of the preceding discussion, implying that the work of God in the lives of the Thessalonians will continue to its completion. This theme prepares for the ethical instruction that will follow in 4:1-12. Also, as with other major sections of the letter, this one closes with the mention of Christ's return (cf. 1:10; 5:23), preparing for the extended discussion of that subject in 4:13-5:11.

1. That He Might Return to Them (3:11)

3:11 Now may our God and Father himself and our Lord Jesus clear the way for us to come to you.
This first part of the prayer brings to a satisfactory close

---

[20]Cf. W. Bingham Hunter, "Prayer," *DPL*, pp. 727-28.

Paul's earlier remarks about his inability to return to Thessalonica (2:17-18). There Paul said that Satan prevented him, but here he offers a confident solution to that problem, for God's power is greater than the adversary's. For this reason Paul emphasizes the role of God in bringing him successfully to Thessalonica: "himself" translates the emphatic personal pronoun αὐτός (*autos*). The implication is that no less powerful a being than God himself will ensure Paul's return. God's role as Father is also appropriate here (cf. 1:1), since God's care for his children is the basis for Paul's confidence that God will enable Paul to visit Thessalonica again. The fact that Paul easily and naturally refers to God the Father and the Lord Jesus in the context of prayer, ascribing the same actions to both, is indicative of Paul's clear concept of Christ's divinity.[21] Bruce clarifies the impact of this statement:

> The unobtrusive spontaneity with which such language is applied to Jesus by more NT writers than one is more eloquent than any formal creedal statement could be. We cannot miss the startling implications of the use of such language by one with Paul's Pharisaic upbringing. His reassessment of Christ, by contrast with his former estimate of him before the Damascus road confrontation, had been revolutionary indeed.[22]

The verb translated "clear," κατευθύνω (*kateuthynō*), may mean "straighten" or "direct," but in either case the concept is the same — that God will reunite Paul with the readers.[23]

---

[21]Cf. comments on 1:1 and 2:13; Wanamaker, p. 141. The fact that the verb here is singular cannot be pressed as evidence that Paul conceived of God the Father and Christ as a single entity because singular verbs occur with compound subjects several times in the Greek New Testament without such an implication and because each is modified by a separate definite article. But the construction does presuppose that the two are closely related, neither completely distinct nor completely identical (James A. Hewett, "1 Thessalonians 3¹¹," *ExpTim* 87 [1975-76] 54-55).

[22]Bruce, p. 74.

[23]Cf. BAGD, p. 422.

Acts 19:21; 20:1-2, consistent with Paul's letters (1 Cor 16:5; 2 Cor 2:13), indicates that Paul did return to Thessalonica, but only after spending considerable time in Ephesus on his third missionary journey.

2. That They Might Abound in Love, and Be Blameless at the Lord's Return (3:12-13)

3:12 May the Lord make your love increase and overflow for each other and for everyone else, just as ours does for you.

The mention of "you" at the end of v. 11 prepares for the shift in subject matter in v. 12; Paul makes the shift by placing ὑμᾶς (*hymas*, "you") in the emphatic position at the beginning of this sentence. The Thessalonians have already been commended for their "labor prompted by love" (1:3), so we can assume that the prayer here is for greater abundance in that love. Two verbs with similar meaning, πλεονάζω (*pleonazō*, "increase") and περισσεύω (*perisseuō*, "overflow") are put to use here to stress the scale which their love should take (cf. 4:9).

That Christians can indeed have such an abundance of love is made clear by the statement that the Lord causes the abundance (cf. Eph 3:16-19). Grounded in the grace-full love of God which climaxes in the cross (cf. Rom 5:6-8; 2 Cor 5:14-15) and empowered by the work of the Holy Spirit (Gal 5:22; Rom 5:5), the Christians' love for one another is in all respects a response to and consequence of God's work.[24] Here also Paul brings home the implicit point in the preceding discussion of his relationship to the Thessalonians: his love for them is to provide the model for their love for one another. It may well be that Paul's concern for their mutual love is in part prompted by the persecution faced by the church, an experience which had the potential to strain their commitment to each other (cf. Phil 1:27-2:4).

---

[24]Roger Mohrlang, "Love," *DPL*, pp. 575-578.

3:13 May he strengthen your hearts so that you will be blameless and holy

Though in the NIV it appears as a separate sentence, this verse is in fact subordinate to the prayer of v. 12, indicating that the result of their abounding love will be the status indicated here. The strengthening (στηρίζω, *stērizō*) of the Thessalonians was the purpose of Timothy's trip in 3:2; that strengthening will continue through God's work augmenting their love for one another. Paul's wish for the Thessalonians' strengthening is clearly important to him, as seen by its repetition in 2 Thess 2:17 and 3:3; the threat of persecution may prompt this emphasis. The object of the strengthening is the heart (cf. 2:4, 17), signifying here as it does commonly in the New Testament the inner person, including such attributes as understanding and will. Strengthening the heart will therefore not necessarily imply escape from the difficulties of the outer person, but more significantly it does ensure the ability to withstand whatever pressures one experiences.

The strengthening is for the specific outcome of blamelessness (ἄμεμπτος, *amemptos*). Again, Paul's example comes into play here, for he referred to his own life as having this quality in 2:10 (see comments there); in 5:23 he will once more pray for it for the Thessalonians. Here the standard of blamelessness is established by God alone: the NIV's "and holy" is literally "in holiness," indicating either the means by which the strengthening occurs (as the NRSV translates it) or, as the order of the Greek text implies, the standard by which their blamelessness will be determined. If this latter sense is correct, the emphasis of holiness here is conformity to the character of the holy God himself, who is distinguished from all others in his absolute purity (cf. Lev 11:44-45; 19:2; 20:7, 26).

in the presence of our God and Father when our Lord Jesus comes

Such a focus is appropriate for the close of the verse: the objective of the strengthening is the believers' appearance before God in judgment at the return of Jesus. In Paul's letters two concepts about judgment are held together. One is that for believers justification by faith means that they have already received through Christ the verdict of innocence (Rom 3:21-26; 5:1; 8:1). That confidence is implicit here as Paul again refers to God as "Father." The other concept is that because a genuine relationship with God through faith always bears fruit, believers will stand before the Lord in judgment, where the reality of their faith will be demonstrated (Rom 14:10; 2 Cor 5:10).[25] Together these perspectives create a powerful sense of responsibility for Christians, free from the fear of condemnation, to put their faith into practice so that in judgment they will prove pleasing to the God who has saved them by his grace.

The reference to the παρουσία (*parousia*, see comments on 2:19) of Jesus rounds out the section, as it does in 1:10, and again focuses the readers on the central subject matter of 4:13-5:11. That believers should stand before God the Father at the return of the Lord Jesus is not surprising, since for Paul the final judgment of God (Rom 14:10) is also the final judgment of Christ (2 Cor 5:10).

with all his holy ones.

The expression "with all his holy ones" is somewhat ambiguous in this context, since it can refer either to angels or to Christians. In favor of the former is the fact that ἅγιοι (*hagioi*), "holy ones," is used often in the Old Testament and Jewish apocalyptic literature to refer to angels (Job 5:1; 15:15; Ps. 89:7-8; Dan 4:34; 7:18; 8:13; Zech 14:5; Tob 11:14; 12:15; *1 Enoch* 1:6-9). Likewise, the Lord's return is commonly associated with angels elsewhere in the New Testament (e.g., Matt 24:31; 25:31). Against it is the fact that *hagioi* is normally used by Paul to refer to Christians (Rom 1:7; 1 Cor 1:2; 2 Cor 1:1; Phil 1:1; Col 3:12). In fact, in 2 Thess 1:10, a passage markedly

---

[25]Cf. Stephen H. Travis, "Judgment," *DPL*, pp. 516-517. Travis rightly notes that the concept of degrees of reward in eternity cannot be conclusively derived from Paul's letters (p. 517).

similar to this one, Christians are the clear referent of "holy ones."

Besides this point, the reference to Christians is supported by the fact that 4:13-18 emphasizes the Lord's association with his people at his return, though they rise to meet him rather than coming "with" him. However, the difference between accompanying and meeting should probably not be pressed for at least two reasons. One is that *parousia*, translated as "comes" in the NIV, signifies presence or visitation more than the action of coming;[26] consequently, the image is probably more of Christ's being immediately present with his "holy ones" rather than their accompanying him from heaven to earth. Secondly, all language referring to the Lord's return, though intended to refer to an actual event yet to come, is by nature figurative; therefore, an image of the Lord meeting his people (4:16-17) can be compatible with an image of coming with them.

The final decision about the meaning of "holy ones" must therefore be made on the basis of the larger context of the statement. Though angels are perfectly intelligible in this setting, and though the term could refer to both angels and Christians together, a specific reference to Christians is closely coherent with the larger discussion in several ways. It would look forward, of course, to 4:13-18, where the reunion of the living and dead in Christ at his coming is emphasized. In the immediate context of judgment, the statement that "all" of these will be with the Lord is consistent with Paul's teaching that all Christians have the responsibility which comes with appearing before the Lord at the end of history (Rom 14:10; 2 Cor 5:10).

Referring to the Lord's people as *hagioi* also would stress that they have been set apart to belong to him and that by implication they live in imitation of their Lord's holiness (cf. 4:3-4).[27] That they should prove "blameless in holiness" then

---

[26]Cf. Walter Radl, "παρουσία," *EDNT*, 3:43-44.
[27]Cf. Horst Balz, "ἅγιος, κτλ," *EDNT*, 1:16-20.

is part and parcel with their identity as the Lord's holy people. Finally, the image of Jesus being present with all of his people points to the notion of shared triumph, signaling the Lord's final deliverance of those whom he has strengthened though every manifestation of hostility experienced in this age (cf. 2 Thess 1:10).

1 THESSALONIANS 4

IV. EXHORTATION (4:1-5:22)

A. EXHORTATION CONCERNING CHRISTIAN LIVING (4:1-12)

1. To Continue in Current Behavior (4:1-2)

¹Finally, brothers, we instructed you how to live in order to please God, as in fact you are living. Now we ask you and urge you in the Lord Jesus to do this more and more. ²For you know what instructions we gave you by the authority of the Lord Jesus.

Paul's explanation of his absence and the visit of Silas and Timothy, woven together as it was with many deliberate words of reminder and example, reaches its climax with the thanksgiving of 3:11-13. The subject matter then shifts to what might be seen as the more explicitly instructional or hortatory section of the letter. Up to this point the demands of Paul's message have been largely indirect: reminders of who the readers are and what they have received as Christians, explanations of Paul's behavior emphasizing his faithfulness as a Christian messenger and implying that his example be followed, interpretation of the readers' persecution in light of the gospel and God's judgment, and so forth. From here, though, Paul will address the readers directly, urging them to think and behave according to the gospel which they have already received.

In a very real sense, every point which Paul makes in this

section is a reiteration or elaboration of some aspect of Christian teaching which the Thessalonians already know. And so Paul begins the section by making this very point. His words of exhortation are a reminder to live according to the instruction which they have already received, to grow according to the pattern of life that is already theirs. Such growth is exactly what he has prayed for in 3:11-13.

The need for such reminders is clear to anyone who has tried to live as a Christian, but it seems to be especially acute for the Thessalonian believers. Much of what Paul offers in this section counters directly the influences of the Thessalonians' pagan neighbors and habits of their own former lifestyle. Paul's concern apparently stems from the very real possibility that, few in number and subject to persecution, these believers would succumb to the pressure to return to their old way of life. Combined with this danger is the threat of despair or complacency that can come through a failure to appreciate the promise of the Lord's return.

The fact that Paul's letter was written after Timothy had delivered a firsthand report about the Thessalonians' positive progress in the gospel (3:6) may suggest that while the church as a whole had remained faithful, some specific problems in these areas had arisen. That impression is reinforced by the language of 4:13 and more particularly by the fact that in 2 Thessalonians Paul will repeat in much stronger terms the earlier warnings about idleness (4:11-12; 2 Thess 3:6-15). Whatever the situation as he writes, however, Paul provides a vital admonition: in thinking and behavior the readers must resist the pressure of their culture in order to flourish in the truth that they have embraced in the gospel.

4:1 Finally, brothers, we instructed you how to live in order to please God, as in fact you are living. Now we ask you and urge you in the Lord Jesus to do this more and more.

As in Phil 3:1, "finally" (λοιπόν, *loipon*) signals not so much the end of the letter as a shift in discussion. Here Paul announces the basic subject matter to follow: faithfulness and growth according to Christian teaching under divine authority. To this end he will both "ask" (ἐρωτάω, *erōtaō*) and "urge" (παρακαλέω, *parakaleō*, cf. 2:3, 12; 3:2, 7). The two verbs are found together in other Greek literature and may represent a commonly used phrase;[1] together they suggest an earnest, vigorous exhortation.

Several terms come together here to emphasize this concept. The Greek text joins v. 1 to the preceding discussion with the particle οὖν (*oun*), normally translated as "therefore" but omitted by the NIV. The particle suggests that the instruction to follow is a consequence of the preceding discussion, a concept that is underlined in the verse by the repetition of several key phrases and concepts from ch. 1-3.

One of the most obvious of these is the address "brothers," occurring for the seventh time in 1 Thessalonians (1:4; 2:1, 9, 14, 17; 3:7; cf. 3:2), which stresses the relationship which the Thessalonians have to each other (cf. 4:9-10) and to Paul and the other missionaries through Christ. The foundation of that relationship and its implications are emphasized with the phrase "in the Lord Jesus." Though this could be taken in an instrumental sense ("we ask and urge you by [the authority of] the Lord Jesus"), it is more consistent with Paul's use of similar phrases elsewhere to understand it as referring to the union between Christ and his people. Because Christians are in solidarity with Christ as those who have died and been raised with him (Rom 6:1-14), living according to that union is their natural obligation. In particular Paul offers the exhortation "in the *Lord* Jesus," stressing the divine authority to which those united with him must submit.

Likewise, the goal of their lives is "to please God," a concept which Paul has introduced previously (2:4, 15). Understanding their new, harmonious relationship with God (cf. 1:4, 9-10), the Thessalonians now seek to fulfill his will in their behavior, just as Paul has set the example for them. "To live in order to please God" is therefore not merely the per-

---

[1]BAGD, p. 312.

formance of an occasional duty but a transformation of lifestyle: both the infinitives "to live" and "to please" are in the Greek present tense, indicating a continuing action. And both depend on the verb δεῖ (*dei*), which expresses obligation, literally, "how it is necessary for you to live in order to please God."

For the readers this lifestyle has already taken root. Paul has already written that they have turned "to serve the living and true God" (1:9) and have "received the word of God" (2:13). The NIV's "we instructed you" is literally "you received from us" (the verb παραλαμβάνω [*paralambanō*] is the same one found in 2:13; see comments there), indicating particularly their hearing and taking to heart the oral teaching about Christian behavior which Paul and his associates had delivered when the church was first established in Thessalonica. Such teaching was probably based largely on the teaching of Jesus (see comments on v. 2 below), so the fact that Paul exhorts "in the Lord Jesus" may be doubly fitting here. Consistent with that teaching, the readers already live in a way that pleases God as the word of God is "at work" in them (2:13). What remains is for their lives to come into closer conformity with what they have received, literally that they would "abound more" (περισσεύω, *perisseuō*; cf. 3:12) in the way that they live in the Lord.

4:2 For you know what instructions we gave you by the authority of the Lord Jesus.

For emphasis Paul now reiterates the passing remark of v. 1 that the Thessalonians had already received these instructions when Paul was with them. The repetition will serve to encourage them in their struggle and, particularly in 4:13-5:11, to clarify previous teaching. Also repeated for emphasis are the concepts of obligation and authority. "Instructions" translates παραγγελία (*parangelia*), a word which indicates more specifically commands or orders.[2] "By the authority of

---

[2]BAGD, p. 613.

the Lord Jesus" is literally "through the Lord Jesus," probably referring to teachings delivered by Jesus to the apostles, material which probably constituted the core of instruction for new converts in the early church even before the gospels were written. The teaching of this section can largely be paralleled with material in the gospels, suggesting that here, as in some other contexts (e.g., Rom 12:14; 13:8-10; 14:14; 15:3; 1 Cor 7:10; 9:14; 11:23-24; 1 Cor 13:2; Phil 2:6-11), Paul consciously alluded to the life and teaching of Jesus in such a way that presumed his readers' familiarity with it.[3] The name "Jesus" here and in v. 1 may well point in this direction also, since it belongs to the Lord in his incarnation as a person of history. The NIV's rendering, "by the authority of the Lord Jesus," takes some liberties which may obscure the connection to Jesus' ministry, but it legitimately stresses another aspect of Paul's expression: as in v. 1, "Lord" is an appropriate title, indicating Jesus' divine sovereignty from which these obligations come.

This repeated emphasis on Christ's authority brings an

---

[3]Cf. the seminal work of Birger Gerhardsson (*Memory and Manuscript. Oral Tradition and Written Transmission in Rabbinic Judaism and Early Christianity* [ET; ASNU 22; Lund: Gleerup; Copenhagen: Munksgaard, 1961], pp. 290-291), greatly expanded and sharpened by David Wenham on Paul's use of material about Jesus ("Paul and the Synoptic Apocalypse," *Gospel Perspectives 2: Studies of History and Tradition in the Four Gospels* [idem and R. T. France, eds., Sheffield: JSOT, 1981], pp. 345-375; *Gospel Perspectives 4: The Rediscovery of Jesus' Eschatological Discourse* [Sheffield: JSOT, 1984], *passim*; "Paul's Use of the Jesus Tradition: Three Samples," *Gospel Perspectives 5: The Jesus Tradition Outside the Gospels* [idem, ed., Sheffield: JSOT, 1985], pp. 39-62; and most recently *Paul: Follower of Jesus or Founder of Christianity?* [Grand Rapids: Eerdmans, 1995]). Other significant contributions on the subject include David L. Dungan, *The Sayings of Jesus in the Churches of Paul. The Use of the Synoptic Tradition in the Regulation of Early Church Life* (Oxford: Blackwell, 1971); Dale C. Allison, "The Pauline Epistles and the Synoptic Gospels: the Pattern of the Parallels," *NTS* 28 (1982) 1-31. The considerable evidence that Paul knew and taught material about Jesus' ministry nevertheless goes unacknowledged in some quarters: cf. Victor Paul Furnish, *Theology and Ethics in Paul* (Nashville: Abingdon, 1968), p. 55; Donfried, *Shorter Pauline Letters*, pp. 36-41.

important focus to Paul's exhortation. In v. 1 Paul uses terms for his own actions which suggest the urgent persuasion of people free to make a choice: he "ask[s] and urge[s]." Such language recognizes the responsibility of the readers to exercise their own will as they respond to Paul's words. But the ultimate source of Paul's instruction is the sovereign Lord; he has supreme authority and so commands obedience from all. In effect Paul offers an urgent appeal for the readers to continue to do what is finally an absolute moral obligation.

2. To Remain Sexually Pure (4:3-8)

³It is God's will that you should be sanctified: that you should avoid sexual immorality; ⁴that each of you should learn to control his own body^a in a way that is holy and honorable, ⁵not in passionate lust like the heathen, who do not know God; ⁶and that in this matter no one should wrong his brother or take advantage of him. The Lord will punish men for all such sins, as we have already told you and warned you. ⁷For God did not call us to be impure, but to live a holy life. ⁸Therefore, he who rejects this instruction does not reject man but God, who gives you his Holy Spirit.

^a*4* Or *learn to live with his own wife*; or *learn to acquire a wife*

Sexual morality in the Greco-Roman world was markedly lax. While marriage was widely upheld as a cultural ideal, sexual fidelity within marriage was not necessarily expected.⁴ Husbands might with impunity seek the company of a mistress, concubine or prostitute; the role of the wife was to man-

---

⁴The first-century Stoic philosopher Musonius Rufus represented the highest ideal of pagan society by allowing intercourse only in marriage and then only for procreation. But the tenor of his exhortations indicates that his standards were not widely observed (*Fragment* 12, *On Sexual Indulgence*, cited in Abraham J. Malherbe, *Moral Exhortation, A Greco-Roman Sourcebook* [Library of Early Christianity; Philadelphia: Westminster, 1986], pp. 152-154).

age the household and provide legitimate children.[5] The situation was intensified by the presence in various places of religious cults which encouraged the engaging of temple prostitutes as an act of worship. The cults of Dionysus and the Cabirus, both well established in Thessalonica, made use of phallic images and often involved drunken sexual carousing.[6] Judaism, on the other hand, unequivocally regarded sexual activity as belonging only in the context of faithful marriage. While in practice the ideal was undoubtedly violated, among Jews strong social strictures stood against premarital or extramarital sex.

Paul's discussion of this issue reflects the Gentile cultural setting assumed from 1:9-10. He bases his discussion of sexuality directly on the concept of knowing God truly. Discipline in sexual matters is not for Paul merely a matter of doing what is best for oneself but of recognizing God's will and his power to enforce it. Immorality therefore represents deliberate ignorance of God and the nature of his call, leaving one subject to God's judgment. As a secondary but still vital point, Paul also stresses that sexual immorality amounts to a deception of one's brothers and sisters in Christ and so violates the bond which unites the church. Altogether, Paul's words are a powerful warning against a powerful temptation.

Paul's teaching in this section has a remarkably foreign accent for modern or postmodern civilization. The individualistic and relativistic worldviews which permeate our time argue that sexual behavior is private and cannot be restricted

---

[5]Cf. Bruce, pp. 82, 87.

[6]Donfried notes the phallic symbolism of the Dionysian cult, popular in Thessalonica, and the high concentration of sexual ethical language in 4:3-9, concluding that something like "the cultic temptations found in Corinth" may lie behind Paul's instructions (*Shorter Pauline Letters*, pp. 13, 48-49). On the Dionysian cult in general see Everett Ferguson, *Backgrounds of Early Christianity* (2nd ed.; Grand Rapids: Eerdmans, 1993), pp. 243-249. Jewett notes that the Cabirus cult involved some superficial similarities to Christianity as well as the important difference in sexual morality (*Thessalonian Correspondence*, pp. 128-130), a combination which may have made its influence especially powerful to the Thessalonian Christians.

by any standard other than the individual's desires and those of the "partner." But Paul begins with the idea that Christians belong to the God who created and redeemed them with a particular purpose and who will judge them accordingly, and that through that relationship they also are bound to one another for mutual love and self-sacrificial service. Paul puts this basis for his specific behavioral instructions at the forefront of this entire section, for it was just as foreign to the Greco-Roman culture as it is to our own.

4:3 It is God's will that you should be sanctified:
This verse is the beginning of a long sentence, ending in v. 6, in which Paul sets forth both the boundaries for the Christian's sexual behavior and the reasons for those boundaries. The sentence begins by stressing that these instructions are God's will. The syntax highlights this idea: literally the sentence begins, "This is the will of God: your sanctification." Simply stated, the concept of sanctification (ἁγιασμός, *hagiasmos*) is to be made holy or treated as holy. In the biblical setting the concept of holiness begins with the holiness of God. God is holy because he is "other," transcendent and distinct from his creation (Isa 6:3). But in the Old Testament the people of God are also referred to as "holy" (Deut 7:6; 14:2, 21; Ps 31:23; 37:28; 50:5).

This implies first that they belong to God and so are distinct and separate from others who are not his. But it also carries with it an obligation that they live in a way that is distinct from their surroundings and expresses their status as God's distinct and beloved possession (Lev 11:44-45; 19:2; 20:7). It is here that the specific concept of sanctification, being made holy, belongs. With this term Paul reminds the readers that because they belong to God, their lives are to reflect that fact as they resist the sexual temptations of the pagan culture that surrounds them, expressing by their discipline and faithfulness the purpose which God had for human sexuality (cf. Gen 2:24).

that you should avoid sexual immorality;

Paul expresses that purpose with two infinitive phrases in vv. 3-4. The first expresses in negative terms what sanctified sexual behavior is, namely avoiding sexual immorality entirely. Paul uses here the broadest and most common term in the New Testament for sexual sin, πορνεία (*porneia*). In contexts like this one which imply no specific focus, this term refers to any sexual activity before or outside of marriage, including premarital or extramarital sex and homosexual activity. "Avoid" translates ἀπέχομαι (*apechomai*), which when used in this sense in the New Testament indicates abstaining entirely from something one used to engage in (1 Thess 5:22; Acts 15:20, 29; 1 Tim 4:3; 1 Pet 2:11).

4:4 that each of you should learn to control his own body in a way that is holy and honorable,

The second infinitive of purpose appears here, expressing the positive aspect of Christian teaching on sexuality. This Paul sums up with the two descriptive terms at the end of the verse.

"Holy" translates *hagiasmos*, rendered "sanctification" in v. 3. Paul's implication is that Christian sexual behavior should express that the Christian belongs to God. His concept is probably stated most clearly in 1 Cor 6:15-20, where he asserts that in sexual intercourse one is joined to one's partner in a way that transcends the physical. Sexual contact outside marriage, therefore, violates the union that the Christian has with the Lord (1 Cor 6:17). Consequently, chastity and fidelity are vivid and necessary expressions of the reality that believers are "in Christ," that the Holy Spirit lives in them, and that they are God's distinct and eternal possession, his "holy" people.

The second term, "honorable," indicates that in the context of marriage sexual relations are to be treated as something profoundly valuable, as one's spouse is treated with the deepest respect and sensitivity. Both terms express Paul's reverence for the foundational concept of Gen 2:24

that marriage, including its sexual component, is an integral part of God's intention for humanity in creation (cf. 1 Cor 6:16). Hence, to behave in any other way is a denial of true knowledge of God, as Paul will state explicitly in the next verse.

Because of the central importance of the two modifiers at the end of the verse, the difficulty in determining the specific sense of the first part of the verse has less impact than it might otherwise. But one interpretation does appear to be more likely, clarifying Paul's point further. As reflected in the NIV's marginal translations, the difficulty comes in understanding what Paul means by τὸ ἑαυτοῦ σκεῦος κτᾶσθαι (*to heautou skeuos ktasthai*), literally, "to possess his own vessel."

One possibility is that "vessel" here is used as a figure of speech for a wife. It appears that in some Jewish literature wives were sometimes referred to figuratively as vessels, particularly in their roles as sexual partners. 1 Pet 3:7 may reflect this usage. In this case "to possess" may mean "to acquire," a specific sense in which this verb is commonly used, so that Paul would refer to the taking of a wife in marriage. This specific sense appears unlikely in the context, however, since sanctification and honor in marrying a wife would address only one aspect of the broader issue of sexual morality that Paul discusses.

Another alternative is to take "to possess" as a figurative expression for sexual relations in marriage or more broadly for married life generally. This interpretation has the advantage of fitting the context's comprehensive discussion of sexual morality. But both of these possibilities necessitate taking "vessel" in a sense which is clearly attested only in Jewish documents, while this text appears specifically to address Gentile Christians, who are not likely to be familiar with a distinctly Jewish expression.

It is more likely, therefore, that "vessel" should be taken in another sense, as a euphemism for the male sexual organ. This use of σκεῦος (*skeuos*) is attested in both Jewish and pagan Greek literature.[7] "To possess" in this case would have the specific sense of "to have power over," a meaning attested elsewhere for this verb. This interpretation yields a sense that is consistent with the larger context: it states in concrete terms that Christians should govern all their sexual behavior in keeping with their standing as God's people. Furthermore, as Karl Donfried has pointed out, this sense would directly counter the Dionysian cult's use of phallic images, familiar to the Thessalonians.[8] The effect is to express vividly the replacement of the culturally established behavior based on selfish indulgence and power with a new kind of behavior based on holiness and honor. Because this last interpretation is most consistent with the language, culture and context, it appears to be most likely. The NIV text follows this interpretation, using "body" as a euphemism in English dynamically equivalent to "vessel."

4:5 not in passionate lust like the heathen, who do not know God;

Further defining the holiness and honor that characterize Christian sexual behavior and driving home the sharp distinction between the old life and the new, Paul here contrasts the pagan attitude toward sexuality with the Christian approach just described. "Passionate lust" translates a Greek expression which literally reads "passion of lust." The combination of expressions suggests a powerful desire focused on the gratification of the self. Such a mindset, Paul says, is contrary to the true knowledge of God characteristic of his people. "Heathen" here translates the Greek ἔθνη (*ethnē*), more commonly translated "nations" or "Gentiles." But here the term is used not to signal any national or ethnic status but to indicate those who do not know God because they have not entered

---

[7]References can be found in J. Witton, "A Neglected Meaning for *Skeuos* in 1 Thessalonians 4.4," *NTS* 28 (1982) 142-143; Christian Maurer, "σκεῦος," *TDNT*, 7:359.

[8]Donfried, *Shorter Pauline Letters*, pp. 49-50.

into a relationship with him through his covenant. It appears, as has been noted above, that Paul addresses mostly Gentile Christians in this section. So the implicit contrast is important. As Christians, these Gentiles have ceased to be "Gentiles" in the sense of being outside of God's covenant (cf. Gal 3:26-29; Eph 2:11-13). They are now members of his covenant people, the Israel of fulfillment, those "in Christ," namely, the church.[9]

"Passionate lust" is symptomatic of ignorance of God in at least two important ways. As discussed above, it first of all betrays ignorance of God's intention for human sexuality as expressed in creation. Paul makes clear elsewhere that sexual immorality, like idolatry, reflects the repression of divine revelation available through creation even apart from the Scriptures (Rom 1:18-32, especially vv. 26-27). Secondly, and more broadly, merely to seek self-gratification in sex is to deny the imperative of self-sacrificial service for others which lies at the very core of the gospel. As the one who did not come to be served but to serve to the point of giving his life for others, Jesus reveals God as seeking always to benefit his people, not himself (Phil 2:5-11; Mark 10:45).[10] Pursuing "holiness and honor" and avoiding "passionate lust" are therefore expressed not only by confining sexual relations to marriage but also by acting within marriage for the service of one's spouse rather than oneself.

Notably, Jesus himself indicated that the desire to gratify the self by exercising power over others in any sphere is characteristic of "Gentiles" (Mark 10:42). The mention of "Gentiles" here may, therefore, indicate a deliberate echo of Jesus' teaching as the Thessalonians had learned it from Paul (cf. vv. 1-2, 6).

---

[9]Richard B. Hays, "Crucified with Christ: A Synthesis of the Theology of 1 and 2 Thessalonians, Philemon, Philippians, and Galatians," *Pauline Theology, Volume I: Thessalonians, Philippians, Galatians, Philemon* (Jouette M. Bassler, ed.; Minneapolis: Fortress, 1991), pp. 235-236.

[10]Cf. the insightful discussion of this point in N. T. Wright, *The Climax of the Covenant* (Minneapolis: Fortress, 1992), pp. 83-84.

4:6 and that in this matter no one should wrong his brother or take advantage of him.

Though some commentators have concluded that Paul shifts subjects from sexual to business ethics or general behavior in this verse, there is little to indicate such a shift. The NIV's translation, which indicates a continuation of the previous discussion, is almost certainly correct; τῷ πράγματι (*tō pragmati*) most naturally signifies the "matter" under discussion, not "business" or "any matter" (AV). As the previous verse views the basis for Christian sexual ethics from a vertical perspective, so here Paul addresses the horizontal aspect. Sexual immorality not only violates the Christian's bond with the Lord but also with fellow believers.

Paul uses two verbs with similar meanings to emphasize this point. "Wrong" translates ὑπερβαίνω (*hyperbainō*), which specifically indicates going beyond the prescribed boundaries and, as used here, causing injury to another. "Take advantage" represents πλεονεκτέω (*pleonekteō*), suggesting the attempt to gain something for oneself at the expense of another, "to cheat," in other words. Both verbs are in the Greek present tense, indicating continuing action; they therefore point to a continual doing of harm through sexual immorality.

"Brother" here almost certainly points to other Christians, reflecting Paul's particular concern for the effect of immorality on the unity and integrity of the church. But it is probably used generically to refer to either men or women (hence the NRSV's "brother or sister"). In light of the statement of v. 5, Paul's point probably includes the idea that by engaging in sexual immorality, motivated by the self-centered desire for gratification, one violates the sacred boundaries of the partner's integrity and wrongfully takes from the partner something for selfish gain. Also cheated are the present or future spouses of both persons engaged in immorality because by the immoral act the exclusive bond of marriage is violated.

The Lord will punish men for all such sins, as we have

already told you and warned you.

If immorality indeed involves the offenses noted in vv. 5-6a, then its wrong must be declared in divine judgment. To that subject Paul now turns. Literally he writes here, "because God is the one who brings justice concerning all these things." Though immorality committed in secret may escape the notice of all but its participants, God brings to light that which is secret (Eph 5:8-14) in a judgment that is sure and final. The idea that sexual behavior is entirely a private matter, that it can be treated casually or that immorality has no victims or consequences is entirely incompatible with the existence of a just and almighty God who both establishes the standards of morality and brings retribution when the standards are disobeyed.

Again Paul draws attention to the fact that the Thessalonians had already received this moral teaching as a part of their initial instruction as Christian converts. Two verbs are used together to emphasize this point: προεῖπον (*proeipon*), meaning simply "to say beforehand," and διαμαρτύρομαι (*diamartyromai*), emphasizing a solemn, serious warning. The fact that Paul has repeated this already-received injunction at the length and with the firm rhetoric found here is indicative of the seriousness of the issue.

4:7 For God did not call us to be impure, but to live a holy life.

The reality of God's judgment set forth in v. 6 should not be taken so much as a threat to the readers as a reminder of how they are to live as God's people. God has "call[ed]" them, a concept which in Paul's use indicates not only that God has brought to them the message of salvation but also that they have responded to it with faith (cf. 1:4-6, 9-10). Holiness is therefore one part of that faithful response. But the great significance of their call is in the one who issues it, namely God himself. To have been called by God obliges the readers to live "worthy" of the call (cf. 2:12), to put into practice the will of the one who issued the call.

The call was not for ἀκαθαρσία (*akatharsia*), "impurity," a term commonly used in the New Testament for sexual sin, suggesting especially that it defiles its participants, making them unusable for sacred purposes. "A holy life" is again *hagiasmos*, "sanctification," repeated from vv. 3-4. Here is the objective of God's call: that his people would reflect his own holiness and so be fitting and suitable as his servants and people. They are ultimately motivated, then, not so much by a fear of judgment as by the implications of judgment. The reality that God judges sexual sin reminds them that their identity as God's possession compels an entirely different kind of behavior. Having been saved from sin and judgment by God's grace, they no longer want to have anything to do with anything associated with God's wrath (cf. 1:10).

4:8 Therefore, he who rejects this instruction does not reject man but God,

A strong inferential particle, τοιγαροῦν, (*toigaroun*, "therefore") introduces this verse, firmly indicating that this conclusion follows necessarily and inevitably from the preceding discussion. The standards of sexual purity are not merely matters of individual interpretation, coming from Paul's human judgment (ἀνθρωπον [*anthrōpon*, "man"] indicates "human" generically here rather than males specifically), or of cultural differences, coming from Jewish culture in contrast to Greek. These instructions are indeed delivered by a human agent, but he is an agent of God, and apostle who represents the one who sends him and speaks with the sender's authority.[11] The nature of God himself, his intention expressed in creation and special revelation, and his relationship to his people demand the sexual purity that Paul has described. Rejection of this teaching therefore cannot be taken lightly; there is no room for opinion in such matters. Paul uses the present tense for the verbs translated "reject," indicating the continuing rejection of the teaching through a sinful lifestyle and the consequent continuing rejection of God. In essence, then, the one who lives immorally lives in a state of hostility to God.

---

[11]Cf. Karl H. Rengstorf, "ἀποστέλλω, κτλ," *TDNT*, 1:415-420.

who gives you his Holy Spirit.

To drive home this point further, Paul again appeals to one of the blessings received by the Thessalonians. The Spirit of God given them in their conversion is the *Holy* Spirit, the one who sets them apart from others and enables them to grow in holiness of life. To continue in immorality is therefore to treat God's inestimable gift with contempt, denying the very purpose for which God gives the gift. Again, the verb "gives" is in the Greek present tense, probably pointing to the fact that God gives the Holy Spirit continually to abide in the lives of believers and so continually to produce holy living.

The language of this statement is similar to several statements of Jesus in the Gospels (Mark 9:37 and parallels; Matt 10:40; Luke 10:16; John 12:44; 13:20). This similarity may indicate that Paul is deliberately echoing these statements to remind the Thessalonians of the teaching which they had already received (see comments on v. 2 above).

This warning about rejecting the teaching on sexual morality may indicate that some in the Thessalonian church had done just that. On the other hand, in addressing the Corinthian church on the same subject, Paul left no doubt that he was aware of specific instances of immorality, denouncing them precisely and unequivocally (1 Cor 5:1-13, especially vv. 1-2). This warning, then, may be prompted not by immoral behavior already in the church but by the strong potential for it in the environment of Thessalonica.

3. To Exercise Brotherly Love (4:9-10)

⁹Now about brotherly love we do not need to write to you, for you yourselves have been taught by God to love each other. ¹⁰And in fact, you do love all the brothers throughout Macedonia. Yet we urge you, brothers, to do so more and more.

The tone of this exhortation is markedly different from that of the preceding section. Here Paul's confidence in the readers is unmistakable. Again noting that this responsibility stems from God himself and has already been received by the Thessalonians, Paul offers a brief reminder, encouraging the readers to grow in the behavior that they have already shown.

Paul alluded to the Thessalonians' love as one of their three cardinal virtues in the initial thanksgiving section (1:3). The centrality of such love in the Christian life is expressed, of course, in all parts of the New Testament. The supreme importance of love, rather than any specific issue or problem related to the Thessalonians' behavior, is the likely reason for Paul's including this discussion.

4:9 Now about brotherly love we do not need to write to you, for you yourselves have been taught by God to love each other.

"Now about," translating the Greek περὶ δέ (*peri de*), because it is paralleled in 1 Cor 7:1, has been taken by some as an indication that Paul is now replying to a letter delivered by Timothy from the Thessalonians. The rather general tone of the instructions which follow suggest, however, that there was no such letter. The expression is most likely an ordinary transition to a new subject.[12]

That subject is named with the term φιλαδελφία (*philadelphia*, "brotherly love"), which prior to the New Testament was used almost exclusively of love between blood relatives.[13] Its use here emphasizes the relationship among Christians created by their kinship in Christ. It implies first of all that Christians recognize the common bond of their shared relationship with God, which in turn motivates them to care for one another as the closest of family members. Paul's habitual use of "brothers" to address the readers (1:4; 2:1, 9, 14, 17; 3:2, 7; 4:1, 13; 5:1, 4, 12, 14, 25; cf. 4:6, 10; 5:26, 27) and his previous discussion of his own affection for them (2:6b-12; 2:17-3:10) are aspects of his expression of this reality. This

---

[12]Cf. Bruce, p. 89.
[13]Wanamaker, p. 160.

love is based on a common relationship and is mutually shared among the believers, but it goes beyond merely reciprocal affection. The familiar term ἀγαπάω (*agapaō*), used in the New Testament for self-sacrificial love regardless of the unworthiness of the object, is also used here to refer to the love between Christians.

Such love has been "taught by God" (a term found only here in the New Testament) specifically in the gospel itself, which is above all the demonstration of the true nature of God's self-giving love. Reconciled to God through his love and so drawn into a relationship with brothers and sisters in Christ, Christians must exercise the same kind of love to one another as an indispensable consequence. No wonder, then, that Paul reminds readers of this central imperative in all of his letters (e.g., Rom 13:9-10; 1 Cor 13:1-14:1; 2 Cor 2:8; Gal 5:22; Eph 5:2; Phil 2:2; Col 3:14; 2 Thess 3:5; 1 Tim 1:5; 2 Tim 2:22; Titus 2:2; Phlm 9). No wonder also that the divine teaching of love through the gospel is paralleled by God's Spirit distributing it to the hearts of believers (Rom 5:5; cf. Gal 5:22). And no wonder that Paul says here that he has no need to write on this subject: this supreme obligation was at the heart of Paul's face-to-face instruction and has been at the heart of the readers' Christian experience ever since. In line with all of these considerations is the tense of the verb "to love" in this verse: it is present, emphasizing continuing, constant love.

4:10 And in fact, you do love all the brothers throughout Macedonia.

What Paul has just described as an obligation is here expressed as a reality. The readers put God's love into practice: the verb ποιέω (*poieō*, "do") used here suggests that their love is expressed in action, and the tense is again present, indicating a continuing action. Their love is not confined to those in their immediate circle but includes fellow Christians outside Thessalonica. These observations indicate that the Thessalonian Christians were already actively communicating and sharing with other churches in Philippi, Berea, and perhaps elsewhere, exercising the universal love of God beyond the boundaries of convenience (cf. Acts 11:27-30).

Yet we urge you, brothers, to do so more and more.

Paul's exhortation is to grow in this practice of love. "To do so more and more" translates the Greek phrase περισεύειν μᾶλλον (*perisseuein mallon*), literally "to abound more." The implication is that already their love abounds, but grounded in the love of God, it must continue to grow without limits. Such growth would include practicing love more consistently, more widely, at greater cost, and through the specific behaviors described in vv. 11-12.

4. To Lead a Quiet, Honest Life (4:11-12)

¹¹Make it your ambition to lead a quiet life, to mind your own business and to work with your hands, just as we told you, ¹²so that your daily life may win the respect of outsiders and so that you will not be dependent on anybody.

The division of the text at this point, reflected in the verse numbering and in the NIV's paragraph break as well as in the outline of this commentary, is somewhat misleading. A distinct element of Paul's exhortation appears here, dealing with Christian behavior in society, especially economic society. But the sentence structure of the Greek text indicates that Paul conceives of this subject as a continuation of the preceding instructions. Verses 11-12 are grammatically dependent on v. 10, presenting additional objects of the verb translated "urge." In essence, then, Paul presents the responsibilities of tranquil citizenship and honest labor as expressions of genuine Christian love, specifically because they remove burdens from others and remove obstacles that might prevent nonbelievers from coming to faith. Such behavior was a part of his own expression of love when he ministered in Thessalonica (2:6b-12).

Diligent labor was held in high esteem by Greco-Roman society. Philosophers of various schools counseled their students to adopt behavior similar to what Paul describes here. Some have argued, in fact, that Paul offers these instructions merely because they represented the respected morality of the time.[14] However, this conclusion can be maintained only if 2 Thessalonians is not an authentic letter of Paul reflecting the situation in the Thessalonian church (cf. the introduction to 2 Thessalonians below), for there a similar exhortation is given but with much greater intensity (2 Thess 3:6-15). But if 2 Thessalonians is authentic, the most reasonable conclusion is that Paul was already aware of an incipient problem with idleness and troublemaking in the church.

Why such a problem arose is difficult to say. In light of the eschatological emphasis of these letters, some interpreters have proposed that certain Thessalonian Christians may have stopped working because they expected that Christ would return very soon. This exhortation does immediately precede the eschatological discussion (4:13-5:11), which is in turn followed by another about idleness (5:14).[15] However, because Paul directly connects to the eschatological teaching of both letters to other issues, we can have no certainty that the idleness stemmed from eschatological misunderstanding. Another alternative is that some may have taken unnecessary advantage of other Christians' generous sharing of material things by quitting their work. Though this reconstruction has the strength of a connection to the immediate context (vv. 9-10), it also can be regarded as no more than a possibility. Human nature is such that some in the Thessalonian church may have abandoned responsible labor without any specifically identifiable cause.

4:11 Make it your ambition

"Make it your ambition" translates φιλοτιμέομαι (*philotimeo-*

---

[14]Cf. Hock, *Social Context*, pp. 42-47.
[15]Cf. Marshall, p. 117.

mai), used only by Paul in the New Testament (Rom 15:20; 2 Cor 5:9). Originally the verb meant to consider something an honor or to aspire to something, but in the first century it was commonly used in a less specific sense of striving after something. At the same time, the term was used commonly in honorary decrees to mean "to act with public spirit."[16] Though Paul may mean no more imply no more than earnest pursuit here, the emphasis of the rest of the statement on what might be called public virtues might indicate that he uses the verb in this last sense.

to lead a quiet life, to mind your own business and to work with your hands,

As the NIV clearly indicates, this ambition has three objects. "To lead a quiet life" translates ἡσυχάζω (*hēsychazō*), implying behavior that does not cause disturbance or conflict. Perhaps mindful of the conflict naturally engendered by the preaching of the gospel, no less in Thessalonica than elsewhere (cf. Acts 17:5-9), Paul enjoins quietness in part as a means of showing that Christianity is not the socially subversive teaching which some perceived it to be (cf. v. 12). As his own behavior had shown the truth of the gospel (2:1-12), so the readers' must also.

But more than the public image of Christianity is at stake, since the practice of Christian love has peace, not conflict, as its objective (cf. 1:1; 5:23). "To mind your own business" translates a Greek expression which implies both negatively that one would not interfere in the affairs of others and positively that one would be responsible for his or her own material support. Idleness is the opposite of what Paul instructs here, since it gives ample opportunity for interference in others' lives (cf. 2 Thess 3:11; 1 Tim 1:13) and refuses self-support. While the responsibility of Christian love includes sharing with those who have need, it also demands that those who can care for themselves should do so.

---

[16]MM, p. 672.

Again, Paul's own example is paramount here, for he supported himself in Thessalonica even though he could have lived by his converts' gifts (cf. 2:9; 2 Thess 3:7-10; 1 Cor 9:1-18). The exhortation for the readers to work with their hands elaborates the positive aspect of the previous instruction, reflecting the fact that most employment in the ancient world involved manual labor or skilled handcrafts.

just as we told you,

None of these instructions were new to the Thessalonians. "We told" represents παραγγέλλω (*parangellō*), which implies not merely instruction but command (cf. 4:2). The lifestyle that Paul commands here is the same that he had commanded before (2:12) and the same that he lived among them.

4:12 so that your daily life may win the respect of outsiders and so that you will not be dependent on anybody.

Paul here indicates a twofold purpose for his threefold exhortation in v. 11. While the NIV's translation here does not follow the Greek text literally, it nevertheless represents an accurate interpretive rendering of the Paul's sense. More literally the text may be rendered, "so that you may walk respectably for outsiders and may have need of nothing." The first purpose focuses on the impact of the church's behavior on the larger world, implying a style of life that will earn the respect even of those who do not share the Christians' moral outlook (cf. Rom 13:13). It is, of course, impossible for Christians not to find themselves in conflict with the unbelieving world at some points (cf. 2:13-16). But at the least they should not provide any unnecessary basis for accusation or scorn (cf. 1 Pet 2:12, 15, 20; 3:13-17; 4:12-16). And more than that, their exemplary public behavior should provide the occasion to share the gospel with unbelievers (1 Pet 3:15). Their labor should likewise provide sufficient means to meet their own needs, freeing their fellow Christians from unnecessary burdens. Both verbs in this verse, appearing in the present tense, stress continuing action.

B. EXHORTATION CONCERNING THE LORD'S RETURN (4:13-5:11)

Eschatology, or the doctrine of the last things, has been a constant, underlying refrain to this point in 1 Thessalonians (1:10; 2:12, 16, 19; 3:13).[17] In this section it becomes explicit. Apparently some misunderstanding had arisen in the Thessalonian church about Paul's eschatological teaching. Specifically it appears that some did not yet understand the implications of Christ's resurrection and coming for believers who had died. More generally it seems that the church had not thoroughly grasped the implications of Christ's coming for day-to-day Christian behavior and attitudes.

This section focuses on these specific problems, clarifying and reiterating the core of teaching which Paul had already given orally to the Thessalonian Christians. Throughout the discussion, Paul's emphasis is not merely on eschatology as a fascinating aspect of Christian teaching but on its implications for the practice of Christianity. In this respect this section is a part of the direct exhortation which began in 4:1 rather than a distinct unit of its own. Paul's purpose is not to satisfy curiosity about the exact events which accompany Christ's return or the exact nature of life in eternity but to remind the readers that their promised future life in Christ has a radical effect on their already-realized present life in Christ. Proper interpretation of this section must therefore focus on the impact of Paul's words on the Christian experience, not on speculation about issues which the apostle does not address.

1. The Dead in Christ and the Lord's Return (4:13-18)

¹³Brothers, we do not want you to be ignorant about those who fall asleep, or to grieve like the rest of men, who

---

[17]For a survey of Pauline eschatology, see Larry J. Kreitzer, "Eschatology," *DPL*, pp. 254-269.

have no hope. ¹⁴We believe that Jesus died and rose again and so we believe that God will bring with Jesus those who have fallen asleep in him. ¹⁵According to the Lord's own word, we tell you that we who are still alive, who are left till the coming of the Lord, will certainly not precede those who have fallen asleep. ¹⁶For the Lord himself will come down from heaven, with a loud command, with the voice of the archangel and with the trumpet call of God, and the dead in Christ will rise first. ¹⁷After that, we who are still alive and are left will be caught up together with them in the clouds to meet the Lord in the air. And so we will be with the Lord forever. ¹⁸Therefore encourage each other with these words.

The Thessalonian Christians appear to have particularly misunderstood what the coming of Christ meant for those believers who had already died. Possible sources for this misunderstanding are not hard to imagine. One contributing factor could be the distinctive Christian teaching on the resurrection. In Jewish teaching prior to Jesus the resurrection is something that takes place at the end of history. But in the Christian gospel, and especially in Paul's letters, Jesus' resurrection shifts the temporal orientation of the resurrection. Jesus is raised not when history ends but as it continues. That resurrection means that those who are united with Christ are raised with him, experiencing from their baptism onward the new life of eternity even while they live in the present world (cf. Rom 6:3-4). It also guarantees that at the end of this present world, which occurs when Christ returns, they will be raised to live in the new world of the age to come (1 Cor 15:20, 23-26). Thus, the resurrection is for believers both an experience already accomplished at their conversion and something yet to be experienced when Christ returns.

For the readers, many of whom were Gentiles (cf. 1:9) unfamiliar with the concept of the resurrection (cf. Acts 17:18, 31-32), the details and implications of this teaching must have been difficult to grasp. But even Jewish Christians probably had trouble making the shift to thinking of the resurrection as something both present and future. It may well be that the Thessalonians understood that they had already been raised with Christ but did not comprehend the concept of a future resurrection with its implications.[18] Or they may have simply thought that Christ's resurrection is the only resurrection in God's plan. Such belief could easily have caused discouragement and despair if a brother or sister in Christ had died since Paul left. As that death ruptured the fellowship of the church, misunderstanding about the resurrection would have left those who were alive with no hope of being restored to the one who was dead. Furthermore, if Paul had taught that all believers would greet the Lord at his return, a death in the church without a resurrection to come would throw the truth of Paul's teaching into question.

Other reconstructions are also possible. Some argue that the Thessalonians believed merely that the dead would not participate in the parousia or would not have the same blessed experience as those who will be alive.[19] However, it is difficult to believe that this alone would cause them to grieve like those without hope (v. 13).[20] Joseph Plevnik has argued that the Thessalonians believed, with many Jews, that for a person to be taken up from earth to heaven (v. 17), that person must be alive. They understood that at Christ's return the living would be taken up but had mistakenly concluded that the

---

[18]Cf. Kreitzer, "Eschatology," *DPL*, p. 257.

[19]A.F.J. Klijn, "1 Thessalonians 4.13-18 and its Background in Apocalyptic Literature," *Paul and Paulinism: Essays in Honour of C.K. Barrett* (M.D. Hooker and S.G. Wilson, eds.; London: SPCK, 1982), pp. 67-73.

[20]Cf. the discussion of alternatives in Marshall, pp. 120-123. Helmut Merklein, who argues that the misunderstanding has to do only with whether the dead in Christ will participate in the Lord's return, is forced to argue that in v. 13 Paul states that Christians should not grieve at all ("Der Theologe als Prophet: zur Funktion prophetischen Redens im theologischen Diskurs des Paulus," *NTS* 38 [1992] 403-409). Cf. the discussion of v. 13 below.

dead could have no part in this.[21] Though this reconstruction does justice to much of the language of this section, it neglects the indications, noted below, that Paul also implies that the dead are present with Christ prior to his return. The best hypothesis remains a more essential misunderstanding of the resurrection stemming from the shift in thinking demanded by this doctrine.

This passage, then, emphasizes that at the coming of Christ those who have died in Christ will suffer no disadvantage. Theirs is no second-class experience: they will be present with the Lord at his coming and experience all of eternity with him. Furthermore, those who grieve the death of a fellow Christian have the assurance that God's people will all be reunited in his presence at Christ's return. The purpose of God to unite all those who belong to him in eternal fellowship with him and each other will in no way be frustrated by death!

The question is often raised as to whether the teaching of this passage and of 1 Cor 15 on the future resurrection can be reconciled with Paul's teaching on life after death in 2 Cor 5:1-10 or Phil 1:20-23.[22] In those latter passages he speaks of what appears to be a conscious life in the Lord's presence immediately after the death of the individual.

A variety of approaches have been taken to reconciling these passages. Some have argued that Paul's thinking changed between the writing of 1 and 2 Corinthians from belief in a resurrection at the end of history to belief in life immediately after death, perhaps because he sought to explain the death of some believers or the delay in Christ's return. This view, aside from its theologically problematic assertion that Paul's apostolic teaching evolved to the point of contradiction, understands these passages rigidly and simplis-

---

[21]Joseph Plevnik, "The Taking Up of the Faithful and the Resurrection of the Dead in 1 Thessalonians 4:13-18," *CBQ* 46 (1984) 274-283.

[22]For a survey of the relevant issues see Larry J. Kreitzer, "Intermediate State," *DPL*, pp. 438-441. On the close relationship between 1 Thess 4:13-18 and 1 Cor 15:1-58 see Merklein, "Theologe als Prophet," pp. 414-419.

tically, not according to the characteristic complexity of the rest of Paul's doctrine.

Another approach argues that the soul or spirit of the dead believer "sleeps" in an unconscious state until the resurrection. But this conclusion is based on a misunderstanding of biblical language for death (see comments on v. 13 below), undervalues Paul's confidence that to be absent from the body is to be at home with the Lord (2 Cor 5:8), and cannot explain specific expressions in Paul's discussion here (see comments on vv. 14-15 below).

More traditionally it has been understood that between death and the resurrection the Christian exists in a "disembodied state," a conscious but incomplete state of blessedness which ends when the believer receives the resurrection body when Christ returns. The traditional view has the virtue of explaining coherently all of Paul's statements about life after death. But whether Paul or any other New Testament writer implies that in the intermediate state Christians exist as disembodied spirits is at best questionable.

Whatever the specifics at this point, the relevant passages in fact offer a different emphasis in context. This text stresses the resurrection at the end of history as the reuniting of believers who have died with those who are still alive. Here the dead, who are already in the Lord's presence, are raised in relation to those from whom they have been separated, namely those alive on the earth, so that all share together in the return of Christ and the eternal fellowship that follows.[23] In 2 Cor 5:1-10 and Phil 1:20-23 Paul stresses the individual's confidence that nothing, death included, can sever his relationship with Christ—that in fact death makes that fellowship even more direct (cf. Rom 14:8). So whatever else a future resurrection may mean for those who die before the Lord returns, these texts assure those united with Christ in his

---

[23]Plevnik approaches this understanding when he observes that the resurrection in this passage is both "a return to *this* life" and "a transformation" ("The Faithful and the Resurrection," p. 282).

death and resurrection that death for them is in every respect a defeated enemy (cf. 1 Cor 15:54-57).

4:13 Brothers, we do not want you to be ignorant about those who fall asleep,

Paul begins the discussion with an assertion of the subject he will address and the purpose for addressing it. The subject is "those who fall asleep," or more literally "those who are sleeping" (τῶν κοιμωμένων [tōn koimōmenōn] is a present participle, indicating continuing action). "To sleep" is a common euphemism for death in both Greek and Jewish literature.[24] To infer from the expression that those who are dead have no consciousness is a patent over-interpretation, since death is referred to as sleep in a wide variety of ancient texts where no such implication is in view. For Christians, however, the term may have been especially useful since it provided the reminder that Christ would awaken those who have fallen asleep in death (cf. Luke 8:52). "We do not want you to be ignorant" represents a kind of emphatic, double-negative expression which is common in Greek rhetoric; it is the equivalent of "we want to inform you" (cf. Rom 1:13; 11:25; 1 Cor 10:1; 12:1; 2 Cor 1:8).

or to grieve like the rest of men, who have no hope.

Paul's purpose for this teaching is to address and change the grief which they will naturally experience, or may have already experienced, when a brother or sister dies. His point is not that Christians who understand this teaching will not grieve at all. That idea is belied by Paul's own experience: in Phil 2:27 he indicates that had his associate Epaphroditus died from a serious illness, Paul would have experienced "sorrow upon sorrow." Rather his point is that grief with hope is fundamentally different from grief without hope; the statement might be paraphrased, "so that you will not have the same kind of grief as those without hope." "The rest of men"

---

[24]Cf. BAGD, p. 437.

are those without that hope which springs from the gospel; theirs is the condition of sinful humanity left to itself (cf. Eph 2:12).[25] "Hope" (ἐλπίς, *elpis*) is, of course, more than optimism or positive thinking. In the context of the Christian gospel it signifies a confidence about the future which is based on God's faithful promises, already in the process of fulfillment through Christ (cf. comments on 1:3). Christians will therefore still grieve at the death of a fellow Christian because their fellowship with that brother or sister has been interrupted. But as Paul will stress, their hope alleviates and transforms that grief because when Christ comes their fellowship will be restored. Death's "sting" (1 Cor 15:55) is removed from grief because the temporary separation of death will yield to the eternal fellowship of the Lord's people (cf. 2 Cor 4:17-18).

4:14 We believe that Jesus died and rose again and so we believe that God will bring with Jesus those who have fallen asleep in him.

Belief in the final resurrection of the dead in Christ, Paul asserts here, is a necessary consequence of the fundamental Christian belief in the death and resurrection of Jesus. In fact, it has been argued that Paul here quotes a common early Christian creed, or statement of belief: the introductory "we believe," the use of "Jesus" instead of Paul's more common "Christ," and the use of ἀνίστημι (*anistēmi*) for "rose," not the ordinary term for Paul, have been taken as evidence of a pre-Pauline origin for this statement.[26]

But whatever its origin, the force of the statement is unmistakable. The first portion of this verse, "We believe that Jesus died and rose again," is presented as a condition in the Greek text, literally "If we believe . . . ." But the "if" in no way implies any doubt that the Thessalonians have faith in Christ's death and resurrection; rather, the sentence structure allows

---

[25]*HCNT*, § 819-820, offers examples of the very limited hope available to grieving pagans of the first century, including a tomb inscription from Thessalonica itself.
[26]Cf. Bruce, p. 96; Wanamaker, p. 168.

Paul to declare the destiny of the dead in Christ as something which follows as a matter of course from the gospel itself. The work of God begun in Christ's death and resurrection has as its objective the uniting of all of God's people in eternal fellowship with him.

As long as those people are separated, some in his presence in heaven and others on earth, and as long as those on earth do not experience the fullness of his presence, God's purpose remains unfinished. Christ's return to earth for those who are alive will address the second part of this unfinished business, as the Thessalonians already realize. Paul here stresses the solution to the first aspect by asserting that when Jesus comes, he will bring his people who have died "with him" to be reunited in fellowship with those who are still alive.

A couple of expressions in this verse deserve particular attention. The Greek term in this verse translated "fallen asleep" (κοιμηθέντας, *koimēthentas*), is in the aorist tense, different from the present-tense expression in v. 13. It more naturally refers to the point of death rather than the state of being dead indicated in the previous verse, appropriately so since Paul refers to those who were Christian believers when they died. Bruce calls attention to the contrast between the figurative use of "sleep" for the death of believers here and the literal expression "died" for Christ. He notes that Paul nowhere uses "sleep" for the death of Christ, perhaps "to stress the reality of his death, as something not to be alleviated by any euphemism."[27] It is probably also significant that Christ will bring the dead "with him." Though it is possible that this expression refers to their being brought to heaven after their resurrection,[28] expressions in vv. 15, 17 (see comments below) suggest another idea: that those who have died did not simply "sleep" in their graves but have since death been with Jesus in God's presence awaiting his return.[29]

---

[27]Bruce, p. 97.
[28]Cf. Wanamaker, pp. 169-170, 175-176.
[29]Donfried notes that grammatically the phrase διὰ τοῦ Ἰησοῦ (*dia tou Iēsou*, "in Jesus," is redundant unless it is taken with "fall asleep" and there-

4:15 According to the Lord's own word, we tell you

Paul indicates here that the teaching he offers is based on the authority of Jesus himself. "According to the Lord's own word" probably refers to the teaching of Jesus about his return, particularly his assurance that at his coming he will gather together all of his people (Matt 24:30-31) to be "with him" (25:10). Of course, Paul does not repeat this teaching verbatim but elaborates on it and applies it to the Thessalonians' circumstances, all under the guidance of the Spirit's inspiration of the apostle; hence he writes "according to the Lord's own word, *we* tell you . . ." (cf. a similar elaboration, expressed in greater detail, in 1 Cor 7:10-15).[30] It is less likely that this "word of the Lord" is some other teaching of Jesus not recorded in the gospels, and much less likely that it is a later Christian prophet's utterance, unrelated to Jesus' own teaching.[31]

that we who are still alive, who are left till the coming of the Lord, will certainly not precede those who have fallen asleep.

The certain assurance that those who have died are at no disadvantage comes into clear focus with this statement. The living will not "precede" the dead at the Lord's "coming" (παρουσία, *parousia*, see comments on 2:19). This observation is not merely a matter of establishing a chronology of end-time events. Rather, it makes clear that the dead will experience every bit as much of the blessing of the Lord's return as

---

fore refers to the relationship with Christ that exists at death (*Shorter Letters*, pp. 50-51).

[30]This explanation of the relationship of "the Lord's word" to "we tell" appears to make more coherent sense of all the evidence than Merklein's argument that the combination introduces a prophetic statement of Paul's own ("Theologe als Prophet," p. 413).

[31]Cf. Wenham, *Eschatological Discourse*, pp. 89-90; *contra* Morris, pp. 140-141; Bruce, pp. 98-99; C.M. Tuckett, "Synoptic Tradition in 1 Thessalonians?" *The Thessalonian Correspondence* (Raymond F. Collins, ed.; BETL 87; Leuven: Leuven University Press, 1990), pp. 176-182; Donfried, *Shorter Pauline Letters*, pp. 36-41.

the living.³² If, as Paul will elaborate, the dead are raised "first" and "then" those who are alive will join them to meet the Lord (vv. 16-17), the dead will participate in every part of the Lord's triumphant return and its rewards. Thus, the "chronology" really serves a larger issue relevant to the concerns of the Thessalonians: God will fulfill his promises to all his people, even those who have died.

The additional description of the living reinforces this point. "Those who are left" translates οἱ περιλειπόμενοι (*hoi perileipomenoi*), commonly used for persons left "behind."³³ Especially in light of "with him" in v. 14, this can imply nothing less than that the dead in Christ have been with him in a way that the living have not. That state ends for them with the Lord's return. By implication then, if there is any advantage, it lies not with the living, as the Thessalonians had feared, but with the dead, who have been in the Lord's presence already. This concept appears to be the opposite of what was offered in some Jewish literature of this period, in which those alive at the end of history have the greater blessing.³⁴

Some have argued that Paul's use of "we" here (ἡμεῖς, *hēmeis*, "we," is emphatic) indicates that he expected to be alive when the Lord would return.³⁵ To draw this conclusion from this point of grammar is at best unwarranted, however. Though Paul's language here certainly holds out the possibility of Christ's return in the near future, as does the entire thrust of his discussion in 5:1-11, we have no direct indication that he believed that the Lord's return would certainly occur in his generation.³⁶ Paul regarded the time of the Lord's

---

³²*HCNT*, § 821, notes that a similar point is made by an abstract illustration in the apocryphal 4 Ezra 5:41-42.

³³Cf. BAGD, p. 648; *GELNTBSD*, § 85.66.

³⁴*HCNT*, § 822, notes from 4 Ezra 13:16-24; *Pss. Sol.* 17:44; 18:5-6; Sir 48:11; *Sib. Or.* 4.187-92 that Intertestamental Jewish literature tended to put the advantage with those "left" at the Messiah's coming.

³⁵E.g. Wanamaker, pp. 171-172.

³⁶Arguments to this effect based on the "present distress" of 1 Cor 7:26, because of which Paul counseled the unmarried not to marry (e.g.,

coming as indefinite and so requiring alertness (cf. 5:2-6), just as Jesus' teaching counseled patient faithfulness in light of possible delay in his return (Matt 25:1-30). Later in this context, as Marshall points out, Paul acknowledges the very real possibility that "we," as in this verse, might be either alive or dead at the Lord's return (5:10).[37] The concept of 2 Pet 3:1-10 is hardly foreign to Paul's thinking!

4:16 For the Lord himself will come down from heaven, with a loud command, with the voice of the archangel and with the trumpet call of God,

The language that Paul uses here would have been familiar to anyone who knew the traditions of Jewish apocalyptic literature. Its roots are in the Old Testament prophets, especially Dan 7:13-14, where a vision of a series of political empires comes to an end with the coming of "one like a Son of Man" on the clouds of heaven. In his interrogation from the high priest Jesus himself used this language to refer to his triumphal return after his crucifixion (Matt 26:64; Mark 14:62; Luke 22:69), but the most significant parallel is in Matt 24:30-31, where the coming from heaven is also accompanied by the trumpet and, as noted above, the gathering of God's chosen people. Taken as a whole, the statement points to the climax and completion of God's saving work in history.

The images found here underline that in this event the final, universal purposes of God are completed. "The Lord himself" is an emphatic expression referring to the Lord Jesus. His descent from heaven is accompanied by a variety of "sound effects." He issues a "loud command," probably the

---

Wanamaker, p. 172), ignore the very real possibility that some immediate temporal crisis, such as a famine, prompted this *ad hoc* advice (cf. Bruce W. Winter, "Secular and Christian Responses to Corinthian Famines," *TynBul* 40 (1989) 86-106, especially pp. 93-94). Though such a crisis would have been viewed as characteristic of the time before the Lord's coming, the length of that time was uncertain for the early Christians (cf. Brown, "The Parousia," pp. 903, 915-917).

[37]Marshall, pp. 127-128.

summoning of the dead as pictured in John 5:25-29. The "archangel" does not appear in the Old Testament (but cf. Dan 10:13; 12:1) and only in one other text in the New (Jude 9). The term suggests a chief angel; its use here stresses that the voice which announces Christ's return comes from the most authoritative of the heavenly creatures.[38]

Trumpets in the Old Testament are used in warfare (e.g., Num 10:9; 2 Cor 20:28) and during festivals and sacrifices, especially the Day of Atonement (Num 10:10; Lev 25:9). Perhaps more significant for this text is the use of the trumpet to call Israel to assembly (Num 10:7) or regather Israel from exile (Isa 27:13), for here the people of God are called to eternal assembly with the trumpet. Also significant is the trumpet sound which accompanies God's manifestation at Mount Sinai (Exod 19:16), as Christ's coming brings the ultimate theophany.[39] Likewise the trumpet is associated with God's judgment on the wicked and his deliverance of his people (cf. Isa 27:13; Zech 9:14); Christ's coming again brings the final judgment and deliverance. The combination of these factors suggests a sudden, dramatic, unmistakable, universal and final event. As Morris notes, this imagery is very difficult to square with the concept of a "secret rapture" in which believers disappear from the world but ordinary life continues otherwise.[40]

and the dead in Christ will rise first.

Paul notes two immediate consequences of the Lord's return. The first is the resurrection of the dead in Christ. That their resurrection is "first" ensures that they are full participants in all that follows. The context does not allow "first" to imply that a resurrection of the wicked will follow after an intervening period of tribulation; rather, it indicates a sequence with the gathering of the living saints in v. 17. The fate of the

---

[38]Cf. Ingo Broer, "ἄγγελος," *EDNT*, 1:15-16.
[39]Cf. Hermann Lichtenberger, "σάλπιγξ," *EDNT*, 3:225-226.
[40]Morris, p. 145.

wicked is not Paul's concern here. It is worth noting that for Paul the statement that the Lord will bring "with him" those who have died (v. 14) and that they will "rise first" when he comes were entirely compatible. The expression "the dead in Christ" first of all should probably be understood as having a meaning distinct from "those who have fallen asleep in him" (v. 14): that phrase emphasized the point of death, whereas this one suggests that these remain in fellowship with Christ even though they have died.[41]

So what does it mean for these who are in conscious fellowship with the Lord to be raised? As Paul states elsewhere, the nature of the resurrected body, suited to a new order of existence, is beyond our present experience and so impossible for us to comprehend (1 Cor 15:35-53). These different statements are contradictory only if understood in the most rigidly literal and materialistic way; they clearly employ figures to convey concepts beyond present human experience. But to say that they are figures in no way denies that they refer to actual events of the future. It is simply to say that the point of all such biblical descriptions is to convey the significance of God's promised future, not to offer a journalist's description of the events.[42]

4:17 After that, we who are still alive and are left will be caught up together with them in the clouds to meet the Lord in the air.

The second consequence is here described. "After that"

---

[41]Murray J. Harris, *Raised Immortal: Resurrection and Immortality in the New Testament* (Grand Rapids: Eerdmans, 1983), p. 161.

[42]Cf. the remark of Marshall regarding the language used in this text (p. 128): "A real event is being described, but it is one which cannot be described literally since the direct activity of God cannot be fully comprehended in human language. The biblical writers have therefore to resort to analogy and metaphor, the language of symbol, in order to convey their message.... Such a view of the passage must be emphatically distinguished from a demythologising interpretation which sees here the mythical presentation of timeless truths, or which regards Paul's statements as antiquated mumbo-jumbo which must be jettisoned by modern Christians."

translates ἔπειτα (*epeita*), literally "then" or "next"; because it follows immediately after "first" in v. 16, this term indicates that Paul describes two events in sequence. The point, however, is not to stress the sequence but its consequence: the dead in Christ will participate fully the Lord's return.[43] Though the reader of the NIV might infer from "still alive" that Christians alive at the Lord's coming are survivors of a violent persecution, Paul's Greek expression makes no such implication. These are simply "the living" as in v. 15. Also as in that verse these have been "left," that is "left behind" because those who have died have gone to be with the Lord. But their separation from the Lord's immediate presence now comes to an end.

What happens to the living is now exactly what happens to the dead; Paul emphasizes this with a repetitive expression, ἅμα σὺν αὐτοῖς (*hama syn autois*), "together with them." Both the living and the resurrected dead are "caught up": ἁρπάζω (*harpazō*; the Latin translation *rapere* is the origin of the modern term "rapture") implies a sudden, even violent action and is used elsewhere by Paul of his own experience being "caught up" to heaven (2 Cor 12:2-3). Its use in the passive voice here implies that God does the action, even if it is accomplished through angelic intermediaries (Matt 13:41). As a result the Lord's people join him "in the clouds." Clouds are an important element in the description of the coming of the Son of Man in Dan 7:13-14 and Matt 24:30, undoubtedly because of their prior biblical association with God's visible manifestation (Exod 16:10; 19:16; 1 Kgs 8:10-11; Isa 19:1; Ezek 1:4, 28; cf. Acts 1:9).

There they "meet" the Lord; ἀπάντησις (*apantēsis*, "meeting") appears here and in Matt 25:9, perhaps because Paul has based this statement in part on that saying as well.[44] While

---

[43]To this extent the assertion of Lothar Schmid that the terms are qualitative rather than temporal is correct ("κέλευσμα," *TDNT*, 3:658-59). However, it is more accurate to say that the *image* of a temporal sequence conveys the qualitative *concept*.

[44]Wenham, *Eschatological Discourse*, p. 89.

it has been argued that this was a technical term for an official meeting of a visiting dignitary,[45] the evidence cited to support such a specific meaning of the word is not conclusive.[46] But the context of the expression certainly bears out that implication here, whether the word carries a technical sense or not. Those who meet the Lord welcome him as the king who has come to reign. That the meeting occurs "in the air" is consistent with the image of the Lord descending with the clouds and further underlines that this event occurs by the power of God himself.

Speculation is rife as to whether the Lord leads his people to heaven or back to earth after this meeting.[47] It must suffice to make two observations at this point: (1) nothing in this text expresses or implies anything on the subject; (2) the point which Paul does stress here is not *where* these events will conclude but *with whom*, as the next sentence indicates.

And so we will be with the Lord forever.

This statement concludes the description of the Lord's coming by making explicit its result. For both the living and the dead in Christ, his return means the completion of all that has been incomplete. The separation of living and dead will be ended as both are united in Christ's presence; the real but not-yet-fully realized relationship between believers on the earth and the Lord in heaven will be fulfilled (cf. 1 Cor 13:12). In every respect God will have been faithful to his promises.

4:18 Therefore encourage each other with these words.

As Paul began the eschatological discussion by expressing the value that this teaching had for the Thessalonian Christians (v. 13), so now he ends this section with a similar statement.

---

[45]MM, p. 53; Wilhelm Mundle, "Come," *NIDNTT*, 1:325.
[46]Michael Lattke, "ἀπαντάω, ἀπάντησις," *EDNT*, 1:115.
[47]For the former opinion see Wanamaker, pp. 169-170, 175-176; for the latter, Marshall, pp. 124-25.

In light of the context, the encouragement that this teaching offers first of all goes to the grieving that their separation from the dead will indeed be overcome. But as Paul has begun the larger section as an encouragement to live in order to please God (4:1), that note may be sounded here secondarily. As Marshall rightly points out, the text emphasizes not the reunion of the living with the dead in Christ but the reunion of all the Lord's people with the Lord himself.[48] That emphasis carries with it the imperative to live as one who spends eternity in the Lord's presence. Thus, the discussion of 5:1-11 will focus more specifically on the relevance of the Lord's coming to the day-to-day life of the Christian.

---

[48]Marshall, pp. 142-143.

1 THESSALONIANS 5

2. The Suddenness of the Lord's Return (5:1-11)

¹Now, brothers, about times and dates we do not need to write to you, ²for you know very well that the day of the Lord will come like a thief in the night. ³While people are saying, "Peace and safety," destruction will come on them suddenly, as labor pains on a pregnant woman, and they will not escape.

⁴But you, brothers, are not in darkness so that this day should surprise you like a thief. ⁵You are all sons of the light and sons of the day. We do not belong to the night or to the darkness. ⁶So then, let us not be like others, who are asleep, but let us be alert and self-controlled. ⁷For those who sleep, sleep at night, and those who get drunk, get drunk at night. ⁸But since we belong to the day, let us be self-controlled, putting on faith and love as a breastplate, and the hope of salvation as a helmet. ⁹For God did not appoint us to suffer wrath but to receive salvation through our Lord Jesus Christ. ¹⁰He died for us so that, whether we are awake or asleep, we may live together with him. ¹¹Therefore encourage one another and build each other up, just as in fact you are doing.

Paul's discussion of Christ's return now shifts from correcting their specific point of misunderstanding to a more general reminder and exhortation about its significance. Two key concepts stand in dynamic tension throughout New Testament teaching on the parousia: the possibility that Christ could return at any time and the prospect that his return will take longer than his people might expect or hope. Though modern scholars have attempted to reconstruct early Christian thinking as having begun with the first idea, later abandoning it for the second when the expectation of Christ's immediate return was disappointed, such a reconstruction fails to do justice to any part of the New Testament as it addresses these topics.[1]

It is precisely because of both sides of this teaching that Paul makes the exhortation here, based on Jesus' own instruction (cf. Matt 24:1-25:46; Mark 13:1-37; Luke 12:35-46; 17:22-37; 19:11-27; 21:1-38), for enduring watchfulness. The Lord will indeed come back, and he could do so at any moment. His followers must therefore live with that expectation and reflect it in their sober behavior. But because he may not come back immediately, they must strengthen each other to remain faithful.

As in the preceding section, the eschatological teaching here is given for its practical value, not for speculation. In particular, Paul has nothing to do with conjecture or hints about the precise time of the Lord's return or signs which may precede it. In fact, the entire course of his argument depends on the time of Christ's coming being uncertain. Instead, he offers this teaching to throw into sharp contrast the attitude, lifestyle and destiny of the Christians in comparison with their pagan neighbors. Understanding how their identity with Christ will affect eternity will in turn define for them how their lives are to be different in the present.

As the emphasis of the preceding section was on the salvation that comes with the Lord's return, so here the emphasis lies on the judgment that comes with that event. Like the tension between imminence and delay, this tension is consistently presented in biblical eschatology. Paul's assurance to the readers is that judgment for them is no threat: Christ's return means condemnation only for those who have rejected

---

[1]Cf. Kreitzer, "Eschatology," pp. 260-261; Brown, "The Parousia," pp. 903, 915-917.

him, the very people who now oppose and persecute the Christians.

5:1 Now, brothers, about times and dates we do not need to write to you,

Paul indicates with this statement that he continues the previous subject while altering the specific focus. Having shown how Christ's return provides comfort for the readers' grief, he now shifts to a reminder of the broader impact that their expectation should have on their behavior. "Times" translates the Greek χρόνος (*chronos*); "dates" represents καιρός (*kairos*). Both are expressions for time with broad ranges of possible meanings. Though they can be used with distinct emphases, no possible differentiation between them has relevance in context. Likewise, the fact that Paul uses the plural does not suggest that he assumes here a specific series of "times and dates" which will be fulfilled in the future. The point lies rather with the combination of both plural terms, underscoring the readers' comprehensive grasp of the nature of the age in which they live. The combination may, in fact, be a common way of referring to the time of final judgment (cf. Acts 1:7).[2]

The reason that Paul has no need to instruct the Thessalonians concerning these "times and dates" is clarified by the verses that follow. Paul does not assert here that they know the time or date of the Lord's return. The discussion that follows clearly depends on the time of his return being indefinite. The statement of Matt 24:26 is entirely consistent with Paul's point here. Instead, Paul emphasizes with this introductory reminder that the Thessalonians understand the character of the era in which they live. Because Christ has come and inaugurated the fulfillment of God's end-time promises, they recognize that they already live in the "last days," the age of fulfillment which is also characterized by deception, unbelief, suffering and persecution. They can therefore understand

---

[2]Bruce, pp. 108-109.

that such things are indications of the imminence of the judgment that will come for those unprepared for Christ's return (cf. 1:10; Matt 24:4-14, 32-35).

5:2 for you know very well that the day of the Lord will come like a thief in the night.

The comparison of the Lord's return to a thief in the night is found in a wide variety of texts in the New Testament (Matt 24:43; Luke 12:39; 2 Pet 3:10; Rev 3:3; 16:15). The distribution of these references through all parts of the New Testament indicates that this aspect of Jesus' teaching was widely circulated among early Christians. In this text and others the comparison stresses that for those who are not his followers, the Lord's return will be unexpected and disastrous. The thief's coming is secretive; those who are unprepared have no idea that he is coming at all. But the context does not permit the inference that he both comes and departs without being noticed, as in the eschatological view that argues for a "secret rapture." The image rather indicates that his coming is not expected prior to the event, but when the thief arrives, catastrophe comes suddenly and decisively on the unprepared.

Continuing the sentence begun in v. 1, Paul stresses that the readers already know what he offers here by way of reminder. Undoubtedly they had received this teaching as part of their larger instruction about Jesus. At a number of points, Paul's language in the following verses resembles passages of the Gospels dealing with Jesus' return.[3]

Paul here uses the expression "day of the Lord" to refer to Christ's return. The phrase has its background in the Old Testament (e.g., Isa 13:6-16; Joel 1:15; Amos 5:18-20; Obad 15-21; Zech 14). There it can signify any great action of God bringing blessing or judgment, but especially God's final and decisive act of judgment and redemption. Only Paul in the New Testament uses this specific phrase to refer directly to

---

[3]Cf. Wenham, *Eschatological Discourse*, pp. 54-55, 110-114.

the return of Christ (1 Cor 1:8; 5:5; 2 Cor 1:14; 2 Thess 2:2).[4] However, the basis for his associating Christ's return with the ultimate fulfillment of God's purpose is clearly set forth in Jesus' own teaching, and the concept of a coming "day" is found throughout the New Testament.[5] So the phrase would be familiar to the readers, as would its association with judgment for unbelievers but blessing for believers. No wonder, then, that Paul writes that the Thessalonians know this point "very well," ἀκριβῶς (akribōs), a word used commonly to stress that something is known accurately or thoroughly.[6]

5:3 While people are saying, "Peace and safety," destruction will come on them suddenly,

Paul's point here is similar to the one made in Matt 24:36-39: Christ will return in a time that appears to be ordinary and comfortable to unbelievers. Paul here describes the unbeliever's general, repeated characterization of life.[7] For such people the situation is "peace and safety." The first term is especially ironic, since from Paul's perspective real "peace" is available only through the Christ whom these have rejected (1:1; 5:23; Rom 5:1; cf. Jer 6:14-15; Ezek 13:10-16). "Safety" underscores the significance of the first term: there appears to be no threat to the peace that the unbeliever perceives. But such is emphatically not the case, for in place of this false security, indeed in the very midst of it, will come "destruction," signifying the complete ruin of their confidence and comfort (see comments on 2 Thess 1:9 below). Underlining

---

[4]Wolfgang Trilling, "ἡμέρα," *EDNT*, 2:121.

[5]Cf. Georg Braumann and Colin Brown, "Present, Day, Maranatha, Parousia," *NIDNTT*, 2:887-895. There is little basis in the NT for seeing the "day of the Lord" as a special time of tribulation immediately preceding the parousia as opposed to the parousia itself; the day always means blessing for God's people. Morris' discussion of whether believers will have to endure the "day" is therefore moot (pp. 151-152).

[6]Cf. MM, p. 19.

[7]The verb is a present subjunctive, signifying a repeated, indefinite action; cf. MHT 3:112.

the unexpectedness is the modifier "suddenly." This term, αἰφνίδιος (*aiphnidios*) is used elsewhere in the New Testament only in Luke 21:34, where the same verb, ἐφίστημι (*ephistēmi*, "comes"), not a common verb for this concept, is used also. The echo of Jesus' teaching is unmistakable.[8] The verb here is in the Greek present tense, stressing the common, repeated experience of all those unprepared.

as labor pains on a pregnant woman, and they will not escape.

The comparison of the Lord's return to labor pains has two apparent points of comparison in context. The first looks back to the first part of the verse: like labor pains, the Lord's return will come suddenly. The second is found in the close of the verse: as with labor, there will be no escape. The verb translated "escape," ἐκφεύγω (*ekpheugō*), appears also in Luke 21:35, again connecting this passage to Jesus' teaching. Paul does use the figure of labor pains in a different sense than is found in Matt 24:8. There Jesus warns the disciples not to view the hardships which they will experience as indications that the end has already come but as the "beginnings of birth pangs," only the most preliminary of events that precede the end. Though Paul obviously uses the same image here to make a different point, he may still be consciously drawing upon Jesus' teachings by way of reminder for the readers.

5:4 But you, brothers, are not in darkness so that this day should surprise you like a thief.

Paul begins this verse with an emphatic pronoun, ὑμεῖς (*hymeis*, "you"), which draws a sharp contrast between those not prepared for Christ's return and the readers of the letter. These, again, are "brothers," those drawn into the fellowship of God's people and so prepared for his final judgment. Such people are not in darkness but light, associated with God and

---

[8]Wanamaker notes that the verse contains several expressions which are exceptional in Paul's letters (p. 180).

his truth.[9] The dawning of the "day" is therefore for them not a catastrophe but a blessing. "Surprise" renders καταλαμβάνω (*katalambanō*), literally signifying to overtake or seize, especially with hostile intent.[10] Paul's point is not that the day of the Lord is no surprise because the readers know when it will come but that when it does come, they can welcome it rather than fear it.

5:5 You are all sons of the light and sons of the day.

From the contrast between light and darkness, Paul will now draw out the exhortation that forms the main thrust of this discussion. As God's people, the readers belong to the light, a common metaphor for God's truth (cf. Ps 27:1; 112:4; Prov 4:18-19; Isa 9:2; 5:20; Matt 5:14; Luke 2:32; John 1:4-9; 1 John 2:8). According to the common turn of phrase in Semitic languages, Paul here calls those characterized by an object as "sons of" that object (cf. Luke 16:8; Eph 5:8).[11] The second expression, "sons of the day" probably connects both backward to the "day of the Lord" (v. 2), indicating that the believers can anticipate that day in confidence, and forward to the contrast with the evil behavior that characterizes the night (v. 7).

We do not belong to the night or to the darkness.

The whole image is reinforced and developed with the negative statement about the night and darkness that follows. As those characterized by light, the people of God have nothing to fear from something that comes as a thief for those in the darkness. As a corollary, their behavior should fit the light to which they belong. And so Paul next sets forth two behavioral implications of belonging to God's light.

---

[9]Hans-Christoph Hahn and Colin Brown, "Light, Shine, Lamp," *NIDNTT*, 2:490-496.

[10]BAGD, pp. 412-413.

[11]Cf. BDF, § 162.6. The Qumran scrolls demonstrate a similar usage, referring to the members of the Qumran sect as "sons of light" (1QS 3:13-15, 20-21; 4:18-19, 22-23; cf. *HCNT*, § 823).

5:6 So then, let us not be like others, who are asleep, but let us be alert and self-controlled.

This verse begins with two Greek particles (ἄρα οὖν, *ara oun*, "so then") combined for emphasis, indicating that the statement which follows is a direct consequence of what precedes.[12] This Paul states as an exhortation, identifying himself along with the readers as under the obligation to act in the way he describes. Because Christians belong to the light, to be "asleep" for them is inappropriate.[13] The comparison here is with the self-sufficient insensibility that characterizes those who do not expect Christ to return.

By contrast Christians are to "be alert." This phrase translates γρηγορέω (*grēgoreō*), which has the literal meaning "to be awake" but often takes the sense of being watchful.[14] This verb is again found in Jesus' teaching on his return (Matt 24:42-43; 25:13; Mark 13:34-35, 37; Luke 12:36-38; cf. Rev 3:2-3; 16:15), stressing the necessity of the disciple to be faithful in the Lord's absence, expecting the Lord's return at any time and so busy in faithful service at all times. The specific way in which Paul urges faithfulness here first is implied by the contrast with those who sleep: the readers are to resist the pressure from their pagan society to conform to its immoral and self-indulgent habits.

That point is further underlined with the addition of "self-controlled," the Greek νήφω (*nēphō*), which literally means to be sober as opposed to drunk. Though Paul's point partly

---

[12]Wanamaker notes that Paul uses this combination elsewhere as he does here, to introduce the ethical implications of a preceding statement (Rom 8:12; Gal 6:10; 2 Thess 2:15; cf. Rom 5:18; 7:3; 8:1; Wanamaker, pp. 183-184).

[13]The verb for "sleep" in vv. 6, 7 and 10, καθεύδω (*katheudō*), is found elsewhere in Paul's letters only in Eph 5:14, where Paul apparently quotes either a combination of OT texts or an early Christian hymn or tradition. It is different from the word in 4:13-15, κοιμάομαι (*koimaomai*), which Paul uses elsewhere in 1 Cor 7:39; 11:30; 15:6, 18, 20, 51. The unusual word is probably used here as an echo of Jesus' teaching, since it is found in Matt 25:5; Mark 13:36.

[14]Johannes M. Nützel, "γρηγορέω," *EDNT*, 1:264-265.

relates to literal soberness, his point is much broader, as the following verses show: he has in mind the keen grasp of spiritual reality that comes from knowing God truly through Christ.[15] Both verbs are in the present tense, stressing that the actions are to be continuing.

5:7 For those who sleep, sleep at night, and those who get drunk, get drunk at night.

At the very least, this verse continues and amplifies the comparisons of vv. 5-6. Both sleep and drunkenness were associated with the night (the latter is less confined to the night in our culture than in Paul's). But clearly, as in v. 6, the expressions here are figurative, suggesting the spiritual insensitivity and absence of clear thinking which result from unbelief. Paul's point may also go further, however. Since drunkenness was associated with revels honoring the Greek god Dionysus, and sometimes in that setting seen as a medium of receiving enlightenment from the god, Paul may here set the Christian's position in sharp contrast with those practices.[16] The implication of the revelation of God received by the Christians is different from such pagan practices, as the following verse emphasizes. There also may be another echo here of Jesus' teaching, since drunkenness is one vice of the unfaithful servants in Luke 12:45.[17]

5:8 But since we belong to the day, let us be self-controlled,

Paul now amplifies the meaning of "self-controlled" or "sober" with the figure of a soldier or sentry, perhaps suggested by the idea of watchfulness. Reiterating the foundational point, that Christians belong to God and his truth, Paul stresses that they must put that identity and truth into practice, using the blessings which they have received in Christ as a

---

[15]Cf. Otto Bauernfeind, "νήφω, κτλ," *TDNT*, 4:936-939.
[16]Cf. Bauernfeind, "νήφω, κτλ," pp. 938-939; Donfried, *Shorter Letters*, pp. 49-50.
[17]Wenham, *Eschatological Discourse*, p. 63.

means of protection against the ungodly influences that surround them. Grammatically "putting on" supports "be self-controlled," setting forth the means by which that self-control is accomplished.[18]

putting on faith and love as a breastplate, and the hope of salvation as a helmet.
As in Rom 13:12 and Eph 6:10-18, Paul compares God's provision for the Christian to armor, and in common with the latter passage, he elaborates by discussing specific pieces of armor. But his point is less on the identification of specific parts of armor with specific ideas than on the concept that God has equipped the Christian with all that is needed for the battle with evil. In this text, even the idea of battle itself is not directly stated. In light of the preceding context, however, it is clear that Paul implies that the readers must continue to struggle against the dominant pagan culture.

In this text Paul highlights God's provision in the three cardinal virtues of 1:3, climaxing with hope as the helmet at the apex of the image. Paul's comparison of the breastplate to faith and love is different from Eph 6:14, which alludes more precisely to Isa 59:17 in connecting righteousness to the breastplate. "Hope of salvation" is an ambiguous phrase here: it may mean either "the hope that comes from salvation" or "the hope that looks forward to salvation." Since the following verse refers to salvation as something yet to be received, the second alternative is probably Paul's specific sense. However, in light of the common misuse of this phrase among some modern Christians, it must be stressed that "hope of salvation" means not just "a chance of being saved" but "a confident expectation of being saved." Paul's point, then, is that by

---

[18]Wanamaker too narrowly delineates the possible range of meaning for the aorist participle here when he asserts that it must indicate an action antecedent to the main verb (p. 185). Aorist participles are by nature capable of having any one of many relationships to their main clauses (cf. BDF, § 339: "The notion of relative past time, however, is not at all necessarily inherent in the aorist participle").

practicing faith, love and hope the readers can overcome the pressures of their environment to conform to pagan standards, thereby proving faithful to the Lord who returns for their salvation.

5:9 For God did not appoint us to suffer wrath but to receive salvation through our Lord Jesus Christ.

Paul now makes explicit the basis for the confidence in salvation expressed in the preceding phrase. He has noted already that Jesus delivers his people from God's wrath (1:10). The contrast here further stresses that point as a source of confidence in the readers' ongoing struggle with their surroundings. "Wrath," God's holy anger against sin, belongs not to the Christians but to those who continue to live in deliberate ignorance of God. God's purpose in extending his call to the readers is to receive (περιποίησις, *peripoiēsis*) salvation (cf. 2 Thess 2:14), made possible through the work of Jesus. If the behavior of the unbelievers reflects their ignorance of God and ultimately brings God's wrath, those who know God and have been delivered from wrath will want to have nothing to do with such conduct. Confidence in salvation, then, should not lead to indifference about how one lives but should motivate the watchful, sober, faithful obedience which Paul encourages here.

The use of "appoint" here raises the question of God's activity in salvation in relation to human response. Reformed exegetes have traditionally taken such expressions to mean that God has appointed some to salvation apart from their fulfilling any condition of salvation. God then causes those people to have faith and practice obedience, including the watchful faithfulness discussed in this section. However, Marshall rightly points out that this concept is nowhere articulated in this passage; Paul does not say that a failure to be watchful indicates that one was never a Christian in the first place. Rather, as Marshall expresses it:

> At this point in the letter Paul is dealing with the fear of his readers that the day of the Lord may overtake them

unprepared for it. He is assuring them that they do not need to know the date and specially prepare for it, because if they are Christians they will be in such a state of preparedness that the day will not come as a day of judgment on their sin. There is certainly a danger that Christians could fall asleep and the final day will surprise them like it will the non-believers; let them beware lest that happens. But God intends for them to be saved, and he has given them many guarantees for this. Let them therefore trust in him, remain faithful and watchful.[19]

5:10 He died for us

The discussion of the previous verse continues, still in support of the admonition of v. 8, but specifically developing the concept of the end of v. 9. Salvation has been made possible specifically through Jesus' death. Paul's understanding of the means by which the cross brings salvation, his "theory of the atonement," is probably expressed most clearly in Rom 3:25: Christ died as a "propitiation," a substitutionary sacrifice satisfying the wrath of God which, according to his justice, must exact a penalty for sin.[20] Hence, "for us" here probably expresses that idea in brief: Jesus died in place of us, as our substitute, taking our penalty. By his death, deliverance from God's wrath is effected.

so that, whether we are awake or asleep, we may live together with him.

But the positive side of salvation is effected as well, as is expressed at the end of the verse. Salvation means not only escaping the penalty of sin but also union with Christ in his resurrection and consequent fellowship with him in the present and the future (Rom 6; 2 Cor 4-5; Gal 2:20). Paul combines terms to make this point emphatically: "together with" translates ἅμα σύν (*hama syn*; cf. 4:17), which in combination stress that the believers are with Christ under all circumstances.

---

[19]Marshall, "Election and Calling," pp. 268-269.
[20]Cf. Morris, *Apostolic Preaching*, pp. 144-213.

The images of wakefulness and sleep are now compared to different objects than in vv. 6-8. Clearly, in light of the earlier discussion, Paul does not here equivocate about whether Christians should remain alert. Instead, he shifts these images back to the comparison found in 4:13-15, where sleep refers to death. This comparison makes Paul's point here all the more clear and serves to tie the larger discussion of 4:13-5:11 together. Nothing can separate the believer from Christ's love and fellowship, not even death itself. Whether alive or dead, Christians can be assured that they belong to God through Christ in every respect. As they look forward to the culmination of that relationship when Christ returns, they live out an alert and faithful life by demonstrating their union with Christ through Christlike behavior.

5:11 Therefore encourage one another and build each other up, just as in fact you are doing.

As in 4:18, so here Paul concludes his eschatological discussion by reminding the readers to recognize the value of the message as a source of encouragement. In both verses Paul uses παρακαλέω (*parakaleō*, "encouragement") as the verb, though with a slightly different emphasis. In 4:18 the emphasis was on the encouragement that ameliorates grief. Here it is encouragement to positive Christian behavior and resistance to temptation. That point is made clear by the addition of "build up," (οἰκοδομέω, *oikodomeō*). Paul often uses this term and related ones, picturing the church and its members as a building under construction by God, a building which will ultimately conform to God's design.

To "build up" one another, then, implies that by practicing and encouraging watchfulness, the Thessalonian Christians will move into closer conformity with God's intention for them. Again, if the particular concern of the context is that the readers not succumb to the pressures of pagan society, the need for encouragement and edification is clear. These responsibilities are to be discharged by each member of the church for the other, as Paul expresses that idea with distinct objects for each verb. And they are to be done continually, as indicated by the Greek present tense with both verbs. Closing the discussion on a note of confidence, Paul indicates that the readers are already following these instructions, as they have received them before (cf. v. 2).

C. GENERAL EXHORTATIONS (5:12-22)

Paul's letters commonly include a loosely organized series of general exhortations near the conclusion, as is found here. Unlike the contents of the previous section, these instructions are not so much aimed at specific issues or problems in the church as at the broader life of the believers. Because of the similarities between this passage and Rom 12:11-18, it has been suggested that Paul has inserted a traditional Jewish-Christian exhortation.[21] However, in the topics addressed, one can still see Paul's concern for the Thessalonian church's particular situation.[22] Even these general instructions are especially fitting for a church in its early stages of development, still acutely vulnerable to confusion about the content of its faith, to internal strife and to pressure from a hostile environment.

1. Behavior in the Christian Community (5:12-15)

¹²Now we ask you, brothers, to respect those who work hard among you, who are over you in the Lord and who admonish you. ¹³Hold them in the highest regard in love because of their work. Live in peace with each other. ¹⁴And we urge you, brothers, warn those who are idle, encourage the timid, help the weak, be patient with everyone. ¹⁵Make

---

[21]Cf. the discussion of this possibility in Wanamaker, p. 191.
[22]Cf. Marshall, p. 146.

sure that nobody pays back wrong for wrong, but always try to be kind to each other and to everyone else.

The first section of general exhortations deals with responsibilities of Christians toward others in the church. The section divides itself into two subsections, each introduced with a first-person, plural verb: "we ask" (ἐρωτῶμεν, *erōtōmen*, v. 12) and "we urge" (παρακαλοῦμεν, *parakaloumen*, v. 14). The first of these is the instruction to respect and submit to leaders (vv. 12-13a), a reminder which may have been especially important for a church still so young in the faith. This concludes with a general command to peace (v. 13b), leading in turn to another series of exhortations about mutual responsibilities in serving one another (vv. 14-15). Prominent here are instructions which seem to address issues indicated elsewhere in the letter, especially the responsibility to support oneself by working (4:11-12), to remain firm in persecution (1:6; 2:13-14; 3:3-5, 8) and to exercise love for each other (1:3; 4:9-10).

Respect for Christian Leaders (5:12-13)

5:12 Now we ask you, brothers, to respect those who work hard among you, who are over you in the Lord and who admonish you.

Paul's instructions here clearly focus attention on those who function as leaders in the Thessalonian church. In critical study of the New Testament for the last two centuries, it has become a commonplace to assert that leadership in the early church evolved from an informal, dynamic, "charismatic" approach, in which those gifted for leadership simply exercised their function, to a formal, static, "hierarchical" approach in which leaders were more deliberately appointed to specific offices, powers and responsibilities. In large measure this model is supported by a comparison of Paul's earlier letters, where terms such as "elders," "overseers" or "deacons" are absent but discussion of gifts and functions are prominent, with 1 Timothy and Titus, widely regarded as post-Pauline pseudepigraphs, or Acts, again taken as a late-first-century work, where titles appear prominently.

While the whole of this issue cannot be addressed here, several observations are in order. First, the fact that Paul's letters are written for specific circumstances strongly argues against reading too much into their silences. The fact that he describes leadership by function instead of title here, for example, does not mean that terms like "elder" or "overseer" were not used in the Thessalonian church. Likewise, the focus on gifts as opposed to titles in 1 Corinthians arises very specifically out of the problems which Paul addresses in ch. 12-14, as the more prominent place of titles in 1 Timothy and Titus arises out of the threat of false teaching addressed in those letters.

Secondly, one cannot assume that the use of a title indicates a shift from functional dynamism to static hierarchy in leadership. "Elder" (πρεσβύτερος, *presbyteros*) and "overseer" (ἐπίσκοπος, *episkopos*) were both widely used in the first century outside the church; adoption of those terms early in the early years of the church to refer to those who exercised leadership would hardly be surprising.

Thirdly, whatever the value of the evidence of Acts or the Pastoral Epistles, other uses of titles for leaders cannot be easily dismissed as late developments. Specifically Phil 1:1 and 1 Pet 5:1-4 argue strongly for the early use of such titles.

Finally, the distinction between functional and official leadership appears to be more a consequence of the hypothesis that church leadership evolved along the lines described by the theory than of what the text actually says. Is the command to respect leaders here genuinely less "official" than the instructions of 1 Tim 3, or are those instructions any less "functional" than these?[23]

---

[23]For an example of the common critical approach to this issue and of the assumptions which underlie it, note the following statements of Joachim Rohde: "In Acts 20:28 . . . this speech does not reflect the organization of the Pauline mission churches, but presupposes rather the offices in

Still it must be recognized that Paul's emphasis on leadership, in 1 Tim 3:1, 5, 10, 13 and Titus 1:9 no less than other passages, is on the function of leadership rather than titles, offices or powers.[24] That function can broadly be termed pastoral, centering on the protection and nurture of fellow Christians in their faith and leading to their maturity. Paul describes that function with three participles here, all governed by one definite article to indicate that he speaks of one group of persons who do all three activities, and all in the present tense to stress continuing action. "Work hard" translates literally and accurately the Greek κοπιάω (*kopiaō*), which indicates laboring to the point of weariness. "Are over you" renders προΐστημι (*proistēmi*). This term is ambiguous in this context: it could suggest either the exercise of leadership and direction (cf. 1 Tim 3:4, 5, 12; 5:17) or of care and assistance (cf. Rom 12:8).[25] However, there is little distinction between

---

Christian congregations at the time of the origin of Acts — at the end of the first century. Likewise the Pastorals do not reflect the organization of the Christian churches in the last years of Paul's life, but that of the period when the deutero-Pauline writings came into existence — at the end of the first century. . . . The ἐπίσκοποι and deacons of Philippians cannot be identified with those of the Pastorals" ("ἐπίσκοπος," *EDNT*, 2:36). For a response to this approach see E. Earle Ellis, "Pastoral Letters," *DPL*, pp. 659-660.

[24]Cf. Robert Banks, "Church Order," *DPL*, pp. 131-137.

[25]Cf. BAGD, p. 707. As a specific sense of the second possible meaning, Wayne Meeks has suggested that Paul here refers to those who were financial patrons of the Thessalonian church (*The First Urban Christians: The Social World of the Apostle Paul* [New Haven, CT: Yale University Press, 1983], p. 134). However, the evidence is at best slim that such people could by virtue of their patronage be said to "labor" or "admonish" as well. Wanamaker argues that those wealthy enough to be financial patrons could support themselves as they exercised leadership and had the social status to reinforce their corrective instruction (pp. 193-195). However, support for this conclusion is also lacking. If Paul's discussion of his self-support through his trade has any relevance to the Thessalonians' situation, we may well question whether patronage was of much relevance to leadership in the church. Secondly, it is not entirely clear from 1 Cor 16:16-18 that Stephanus, the most widely cited example of a "patron" in Paul's letters, in fact financially supports the Corinthian church.

those two senses in Paul's lexicon, since according to Christ's model authority is always exercised in self-sacrificial service which seeks others' benefit (cf. 1 Cor 9:1-23; Phil 2:1-11; Mark 10:35-45; John 13:1-20). No wonder, then, that Paul describes this function as being "in the Lord": leaders function in this way because of the union with Christ shared by the entire church. The third term, νουθετέω (*noutheteō*, "admonish") indicates instruction in correct belief and behavior, especially as it addresses some problem or deficiency (cf. v. 14; 2 Thess 3:15).[26]

The readers are told first of all to "respect" these leaders. Literally the Greek term οἶδα (*oida*) here means "to know," but in context it implies a recognition of the vital function for which these leaders have been gifted and, consequently, cooperation with and submission to their nurturing work. Possible but less likely are the meanings "take an interest in" or "care for," particularly in light of the complementary instruction of the next verse.[27]

5:13 Hold them in the highest regard in love because of their work.

This sentence in the NIV is actually a continuation of the sentence in the previous verse, naming an action coordinated with "respect." The action is expressed in the Greek present tense, indicating a continuing action. Paul uses an emphatic adverb, ὑπερεκπερισσῶς (*hyperekperissōs*) to describe the regard that the church should have for its leaders. This regard is based, however, not on submission to power but self-giving love (ἀγάπη, *agapē*) and respect for the vital nature of the work which these leaders perform.

What specific purpose did Paul have for these instructions? It may be that a particular faction of the Thessalonian church, perhaps the "idle" of v. 14, was not in submission to the leaders.[28] But the broad terms in which the instructions

---

[26]Cf. *GELNTBSD*, §§ 33.231, 418, 424.
[27]BAGD, p. 556.
[28]Cf. Marshall, pp. 149-150.

are given may indicate less a problem in respect for leaders than the importance that it had for the situation. As an infant church whose nurture had been cut short by Paul's hasty departure and which faced ongoing persecution, the congregation's stability and growth depended largely on its loving submission to those with the gifts and maturity to lead it. The work of leadership, always important, carried a special premium under these circumstances.

Live in peace with each other.
Coming at the end of the instructions about the relationship to church leaders and before the "we urge you" that marks off the next section, these words probably are intended by Paul to address further the leadership issue. "Peace" is, of course, a primary consequence of being a Christian (1:1) and belonging to "the God of peace" (5:23). It must be put into practice continually (the verb is again in the Greek present tense) in all aspects of the church's life. But Paul's placing the instruction here may reflect his recognition that maintaining genuine harmony and cooperation is especially crucial in relationships between spiritual leaders and those in their care.

Service and Forgiveness (5:14-15)

5:14 And we urge you, brothers, warn those who are idle,
"We urge you, brothers" parallels the beginning of v. 12 and signals a new set of instructions for life in the church. Here the focus is on mutual responsibilities of all Christians toward each other. Four brief commands, all in the present tense to emphasize continuing action, follow in quick succession. Paul has structured this statement as a sharp and memorable reminder of how responsible Christian brotherhood will be lived out in the circumstances faced by the Thessalonian church.

The first command raises an interpretive problem. "Warn" here translates νουθετέω (*noutheteō*), rendered as "admonish" in v. 12, but here with the same sense of offering correction, a mutual responsibility here given to all the Thessalonian Christians, not just the leaders. The difficulty comes with the term translated "idle," ἄτακτος (*ataktos*). Literally the term means "disorderly," but its specific sense, as is the case with all words, varies with its context. The immediately surrounding discourse gives little reason to take the word in anything other than its broadest sense.

However, the cognate words ἀτακτέω (*atakteō*) and ἀτάκτως (*ataktōs*) appear in 2 Thess 3:7 and 2 Thess 3:6, 11 respectively, where they clearly refer to those in the church who do not support themselves. On that basis, the word here should almost certainly be taken with the sense reflected in the NIV (cf. 4:11-12), a meaning attested in some uses of the word outside the New Testament also. This idleness should be understood as not so much laziness but rebellious irresponsibility or willful idleness: those who do not work are abandoning the charge that is theirs as Christians.[29]

encourage the timid, help the weak, be patient with everyone.

The following commands are straightforward in meaning, though still related to the circumstances of the Thessalonian church. The "timid" are ὀλιγόψυχος (*oligopsychos*), a word which probably points to a state of discouragement.[30] They are to be "encouraged"; παραμυθέομαι (*paramytheomai*) indicates especially the comfort or encouragement given to those in grief or pain.[31] In the next command "weak" could refer to those suffering physical illness, but in light of the preceding almost certainly indicates those who are weak in faith. Taken together, these two commands suggest the kind of response especially necessary in the face of persecution.

The fourth command rounds out the series. "Be patient"

---

[29]Gerhard Delling, "τάσσω, κτλ," *TDNT*, 8:47-48.
[30]Cf. MM, p. 445; Albert Dihle, *et al.*, "ψυχή, κτλ," *TDNT*, 9:665-666.
[31]Cf. *GELNTBSD*, § 25.153.

translates μακροθυμέω (*makrothymeō*), which indicates particularly the restraint of anger, in the New Testament especially enjoined on believers because God has offered forgiveness in place of wrath.[32] The readers must extend such patience to all because God has extended his patience to all. This instruction is, of course, applicable under all circumstances, but it may have had special relevance for Christians facing the pressures of persecution.

5:15 Make sure that nobody pays back wrong for wrong, but always try to be kind to each other and to everyone else.

The same pressures and the same compelling truths underlying the command for patience also support this command. Seeking retribution is excluded here as elsewhere in the New Testament (e.g., Matt 5:38-48) both because of God's offer of forgiveness noted above and because of his promise of judgment on the unrepentant (cf. 2 Thess 1:6-10). So in imitation of God's forgiveness and with consideration for his role as ultimate judge, Christians are to shun retribution under all circumstances.

Several features of this verse underline this point. Both imperatives, "make sure" and "try," are in the present tense, implying continuing action. The first is from ὁράω (*horaō*), "watch," suggesting a constant vigilance against this temptation. "Pay back" quite literally translates ἀποδίδωμι (*apodidōmi*), which is used to indicate repayment of an obligation. Though it might be seen as such from other vantages, from the perspective of the gospel vengeance is never an obligation. "Try" translates διώκω (*diōkō*), a strong expression often meaning "pursue" and so implying here an active, ardent effort to do good in place of evil. This responsibility belongs first to the community of faith, but because God has forgiven those hostile to him, Christians must extend this attitude to those outside their fellowship as well — even, by implication, to persecutors.

---

[32]Cf. Ulrich Flakenroth and Colin Brown, "Patience, Steadfastness, Endurance," *NIDNTT*, 2:764, 768-72.

2. Constants of Christian Behavior (5:16-18)

¹⁶Be joyful always; ¹⁷pray continually; ¹⁸give thanks in all circumstances, for this is God's will for you in Christ Jesus.

This brief section sets forth in terse and memorable fashion three imperatives which are to characterize the Christian's life at all times. The short, parallel imperatives here are similar to other Pauline exhortations (cf. Rom 12:9-13). In tone, and in some respects in content, these brief instructions reflect what Paul has shown of his own behavior in 1:2-3:10.

The three commands in these verses are expressed in parallel form: each begins with a different adverb or adverbial prepositional phrase emphasizing that the action is to be constant, and in each the command is expressed with a single verb in the present tense, indicating a continuing action. "Be joyful" is literally "rejoice" (χαίρω, *chairō*), the consequence of having received God's salvation and therefore an attitude unaffected by outward circumstances (cf. 2 Cor 4:16-18; Phil 3:1; 4:4; Col 1:24). Constant prayer is likewise a feature of Christian life as it expresses confident dependence on God's provision (cf. Phil 4:13). The reality of salvation as both a present and a future experience yields the constant thanksgiving enjoined here; in all things the person of faith can have assurance that God's purpose is being achieved (cf. Rom 8:28-39).

3. Responding to Christian Prophecy (5:19-22)

¹⁹Do not put out the Spirit's fire; ²⁰do not treat prophecies with contempt. ²¹Test everything. Hold on to the good. ²²Avoid every kind of evil.

The exercise of the gift of prophecy is a distinguishing feature of the early church. Acts identifies prophecy as the consequence of the pouring out of the Spirit promised in Joel (Acts 2:17-18) and draws attention to the exercise of the prophetic gift at critical points in the church's development (Acts 11:27-30; 13:1-3; 15:32; 21:8-14). Paul indicates that prophecy is the most crucial gift to be exercised for the edification of the Corinthian church (1 Cor 14:1-4, 39), though this gift is partial and temporary (1 Cor 13:8-12). In Ephesians Paul links prophets to apostles as the "foundation" of the church (Eph 2:20; 3:5; 4:11).

For Paul and other New Testament writers "prophecy" refers to speech which has been directly inspired by God. Though it could involve prediction of the future, any divinely-inspired message could be called prophecy. The explicit examples of prophecy in Acts all involve specific, practical instructions or warnings to the church at a particular place and time (see references above). Paul's discussion of prophecy probably includes such "occasional" oracles, but his statements that prophets stand at the church's foundation and that the mystery of Christ has been revealed to them (Eph 2:20; 3:5) indicate that Christian prophets delivered doctrinal as well as practical messages.

At this point controversy arises as to the modern relevance of Christian prophecy. Should Christians expect to prophesy today as did the first-century prophets? If so, should they expect to receive additional doctrinal revelation? Despite the attempts of some exegetes to limit early Christian prophecy to non-doctrinal, occasional matters only, the use of "prophet" in Ephesians almost certainly indicates that the gift involved some doctrinal revelation. But if doctrinal revelation is seen as continuing in every generation of the church, Paul's statement about the foundation is clearly compromised. The central concept of the gospel, that in Jesus Christ the purpose of God in history has been uniquely and fully accomplished, carries with it the implication that the message of Christ, revealed to those first "apostles and prophets" closely associated with Christ's appearance in history, is likewise unique and full.

It therefore appears that Paul's statement that prophecy would "cease" (1 Cor 13:8-10) has in fact been fulfilled with the close of the apostolic age. Pentecostals and Charismatics may argue this point with "cessationists," but the foundational, apostolic and prophetic deposit of doctrine must in no way be obscured by any exercise of modern-day "prophecy," whether genuine or otherwise.[33]

This section briefly reminds the Thessalonian Christians of the imperatives for the proper exercise of this gift. It stresses, on the one hand, that prophecy be exercised fully and accepted readily. Certainly this gift would have been important for a young church still digesting the basics of the gospel message. But at the same time Paul cautions against merely accepting any utterance claiming to be prophetic as a genuine message of God. Donfried has suggested that the Thessalonian Christians may have easily confused genuine Spirit-inspired utterances with the claims to divine enlightenment in the Dionysian revels.[34] Whether this is the case or not, a credulous church could easily have been deceived by a false claim to prophetic inspiration. In fact, such a thing appears to underlie Paul's discussion in 2 Thess 2:1-12.[35]

In place of naive acceptance of everything claiming to be prophecy, Paul calls for the testing of prophecy. In this respect his words are no less applicable today, even among Christians who do not believe that the gift of prophecy still operates in the church as it did then. The need to test all kinds of ideas from all kinds of sources — including claims to modern-day miraculous gifts of the Spirit — is just as necessary now as it was then, and the stakes are just as serious. And

---

[33]For a survey of the issues concerning prophecy in the early church, see Cecil M. Robeck, Jr., "Prophecy, Prophesying," *DPL*, pp. 755-762. For a thorough presentation of the so-called "cessationist" view of prophecy and other miraculous gifts, see Richard B. Gaffin, *Perspectives on Pentecost: Studies in New Testament Teaching on the Gifts of the Holy Spirit* (Phillipsburg, NJ: Presbyterian and Reformed, 1979).

[34]Donfried, *Shorter Pauline Letters*, pp. 49-50.

[35]There is nothing aside from the conjectures of modern scholars about the sociological dynamics of the Pauline churches to support the idea that vv. 12-13 and vv. 19-22 reflect a conflict in the Thessalonian church between official leaders and charismatic prophets (*contra* Jewett, *Thessalonian Correspondence*, pp. 174-175; Wanamaker, pp. 202-203).

the standard by which the test is made, now as then, can be nothing other than the apostolic gospel, delivered to us through the New Testament itself.[36]

Yielding to the Spirit's Work (5:19-20)

5:19 Do not put out the Spirit's fire; 5:20 do not treat prophecies with contempt.

These twin imperatives express Paul's encouragement to heed the prophecies received by the church. The first focuses particularly on the Spirit's role in inspiring the prophet. Paul's expression is literally, "Do not quench the Spirit," by implication comparing the Spirit's work to a fire that could be doused with water. That Paul has the Spirit's work in prophecy in mind is made clear with the next command. "Treat with contempt" translates ἐχουθενέω (*exoutheneō*), which implies disdain and utter rejection. To ignore or disobey God's inspired instruction would be most perilous for this young congregation. Both commands are expressed in the Greek present tense, indicating continuing action.

Testing Prophecy (5:21-22)

5:21 Test everything. Hold on to the good. 5:22 Avoid every kind of evil.

These words, like v. 19, could be taken in a general sense, but combined with v. 20 they appear to address again the specific issue of prophecy. "Test" here translates δοκιμάζω (*dokimazō*), which implies in particular a test to prove genuineness.[37] How prophecies are to be tested is something that Paul does not articulate here; he apparently assumes that the

---

[36]Cf. Marshall, pp. 159-160.

[37]On the possible connection between this statement and a saying attributed to Jesus in the early church fathers but not found in the Gospels (γίνεσθε τραπεζῖται δόκιμοι [*ginesthe trapezitai dokimoi*], "Be approved money changers") see Joachim Jeremias, *Unknown Sayings of Jesus* (London:

readers have already been instructed in this matter. But we can infer that the test would involve at least a comparison of the prophecy's content to what the readers had already received in the gospel (cf. Matt 24:4-5, 11, 23-27; Mark 13:5-6, 21-23; Luke 17:23; 21:8-11; 1 Cor 12:1-3, 10; 14:29; 1 John 4:1-3). Paul's own "test" in 2 Thess 2:1-12 of a supposed prophecy about the Lord's return having already occurred is of this kind, based on the gospel's affirmation that Christ's return will mean the end of every manifestation of evil (see discussion below).

The results of the test are expressed in the two commands that follow. These are expressed in parallel fashion. "Hold on" translates κατέχω (*katechō*), literally "hold fast to"; "avoid" renders ἀπέχω (*apechō*), literally "hold away." As if to underline the importance of the negative command, Paul adds the phrase "every kind," subtly suggesting the broad range of threats to the believers' faith.

V. CONCLUSION (5:23-28)

²³**May God himself, the God of peace, sanctify you through and through. May your whole spirit, soul and body be kept blameless at the coming of our Lord Jesus Christ. ²⁴The one who calls you is faithful and he will do it.**

²⁵**Brothers, pray for us. ²⁶Greet all the brothers with a holy kiss. ²⁷I charge you before the Lord to have this letter read to all the brothers.**

²⁸**The grace of our Lord Jesus Christ be with you.**

Paul's letters generally end with a combination of the elements seen here: a benediction or prayer for God's blessing (a "wish-prayer"; cf. discussion of 3:11-13 above), a request for

---

SPCK, 1958), pp. 89-93. There is evidence to suggest that this is a genuine saying of Jesus and that Paul alludes to it here, though by no means is the evidence sufficient to prove either postulate.

prayer for himself, a word of greeting, instructions about the reading of the letter, and a pronouncement of blessing. Though such conclusions are loosely structured and contain stock elements, they nevertheless express the close relationship which Paul has with the churches and his confidence in God's protection and blessing for them and for him while they are separated.

A. BENEDICTION (5:23-24)

5:23 May God himself, the God of peace, sanctify you through and through.

Paul's prayer highlights the connection between God's peace and his work in making his people holy. For Paul this was apparently a significant connection: to be at peace with God and others could come only through holiness.[38] Holiness is, of course, already an attribute of the readers, as they have been made God's people through Christ (3:13). It is also their ongoing responsibility to live in holiness (4:3-4, 7).[39] Here, then, is the final assurance that God will indeed bring to completion the work which he began at their conversion and continues as they live their lives as Christians. Paul stresses this idea with the adverb ὁλοτελής (*holotelēs*, "through and through"), a compound word which emphasizes the utter completion of the process.

A controversial theological issue hinges on the interpretation of this statement, namely the idea of "entire sanctification," that God gives to some a second act of grace by which they are made incapable of sinning. Exegetically this conclusion is drawn from the use of the aorist tense here, which, it is argued, indicates a single, momentary action. Even if this

---

[38]Cf. the discussion in Jouette M. Bassler, "Peace in All Ways," *Pauline Theology, Volume I: Thessalonians, Philippians, Galatians, Philemon* (*idem*, ed., Minneapolis: Fortress, 1991), pp. 81-82.

[39]Cf. Stanley E. Porter, "Holiness, Sanctification," *DPL*, pp. 397-402.

were the case, Paul could be referring to the moment of the Lord's return, as the end of the verse shows. However, it is simply not true that the aorist tense alone indicates a one-time action, as many counter-examples demonstrate.[40] The aorist tense leaves the specific manner of action to the context; Paul elsewhere envisages an ongoing process of God's work in the believer's life, climaxing at the return of Jesus (e.g., Phil 1:6, 9-11).

May your whole spirit, soul and body be kept blameless at the coming of our Lord Jesus Christ.

The connection of this prayer with the last one (the two clauses are joined with a coordinating conjunction *kai* in the Greek text, untranslated in the NIV) clarifies that Paul sees both these actions as belonging to Christ's coming. The final result of the "entire sanctification" of the preceding clause is something to be anticipated by all Christians when the Lord returns, not an experience received by a few Christians in this life.

The assurance that God will complete his sanctifying purpose is coupled to the assurance that he will protect and preserve believers comprehensively through the trials of this age, bringing them safe and whole to the goal which the Lord has for them. Paul's language here emphasizes that God protects and preserves believers in every aspect of their being. "Whole" translates ὁλόκληρος (*holoklēros*), used here as an adverb at the beginning of the clause to stress that God's protective work is absolutely thorough. This word obviously is a compound sharing the same initial root word found in ὁλοτελής (*holotelēs*, "through and through"), further strengthening the emphasis in both clauses.

That idea is further underlined with the combination "spirit, soul and body." Much discussion of this phrase has concerned whether it indicates that human beings are

---

[40]"Reigned" in Rom 5:14; "loved" in Eph 2:4; "remained" in Gal 1:18; etc. Cf. Frank Stagg, "The Abused Aorist," *JBL* 91 (1972) 222-31.

trichotomous, consisting of three distinct aspects described by these terms, or dichotomous, really consisting of two aspects, body and spirit. In favor of the former interpretation is the fact that all three terms are used here; in favor of the latter is the difficulty in distinguishing clearly between the meaning of "spirit" (πνεῦμα, *pneuma*) and "soul" (ψυχή, *psychē*). However, it must be conceded that Paul is not discussing the precise nature of humanity but is offering assurance of God's protection. The combination of three terms here is probably only intended as a means of underlining the comprehensive nature of that protection; it is no more a systematic presentation of human nature than is the combination "heart, soul, mind and strength" in Matt 22:37; Mark 12:30; Luke 10:27. Paul, like the other New Testament writers, repeatedly indicates that God's purpose is to save the whole person, not just some part.[41]

The nature of that salvation and preservation is expressed with "blameless" (ἀμέμπτως, *amemptōs*), connected earlier in this letter to the concept of holiness or sanctification (2:10; 3:13). God's work in both removing the penalty of sin, complete at conversion, and its power in the Christian's life, an ongoing process of growth, will ultimately lead to the fulfillment of his purpose, the elimination of every aspect of sin and its effects from his people. Regardless of the circumstances faced by the readers, they can be assured that God's love and power will not fail them in this regard.

5:24 The one who calls you is faithful and he will do it.

Reiterating the focus on God's preserving work, Paul points to the nature of God as the final source of assurance. God's faithfulness is a basic assumption of everything that the gospel teaches; he is true to his promises and utterly able to fulfill them. By focusing on the believers' call from God, Paul reminds them of their ongoing relationship with God and

---

[41]Cf. Bruce, p. 130; J. Knox Chamblin, "Psychology," *DPL*, pp. 769-770, 772-774.

established by his power. "Calls" translates a present participle and so stresses that God continually calls Christians as his people. And so that ongoing process he will certainly complete for eternity (cf. Phil 1:6). Therefore, the readers' confidence in difficulty is based supremely on the utterly certain faithfulness of God.

B. FINAL WORDS (5:25-28)

5:25 Brothers, pray for us.

Paul asks for prayers on his behalf at the end of other letters, sometimes expressing concerns that arise out of the specific circumstances of his ministry (2 Thess 3:1; Rom 15:30-32; Eph 6:19-20; Col 4:3). Just as Paul prays for the readers (cf. 1:2-3; 3:11-13; 5:23), so he asks them to pray for him. To do so is a necessary consequence of the brotherhood expressed with the familiar noun of direct address here. And it voices the faith expressed in the previous verse: the assurance of God's faithfulness carries with it the responsibility to depend on God in all things and to confess that dependence through prayer.

5:26 Greet all the brothers with a holy kiss.

Brotherhood expressed to God in prayer for others is also to be expressed to one another directly. The significance of the kiss in the Greco-Roman world is not entirely clear; it appears to have been practiced more widely and openly in some circles than in others. What is clear is that outside the New Testament, we have no examples of ethical teachers who specifically commanded or encouraged the people of a community to greet one another with a kiss. It may well be, then, that this repeated New Testament command (Rom 16:16; 1 Cor 16:20; 2 Cor 13:12; 1 Pet 5:14) attests to an innovative and striking practice among early Christians, one that expressed a bond that stretches beyond the usual social boundaries.[42] There is evidence to

---

[42]Cf. William Klassen, "Kiss (NT)," *ABD*, 4:89-92. Evidence from the early

suggest that the kiss was a regular part of Christian worship, incorporated into the observance of the Lord's Supper, at least as early as the second century and perhaps before.[43] Since "brothers" (generically including "sisters" also) are particularly those to be so greeted, it appears that Paul uses the modifier "holy" to indicate that the kiss expresses the mutual relationship of believers as those who belong to God.

In modern western culture the kiss may not be an appropriate means of expressing Christian fellowship as it is generally confined to family or sexual relationships.[44] Marshall's remark about the application of this verse is trenchant:

> What is important is that the members of the church should have some way of expressing visibly and concretely the love which they have for one another as fellow-members of the body of Christ. The manner of expression may vary in different cultures; but it is doubtful whether doing nothing at all, as modern western Christians tend to do, really fulfills the spirit of the injunction.[45]

5:27 I charge you before the Lord to have this letter read to all the brothers.

Paul's self-consciousness of his apostolic authority is very much in evidence with this instruction. As one who speaks under the inspiration of God, his words carry an import and authority which makes them relevant to the entire Thessalonian church and, by implication, to other churches as well. Because his teachings as an apostle carry the authority of the Lord himself, they are to be heard and followed by Christians

---

church fathers indicates that later generations of Christians extended the holy kiss across social lines (R. E. Perry, "Kiss," *ZPEB*, 3:831-832).

[43]Cf. Bruce, pp. 133-135.

[44]Morris notes that the indiscriminate practice and abuse of the kiss in later centuries led church councils to place various restrictions on it (pp. 185-186).

[45]Marshall, p. 165.

generally, not only those who first received the letter. Similar authority is reflected in, among other things, the remark which Paul makes about the circulation of his letters in Col 4:16 (cf. 2 Pet 3:15-16), the wide scope of the address in 1 Cor 1:2 ("with all those everywhere who call on the name of our Lord Jesus Christ") and the apparent counterfeiting of his letters by opponents (2 Thess 2:2; 3:17).[46]

The issue of the "canonization" of the New Testament, the delineation of what constituted Scripture for the church, is complex, involving a series of historical developments in the early centuries of Christianity. But the core of the later developments is to be found here in Paul's consciousness that his words carried divine authority. Certainly he may have had in mind a specific issue in the Thessalonian church that made the reading of this letter important for all; the suggestion that he wanted the "idle" (v. 14) to hear it has some merit.[47] But whatever its proximate cause, the dramatic expression here points to Paul's consciousness of authority for the document: "charge" literally indicates a call for the recipients of the letter to swear by the Lord's own authority to read the letter to all.[48] Such reading would, of course, be aloud, so directing that it be read "to all" would point to a reading in the Lord's Day assembly of the entire church, another formative factor in the early foundation of the canon.[49] It is especially notable that these points are articulated in what may be Paul's earliest extant letter.

The shift from first-person plural to singular here is noteworthy. It may indicate that at this point Paul took up the pen from his amanuensis and wrote the words himself (cf. 2 Thess 3:17).

5:28 The grace of our Lord Jesus Christ be with you.

As Paul begins with a word about grace (1:1), so he con-

---

[46]Cf. Donald Guthrie, *New Testament Introduction*, pp. 996-1000.
[47]Bruce, p. 135.
[48]Cf. BDF, § 149.
[49]Morris, pp. 186-187.

cludes with it here (cf. 2 Thess 3:16; Rom 15:33; 16:20; 2 Cor 13:11; Phil 4:9). While it would be wrong to put too much weight on what was for Paul a standard closing formula, the fact that he begins and ends with this theme no doubt reflects the supreme importance of grace to Paul's experience and doctrine.

THE BOOK OF
2 THESSALONIANS

INTRODUCTION

The pressures of persecution, apparent in 1 Thessalonians, have intensified in this letter. In its three brief chapters the reader perceives the vital importance for suffering believers of confident hope in the Lord's return. Likewise intensified is the problem of idleness. In the face of abuses of Christian generosity, 2 Thessalonians gives a sharp reminder of the individual Christian's duty to live as a responsible member of the community, hard-working and self-supporting.

Much of what was said about the circumstances and organization of 1 Thessalonians can also be affirmed of the second letter (see introduction to 1 Thessalonians above). But unlike 1 Thessalonians, this letter presents two major critical problems. Brief attention will be given to these below.

AUTHORSHIP

Unlike 1 Thessalonians, the second letter has widely been taken as a pseudepigraph, composed after Paul's death by one of his followers who used 1 Thessalonians as a model. Several lines of evidence have been cited to support the hypothesis that 2 Thessalonians is not an authentic letter of Paul.

One of these concerns the letter's eschatology. While 1 Thessalonians emphasized that the Lord's return was imminent, that is, that it could occur at any time (5:1-11), 2 Thessalonians appears to propose a series of preliminary signs which must occur before the Lord can return (2:1-12). If this is indeed the case, then, it is argued, that the tension between the two letters is such that Paul could not have written both.

More particularly, it is often argued that the less imminent expectation of 2 Thessalonians reflects a later period in the life of the church, when the vivid expectation that the Lord would return within the lifetime of the first generation of Christians had been disappointed. If so, then it is clearly a production of the generation after the apostle Paul.

Secondly, it is argued that the tone of 2 Thessalonians is considerably colder and more formal than 1 Thessalonians. As an example, "we ought to thank" in 2 Thess 1:3; 2:13 is regarded as less warm than "we thank" in 1 Thess 1:2. Likewise, the repeated use of "command" in 2 Thess 3:6, 12 is said to reflect a less intimate relationship between the writer and the readers. Such a shift in tone is thought to be unlikely if Paul had written both letters, especially if 1 Thessalonians was written first, but is entirely to be expected if the second letter was a pseudepigraph.

Thirdly, the background of the readers appears to be different. 1 Thess 1:9 appears to indicate a predominantly Gentile audience, but in 2 Thessalonians references to the final judgment (1:6-10) and the man of lawlessness (2:1-12) appear to assume knowledge that could be expected only of Jews. It is consequently argued that the second letter was not written for the same church, indicating that the addressee and so also the author named in the salutation are fictions.

Combined with these concerns is the literary style of 2 Thessalonians. In some respects it closely resembles 1 Thessalonians, following a similar outline (including a double thanksgiving: 1 Thess 1:2-10; 2:13-16; 2 Thess 1:3-12; 2:13-17) and discussing similar themes (eschatology, idleness). However, it has been argued that the sentence structure of 2 Thessalonians is significantly different from the undisputed letters of Paul. In particular, 2 Thess 2:3-12 is a more complex sentence than is found elsewhere in Paul's letters, constructions with the genitive are more frequent, and subordinating conjunctions are more numerous.[1] Likewise it is argued that a

---

[1]Daryl Schmidt, "The Syntactical Style of 2 Thessalonians: How Pauline Is

number of terms and concepts from Paul's authentic letters are used in a different sense in 2 Thessalonians.[2] The combination of similarity and dissimilarity is said to point to a post-Pauline imitator, who at some points incorporated elements of Paul's style and substance from 1 Thessalonians and at others reflected followed his own course.

The force of these arguments is considerable, and a large number of contemporary scholars have been persuaded by them to reject Pauline authorship of this letter. However, the idea that 2 Thessalonians is pseudepigraphical is itself problematic. It is first of all difficult to understand why someone would write 2 Thessalonians and ascribe it to Paul, since presumably it contained nothing so controversial as to demand the apostle's authority for its acceptance. Furthermore, if written by a later imitator, that person knew only 1 Thessalonians, since the major parallels are only with that letter. Such a situation would be surprising for a second-generation disciple of Paul. The reference to the temple in 2:4 gives no indication that the Jerusalem temple has been destroyed by the Romans, again surprising if the letter were written near the end of the first century when the fall of Jerusalem was well known. Furthermore, 3:6-15 give every appearance of having been written to a specific congregation in response to a particular problem. It would be most unusual for a letter to be written to specific church in the name of Paul after his death and not be detected as a pseudepigraph. And if all in the church recognized the fiction and accepted it as such, we must explain how the later church forgot the origins of the letter, since all external evidence affirms that Paul is the author (Marcion, c. A.D. 150, and the Muratorian Canon, c. A.D. 180, both ascribe it to Paul). These considerations make the hypothesis of pseudepigraphy less than likely.

It?" *The Thessalonian Correspondence* (Raymond F. Collins, ed., BETL 87, Leuven: Leuven University Press, 1990), pp. 383-393.

[2]For a summary of such arguments see Wanamaker, pp. 25-27.

In fact, each argument for pseudepigraphy can be explained on the hypothesis that Paul wrote 2 Thessalonians himself. The eschatological tension in fact has less to do with a lessening of expectancy than is often allowed. Exegesis of 2:1-12 in the comments below will indicate that what Paul discusses here is probably not a series of preliminary signs but the present reality that evil and the Evil One appear to dominate and that such dominance is itself proof that the Lord has not yet returned. In this case, there is absolutely no tension between the eschatology of the first and second letters. However, even if this interpretation should be wrong, it is not impossible that Paul would express a different perspective on the Lord's coming in 2 Thessalonians and not view it as contradictory, just as he does in 1 Cor 15:1-58, which stresses the general resurrection, and 2 Cor 5:1-10, which stresses individual immortality.

Likewise, the change in tone between the two letters can be explained by the change in circumstances. In 1 Thessalonians part of Paul's concern was to reassure the readers of his affection for them despite his absence. That need having been met, the second letter — preoccupied with the persecution of the church, the problem about the Lord's return and the idleness of some members — reflects less of the personal warmth emphasized in the first. Furthermore, if Paul used a different amanuensis for each letter, or if Silas and Timothy had different roles in the composition of each letter, the tone and style could easily have changed.

The change from a Gentile to a Jewish background is more apparent than real. As noted in the introduction to 1 Thessalonians, that letter includes a number of phrases which assume knowledge of the Old Testament and Judaism. The Jewish orientation of the second letter is more explicit but hardly necessitates a different audience. This observation also obviates the need for other hypotheses, such as that Paul sent the two letters to two different factions of the church, one Gentile and the other Jewish, or that he sent the first letter to the church at large and the second to the leaders of the church.[3]

The stylistic differences between 2 Thessalonians and the other letters of Paul are real, but they can be exaggerated. The complexity of sentences and concentration of subordinating conjunctions are in fact not two matters but one, since complex sentences require subordinating conjunctions. The sentence of 1:3-12 is exceptional, but it is approximated in Ephesians and Colossians.[4] The authorship of those letters is also disputed, but to base an argument for one letter's inauthenticity on its similarity with another questioned letter is to build a supposition on another supposition. It would be fairer to admit that in a short letter like 2 Thessalonians, a few unusual expressions may create a false impression of stylistic variance. Furthermore, it is admitted by all that Paul's style changed with each letter. Only in Romans, for example, do we find the rhetorical question, "What shall we say then?" (3:5; 4:1; 6:1; 7:7; 8:31; 9:14, 30), and no one disputes the authenticity of Romans on that basis.[5] Alleged differences in the use of key terms and presentation of concepts have likewise been exaggerated. Paul's usage elsewhere is often more flexible than some critics will allow. And 2 Thessalonians contains some Paulinisms which would have been difficult for an imitator to compose.[6] The combination of similarities and differences between the two Thessalonians letters and between the second and the rest of the Pauline corpus is at least as consistent with the hypothesis that Paul wrote both under changing circumstances as it is with the hypothesis of a pseudepigrapher.

Thus, though the controversy over the authorship of this letter is likely to continue among scholars, the arguments

---

[3]The Latter is the hypothesis of E. Earle Ellis, *Prophecy and Hermeneutic in Early Christianity* (Grand Rapids: Eerdmans, 1978), pp. 19-21.

[4]Schmidt, "Syntactical Style," p. 385.

[5]For a series of such examples see Jewett, *Thessalonian Correspondence*, p. 12.

[6]Marshall notes εἴπερ (*eiper*) in 1:6, ἄνεσις (*anesis*) in 1:7, and ὑπεραυξάνω (*hyperauxanō*) in 1:3 (p. 32).

against Paul's authorship are not sufficient to overturn the testimony of the letter itself and of the early church. By nature of the case, evidence to prove the authenticity of an ancient document always falls short of absolute proof. But those who have accepted 2 Thessalonians as a genuine letter of Paul can do so with integrity, knowing that the balance of evidence favors their conclusion.

ORDER AND CIRCUMSTANCES OF WRITING

The traditional assumption has always been that 2 Thessalonians was written not long after 1 Thessalonians, while Paul was still in Corinth. Paul had apparently received a report, perhaps from Timothy after the delivery of the first letter, of ongoing problems in the Thessalonian church. The persecution had not abated, misunderstandings about the Lord's return continued, and the willfully idle had not repented. Therefore, Paul composed a second letter to address the developing situation, probably only months after writing the first.

There have been several scholars who have questioned the traditional order, however, postulating that 2 Thessalonians was in fact written first. The traditional order of Paul's letters, these have argued, is based not on chronology but length, longer letters of Paul being placed before shorter ones in the canon. Therefore, internal considerations alone, the evidence of the letters themselves, must determine the order of writing.

The most recent and important advocate of the priority of 2 Thessalonians is Charles Wanamaker. His argument, which in the main follows a line marked out by others, may be summarized as follows. First, the persecution of 2 Thess 1:4-7 appears to be a matter of the past in 1 Thess 2:14. Secondly, the idlers of 2 Thess 3:6-15 appear to be a new problem, while 1 Thess 4:10-12 and 5:14 address it as something well known and already under control. Thirdly, the signature of 2 Thess

3:17 appears to be more fitting in Paul's first letter to the church. Fourth, the eschatological teaching of 1 Thess 4:13-5:11, especially in light of the remark in 5:1 that the readers had no need of such instruction because they had received it before, is more coherently explained if it is an elaboration on 2 Thess 2:1-12, especially if some implications of that passage had been misunderstood. On the other hand, if the church had already received 1 Thess 4:13-5:11, it is difficult to see how they would have concluded that the day of the Lord had already come (2 Thess 2:2), since the dead had not yet been raised and united with the living in the Lord's presence (1 Thess 4:17). Therefore, Wanamaker argues with earlier advocates of the hypothesis that 2 Thessalonians was written by Paul after he received a vague report about problems in the Thessalonian church and was delivered by Timothy in the visit described in 1 Thess 3:1-10.[7]

While Wanamaker has succeeded in showing how little evidence there actually is for the priority of 1 Thessalonians, the case for the priority of 2 Thessalonians is far from proved. External evidence must be weighed also: Marcion apparently referred to 1 Thessalonians as the first letter despite the fact that he did not arrange his canon by length.[8] As far as internal matters are concerned, if 2 Thessalonians was the first letter, it is surprising that Paul makes no reference to it in 1 Thessalonians as a part of his passionate discussion of his prior work with the Thessalonian church (2:1-12) and his attempts to return to them since his departure (2:17-20). Wanamaker suggests that the mention of Timothy's visit may be a tacit reference to it, since Timothy can be assumed to have carried some letter from Paul on this visit.[9] Still, one might expect a more specific mention of so substantial a letter as 2 Thessalonians had it been written first. On the other hand, the references to letters in 2 Thess 2:2, 15; 3:17 are at

---

[7]Wanamaker, pp. 37-45, 269 and *passim*.
[8]Guthrie, *Introduction*, p. 600.
[9]Wanamaker, p. 44.

least consistent with the idea that 1 Thessalonians had already been received, though they do not demand it.

If 1 Thessalonians is prior, as the slight balance of probability suggests, we can assume that the persecution of the church, which may have abated after Paul's departure, has heated up again, or at least that the church is in greater turmoil because of it. Likewise, we must assume that the church's misunderstanding of the Lord's return in 2:2 occurred despite the logical force of 1 Thess 4:13-18. Also, the idle who were warned briefly in 1 Thess 4:11-12 and 5:14 did not heed that warning. Such developments will surprise those who assume that human behavior is always reasonable and orderly, but those who have experienced the give and take of pastoral leadership will recognize that churches and Christians, like stocks, seldom move in a straight line. Against such a background Paul dictated his second letter, seeking to correct the church's course and reinforce its growth.

THEOLOGICAL VALUE

2 Thessalonians focuses primarily on three issues: persecution, the Lord's return, and the problem of idleness. Each has remarkable relevance for today's church.

Persecution is perhaps less a part of the experience of Christians in North America than in other parts of the world. Nevertheless, for many Christians it remains a real threat. More broadly, all believers experience the hostility of unbelievers at various points, and all can be subject to the hurt of their ridicule, even if they are relatively safe from physical violence. 2 Thessalonians provides the important reminder that God notices such suffering and promises to bring vindication for his people. The suffering of the church will one day end.

Likewise, the pervasive dominance of evil, obvious to every modern observer, will one day end as well. Whatever the precise nature of the "man of lawlessness" (2:3), Paul certainly focuses attention on his present activity (2:9-12). Christians who wonder whether their faith is true when they see the opponents of Christianity with the upper hand have their answer in this letter. Evil will continue to run rampant in this age, but when Christ returns, he will utterly destroy every manifestation of it and the One who stands behind it. The goodness and faithfulness of God can be trusted to answer every aspect of injustice in this age.

Unemployment, underemployment and wide gaps in income are no less a social reality now than they were for Paul's readers. And so the need for Christian charity continues as it did in the first century. But the dangers inherent in such sharing are still real as well. Paul's reminders about the need for personal responsibility and self-support (3:6-12), coupled with the reminder to continue in good works of generosity (3:13) are messages to be heeded as today's church considers its role in addressing the pressing issues of poverty and the failures of the secular welfare state.

The observation that problems had intensified since Paul wrote his first letter contains a pertinent message in itself. Even in Paul's ministry, the life of the church was characterized by trouble as much as progress. Yet through such trouble the work and will of God are accomplished. Christians frustrated by the one-step-forward-two-steps-back trajectory of the church can take heart that in similar circumstances the great apostle still found much for which to give thanks and boast (1:3-4; 2:13-14). God's will, which will be fully realized only when Christ returns, is even now being worked out in the life of the church, even when outwardly it appears defeated.

OUTLINE

I. GREETING — 1:1-2

II. OPENING THANKSGIVING, ENCOURAGEMENT AND PRAYER — 1:3-12

    A. Thanksgiving for the Thessalonians' Growth and Endurance in Persecution — 1:3-4

    B. Encouragement in Light of God's Judgment — 1:5-10

    C. The Content of Paul's Prayer — 1:11-12

III. INSTRUCTION ON THE LORD'S RETURN — 2:1-12

    A. The Day of the Lord Not Yet Present — 2:1-2

    B. The Apostasy and the Man of Lawlessness — 2:3-12

        1. The Apostasy and the Revelation of the Man of Lawlessness — 2:3

        2. A Description of the Man of Lawlessness — 2:4

        3. Reminder of Oral Instruction on the Subject — 2:5

        4. The One Who Restrains/Prevails — 2:6-10

        5. God's Consequent Actions — 2:11-12

IV. RENEWED THANKSGIVING, ENCOURAGEMENT AND PRAYER — 2:13-17

    A. Thanksgiving for the Salvation of the Thessalonians — 2:13-14

    B. Encouragement to Remain Faithful to the Traditions Delivered by Paul — 2:15

    C. Prayer for the Lord's Encouragement and Strength — 2:16-17

V. EXHORTATIONS — 3:1-16
  A. General Exhortations — 3:1-5
  B. Exhortations Regarding Church Discipline — 3:6-15
    1. Exclusion of the Willfully Idle — 3:6-13
    2. Exclusion of the Disobedient — 3:14-15
VI. CONCLUSION — 3:16-18

2 THESSALONIANS 1

I. GREETING (1:1-2)

¹Paul, Silas[a] and Timothy,
To the church of the Thessalonians in God our Father and the Lord Jesus Christ:
²Grace and peace to you from God the Father and the Lord Jesus Christ.

[a] *1* Greek *Silvanus*, a variant of *Silas*

1:1 Paul, Silas and Timothy, To the church of the Thessalonians in God our Father and the Lord Jesus Christ:
The opening greeting of this second letter is identical to the first letter's in all but two points. Paul's relationship with his co-workers, the readers' identity as the assembly of God's people united with God and Christ, and their blessing of God's grace and peace are again prominent (see comments on 1 Thess 1:1 above). One difference comes in v. 1, where God is specifically "our Father" as in most of Paul's other salutations (Rom 1:7; 1 Cor 1:3; 2 Cor 1:2; Eph 1:2; Phil 1:2; Col 1:2; Phlm 3; Gal 1:3 reads thus in some manuscripts) instead of "the Father" as in 1 Thess 1:1. But little significance can be attached to the change.

1:2 Grace and peace to you from God the Father and the Lord Jesus Christ.
The second difference comes at the end of v. 2, where the source of grace and peace are specified as in the other extant letters of Paul (cf. Rom 1:7; 1 Cor 1:3; 2 Cor 1:2; Gal 1:3; Eph

1:2; Phil 1:2; Col 1:2; 1 Tim 1:2; 2 Tim 1:2; Titus 1:4; Phlm 3). As in v. 1 and 1 Thess 1:1 above, Paul, who was steeped in Jewish monotheism, attributes such gifts to both God and Jesus with absolute ease and naturalness. Such is possible for him because he regards Jesus as fully divine (see comments on 1 Thess 1:1 above).

II. OPENING THANKSGIVING, ENCOURAGEMENT AND PRAYER (1:3-12)

As in 1 Thess 1:2-10 and in most of Paul's other letters, 2 Thessalonians begins with a statement of thanksgiving, focusing on the readers' devotion to Christ. Here Paul also offers a prayer for the readers, commonly attached to the thanksgiving in other letters but separated in 1 Thessalonians by Paul's discussion of his ministry with the church (1 Thess 3:11-13; cf. Phil 1:3-11; Col 1:3-14; Phlm 4-7; Eph 1:15-19; 2 Thess 2:13-14).[1]

The difference in tone between 1 and 2 Thessalonians is immediately noticeable in this section. The warmth and enthusiasm of the first letter are less evident here, where the style appears more formal. This difference can easily be exaggerated, but some difference in tone between the passages is conceded by all. While it is impossible to account for the change entirely, much of the difference can be attributed to the shift in subject matter. In 1 Thessalonians, Paul's concern was largely for his ongoing relationship with the church. Under such circumstances, an extra measure of personal warmth would be expected.

Some have speculated that in response to the more direct praise in the first letter, the Thessalonians had protested through Timothy that they were unworthy.[2] Others have suggested parallels in liturgical language or discussions of suffer-

---

[1] Cf. Peter T. O'Brien, "Letters, Letter Forms," *DPL*, pp. 550-553.
[2] Bruce, p. 144.

ing in apocalyptic literature (Rev 3:4; 5:9, 12).[3] In any case Paul's purpose in this letter has less to do with personal relationships (though they remain "brothers," v. 3) and is more narrowly confined to specific problems in the church. One of these, the church's understanding of the Lord's return in light of their present suffering (cf. 2:1-12), Paul begins to address here. The nature of this subject may have produced a more formal style as well. The use of the opening section to make a preliminary announcement of his themes is also seen in other letters (e.g., Phil 1:3-11).

Though it contains distinct sections, these verses constitute a single, long sentence in the Greek text. For Paul these verses were tightly bound together.

A. THANKSGIVING FOR THE THESSALONIANS' GROWTH AND ENDURANCE IN PERSECUTION (1:3-4)

³We ought always to thank God for you, brothers, and rightly so, because your faith is growing more and more, and the love every one of you has for each other is increasing. ⁴Therefore, among God's churches we boast about your perseverance and faith in all the persecutions and trials you are enduring.

The focus in this first section of the sentence is on the persecution experienced by the readers and God's answer to it. Paul had mentioned persecution in the first letter (1 Thess 1:6) but here makes it more prominent, emphasizing especially both the readers' and God's responses to it, underlining the larger meaning it had for their Christian experience. Though Paul offers thanks in vv. 3-4 for some of the same characteristics as in 1 Thess 1:2-3, the greater focus on persecution here starkly displays the readers' Christian virtues

---

[3]Roger D. Aus, "The Liturgical Background of the Necessity and Propriety of Giving Thanks According to 2 Thes 1:3," *JBL* 92 (1973) 432-438.

against the background of their suffering. This emphasis may reflect an intensification of the persecution in Thessalonica since the first letter. However, in light of the evident problem in understanding the relationship of the Lord's coming to their suffering, Paul probably emphasizes this theme in anticipation of the discussion of 2:1-12.

1:3 We ought always to thank God for you, brothers, and rightly so, because your faith is growing more and more, and the love every one of you has for each other is increasing.

This statement of thanksgiving has many features in common with 1 Thess 1:2-3 (see comments above). The focus of Paul's thanksgiving is again on the readers' demonstration of the cardinal Christian virtues, particularly faith and love. Perhaps reflecting the fact that this is now his second letter, Paul mentions particularly their growth in these areas, in part a fulfillment of his prayer for the church in 1 Thess 3:11-13. The word translated "is growing more and more" is ὑπεραυξάνω (*hyperauxanō*), found only here in the New Testament. It is an intensification of the more common verb signifying growth, perhaps coined by Paul himself.[4]

In context Paul probably uses the intensive form to emphasize the contrast between the readers' growth and their difficult circumstances. Paul uses a different verb, πλεονάζω (*pleonazō*, "is increasing") to indicate their growth in love, but no distinction in meaning should be pressed, since the difference is probably to avoid repetition. Both verbs are in the present tense, indicating that the growth is a continuing action. The whole statement is reminiscent of Jesus' parables which emphasize the growth of God's kingdom from small, insignificant beginnings (Matt 13:31-33; Mark 4:26-32; Luke 13:18-21; cf. 2 Cor 10:15).

Inferences from silence are notoriously debatable, but the prominence of "hope" in 1 Thess 1:3 makes that term's omis-

---

[4]Cf. *GELNTBSD*, § 78.5-6.

sion here striking. Its absence does not imply that the Thessalonians do not have hope, and most of the first two chapters concentrate on the content of their hope, the return of Christ. However, it is possible that Paul does not name hope as a basis for thanksgiving because confusion about the day of the Lord (2:2) has temporarily damaged the readers' hope.

Paul does not state directly that he gives thanks but combines expressions to indicate that such thanksgiving is necessary and right. "Ought" represents ὀφείλω (*opheilō*), which indicates obligation or necessity;[5] "and rightly so," literally "as is fitting" (καθὼς ἄξιόν ἐστιν, *kathōs axion estin*), reinforces that point with a complementary expression. Though the indirect statement is perhaps less personal than the one in 1 Thess 1:2, it is stronger in expressing that such thanksgiving is Paul's solemn duty, even when the circumstances are less than joyful.

1:4 Therefore, among God's churches we boast about your perseverance and faith in all the persecutions and trials you are enduring.

As in 1 Thess 1:7-10 Paul stresses that the Thessalonians' living out of the gospel has been reported as an edifying message to other churches. By using "boast" to refer to these reports, Paul implies that his own work has had their growth and faithfulness as its objective. This statement echoes 1 Thess 2:19-20 (see comments above) as well as remarks in later letters (e.g., 1 Cor 15:31; 2 Cor 1:14; 7:4, 14; 8:24; 9:2; Phil 1:26; 2:16). In other passages Paul expresses the same concept with other terms (e.g., "reward," 1 Cor 3:14). In all of these cases Paul's boast is ultimately not in his own achievements (cf. Rom 3:27; 2 Cor 10:17) but in the results of God's grace, by which he has been given the ministry which bears

---

[5]BAGD, pp. 598-599. Aus notes that this word is considerably less "cool" than other words for obligation, so its impact on the tone of the passage should not be exaggerated ("Liturgical Background," p. 438).

this fruit. To make this boast "among God's churches" (see comments on 1 Thess 1:1 above) is therefore to share more of the good news among the people who belong to God because of that message.

To see suffering as an occasion for boasting requires a keen eye of faith. Using such an eye, Paul focuses particularly on the readers' "perseverance and faith." The first term, ὑπομονή (*hypomonē*; cf. 1 Thess 1:3), stresses active endurance under difficulty and pressure; it is patience put into practice in suffering.[6] The second, πίστις (*pistis*) refers in this context particularly to constancy in faith, or faithfulness: the readers have maintained their position in Christ despite the difficulties it has brought to them.[7] These two terms are obviously similar in meaning, and Paul draws them even more closely together by modifying both with a single definite article. Endurance and faith are the Thessalonians' one response to persecution.

The readers' suffering is also expressed with a pair of terms. "Persecutions," διωγμός (*diōgmos*), indicates specifically the sufferings inflicted by others because of their opposition to one's beliefs.[8] "Trials," θλῖψις (*thlipsis*) can refer more broadly to any kind of suffering but is frequently used in the New Testament to refer specifically to persecution that comes because of one's faith (cf. 1 Thess 3:3-4 and comments above). The combination probably emphasizes the severity of the readers' sufferings, and no distinction between the words is stressed. These troubles continue for the readers even as Paul writes: his verb is in the present tense, accurately translated as "are enduring" in the NIV.

Two unusual expressions occur here. One is that "we" is intensive, literally "we ourselves" (αὐτοὺς ἡμᾶς, *autous hēmas*). An obvious explanation for this emphasis is not forthcoming,

---

[6]Ulrich Falkenroth and Colin Brown, "Patience, Steadfastness, Endurance," *NIDNTT*, 2:764, 772-776.

[7]BAGD, p. 662.

[8]BAGD, p. 201.

but it may be that Paul emphasizes that he takes the unusual step of boasting about them to others.[9] The second is the expression "churches of God." Normally Paul uses the plural "churches" when he specifies the churches in a particular geographical area and the singular when he refers to the "universal" church. Whether this means, as Wanamaker suggests, that Paul refers here to churches without geographical limitation remains uncertain.[10]

B. ENCOURAGEMENT IN LIGHT OF GOD'S JUDGMENT (1:5-10)

[5]All this is evidence that God's judgment is right, and as a result you will be counted worthy of the kingdom of God, for which you are suffering. [6]God is just: He will pay back trouble to those who trouble you [7]and give relief to you who are troubled, and to us as well. This will happen when the Lord Jesus is revealed from heaven in blazing fire with his powerful angels. [8]He will punish those who do not know God and do not obey the gospel of our Lord Jesus. [9]They will be punished with everlasting destruction and shut out from the presence of the Lord and from the majesty of his power [10]on the day he comes to be glorified in his holy people and to be marveled at among all those who have believed. This includes you, because you believed our testimony to you.

Though it can remain an abstraction for those without difficulty, the problem of evil is a burning question for those who are suffering. "Why is this happening?" is perhaps the most troubling question that human beings must confront. For those who suffer because of their faith, the question is

---

[9]Wanamaker, p. 218.

[10]Ibid. His conclusion from this detail that persecution was exceptional for Paul's churches is a *non sequitur*.

even more intense. Christians who believe themselves to be the people of God, those who have received God's salvation and are experiencing the fulfillment of his eternal promises, have an even more difficult question to answer. If God is really on their side, if he is really loving and powerful, why do they suffer?

Paul has already provided much of the answer in 1 Thess 3:3-4: Christians suffer inevitably as a result of their identity, because they are united with the Christ who suffered in fulfillment of God's purpose. Here Paul reiterates that point in v. 5. But here he goes on to explain more. If God allows his people to suffer at the hands of those who have deliberately refused him and his message, if he in effect allows the innocent to suffer at the hands of the wicked, is he really a righteous and powerful God?

In answer to this question, Paul reminds the readers that the present situation is not the final situation. Though it may seem that evil consistently triumphs over good, there remains a final reckoning in which God will bring fitting punishment on those who have persecuted his people. Until that time, the readers can take encouragement in their confidence that God in the end will vindicate his people by repaying their antagonists decisively. God is both just, judging sin wherever it exists, and powerful, able to bring his sentence to bear on evildoers. The Thessalonian church may appear to be a small, insignificant group of people whose enemies have the best of them, but the end of history will show what the unseen reality has always been.

Paul's concept of God's justice here is retributive: evildoers are repaid in kind for the evil which they have done. This notion, once fundamental in western legal thought, is now rejected in many circles. More recently evil has been seen according to the model of disease, and so punishment has been viewed as therapy or rehabilitation. Consequently many modern or postmodern people are uncomfortable with the language of this passage. But for Paul evil was not merely a sickness but a consequence of conscious rebellion against

God and submission to his adversary (cf. Eph 2:1-3).

In Paul's thought forgiveness is therefore costly; God's justice demands appropriate payment for sin, namely the death of Jesus. Only in light of God's justice can the full extent of his love and forgiving grace be seen: through his Son he himself provides the substitutionary payment for human sin (cf. Rom 3:23-26). If some then refuse his offer and even oppose it, they are fully responsible for their actions, and God's justice demands a retributive punishment for them (cf. 1 Thess 1:10; 2:16). For God to do less would mean for him to tolerate evil, especially evil directed toward the very people whom he has saved. If God is truly good, then he must pronounce sentence on evil.

The eschatological view that Christ will return secretly to remove the church from tribulation and later return again to judge the wicked does not fare well in this passage. Paul's language indicates that relief for the believer and retribution for the unbeliever are simultaneous. As elsewhere in the New Testament, the parousia is a single, indivisible act bringing both blessing and judgment (cf. 1 Thess 5:1-11).[11]

Several factors have suggested to some that in vv. 7b-10 Paul has incorporated a traditional formula, including a concentration of Old Testament references, a shift from the second to the third person, and the uses of parallelism.[12] While it is possible that Paul uses a pre-formed tradition here, the content is so consistent with the context and his own thought that his own free composition of this material seems more likely.

This section actually continues the Greek sentence begun in v. 3, though in translation it has been divided into shorter sentences for readability. Here the reason for thanksgiving even in suffering is made clear.

---

[11]Vern S. Poythress, "2 Thessalonians 1 Supports Amillennialism," *JETS* 37 (1994) 529-538.

[12]Wanamaker, p. 232.

1:5 All this is evidence that God's judgment is right,

Though one might think that belonging to God's people would ensure a life without trouble, Paul declares that the opposite is true. To belong to God means to suffer in this age, which is ruled by his great adversary, even as Christ himself suffered. But this suffering belongs in the context of God's promised triumph over sin and judgment against it. Hence, Paul can say that suffering in the present is an indication or "evidence" (ἔνδειγμα, *endeigma*) of God's righteous judgment. The specific evidence to which Paul refers could be the Thessalonians' endurance, the persecutions which they receive, or a combination (v. 4).

In favor of the former is the use of a related word in Phil 1:28, where the reference is clearly to the Philippians' endurance. In favor of the persecutions is the fact that Paul mentions them nearer to "evidence." However, the following context, discussing as it does both the punishment to come on the persecutors and the relief to come to the Christians, favors a broader combination of the two. Paul's point, then, is that the persecution and the readers' response to it demonstrates that God's determination to bring retribution on his opponents and relief to his faithful people is necessary for justice to prevail.

While Paul is about to focus on the future judgment, the language here suggests that the judgment has already begun. Like other aspects of God's promised future, judgment is also a present reality, which may be realized here in several respects.[13] One is the believers' endurance, which demonstrates that they have received the grace which has already pronounced them innocent (v. 12) and aligns them with the faithful of the past (1 Thess 2:14-15). By contrast the persecutors show by their rejection of God's grace and solidarity with God's enemies of the past that they are already under judgment (1 Thess 2:16). In the larger sense, the fact that the believers find themselves persecuted in a world still under the

---

[13]Cf. Stephen H. Travis, "Judgment," *DPL*, pp. 516-17.

sway of evil (cf. 2:3-12 and comments below; 1 Cor 2:8; Eph 2:2; 6:12) shows that they belong to the God who will in the future reestablish the fullness of his reign. It is also possible that Paul views their present suffering as an aspect of God's discipline of his children, which leads ultimately to their salvation (Rom 5:3-5; 1 Cor 11:32; 2 Cor 6:9).[14] Their present identities, as demonstrated by their behavior and circumstances, will be fully revealed and ratified in the judgment to come.

and as a result you will be counted worthy of the kingdom of God, for which you are suffering.

A second result of this situation (the sentence structure suggests that "as a result" should connect the clause to v. 4 rather than to the beginning of v. 5) is being counted worthy of God's kingdom. As union with Christ inevitably brings suffering for one's faith (1 Thess 3:3-4), it also indicates that the sufferer genuinely belongs to the kingdom which Christ rules (cf. 1 Thess 2:12 and comments above). The readers' citizenship in the kingdom of God is both a present reality and a promise of the future. Thus, they continue to suffer for it now ("you are suffering" translates a present-tense verb), but they can both endure and triumph because they already belong to the kingdom and because they look forward to the full realization of God's rule when his enemies will be defeated fully and finally (cf. 1 Thess 2:16).

It should be noted carefully that Paul speaks of being "counted worthy," clearly implying the action of God who accounts worthiness according to grace and not merit (cf. v. 12). The readers' perseverance does not earn God's approval but shows that they genuinely trust in his grace to supply it. Likewise, "of the kingdom" implies not "in order to gain the

---

[14]Cf. Jouette M. Bassler, "The Enigmatic Sign: 2 Thessalonians 1:5," *CBQ* 46 (1984) 498-510. Bassler's assertion that chastisement is more likely than the concept of future retribution flies in the face of the context, where retribution is prominent but chastisement is at best indistinct, though she rightly notes that the text probably intends some reference to the present aspect of judgment which may include chastisement.

kingdom" but "on behalf of the kingdom"; it assumes membership in the kingdom in the present rather than holding it out as a prospect for the future.[15]

1:6 God is just: He will pay back trouble to those who trouble you

God's justice is defined here in unequivocally retributive terms. Though the NIV's rendering of this verse departs considerably from the Greek sentence structure, it captures the sense well. Literally the verse could be translated, "If indeed it is just with God to pay back trouble to those troubling you"; the conditional "if" is firmly assumed to be true.

The concept of retribution has significant biblical background. The principle of *lex talionis* in Exod 21:23-25 establishes the principle of retribution. "An eye for an eye" was first of all a limitation on the extent of punishment, forbidding, for example, the sentence of "a life for an eye." Secondly, the principle did not allow any aggrieved person to take vengeance to this extent; rather, God himself is the one who would bring retribution (Deut 32:35), even if his judgment was mediated through human agents according to Israel's law. In Rom 12:19 Paul quotes this second passage as a reminder not to seek personal vengeance (cf. Acts 23:3). But that restriction on taking justice into one's own hands depends on the assurance that God will bring retribution. This assurance is exactly what the present text offers: "pay back" translates ἀνταποδίδωμι (*antapodidōmi*), which also appears in Rom 12:19, and is underlined with the repetition of "trouble." This retributive emphasis is tied closely to the preceding discussion: "trouble" here translates *thlipsis* and its cognate θλίβω (*thlibō*), the former appearing in v. 4 with the translation "trials."

---

[15]Cf. Murray Harris, "Prepositions and Theology in the Greek New Testament," *NIDNTT*, 3:1196-1197.

1:7 and give relief to you who are troubled, and to us as well.
For the readers the future punishment of their adversaries is a comforting prospect for two reasons. First of all, it means their vindication, as implied in the previous verse. They can be encouraged, not because they will delight in the pain which their opponents will experience but because their punishment will mean the believers' vindication — it will demonstrate that they were indeed God's people and their enemies were his enemies. Second is the assurance of this verse, that their suffering will end with Christ's return as judge. As those who are troubled (*thlibō* as in v. 6), the readers will receive "relief," ἄνεσις (*anesis*), signifying a cessation of their suffering (cf. 2 Cor 8:13).[16]

Though for readability the NIV supplies another verb, "give," here, "relief" is in fact also the object of "pay back" in v. 6. This relief is, in other words, the just retribution which the faithful receive for their endurance of tribulation (cf. Rom 8:18; 2 Cor 4:7-18). Briefly reminding the readers that they are not alone in their suffering for the kingdom, Paul inserts "and to us as well," literally "with us." The Thessalonians had, of course, firsthand familiarity with Paul's sufferings (1 Thess 1:6; 2:2, 16; Acts 17:5-9). As persecution is by nature the experience of all Christians (1 Thess 3:3-4; 2 Tim 3:12), both the apostle and his converts can expect it. But without the assurance that God will bring an end to it with the punishment of the persecutors, the reality of his justice and his commitment to his people could not be maintained.

This will happen when the Lord Jesus is revealed from heaven in blazing fire with his powerful angels.
The description of Christ's return here, in contrast to the one in 1 Thess 4:16-17, provides details that emphasize his power as victor and judge. His revelation (ἀποκάλυψις [*apokalypsis*], rendered as a verb, "is revealed," in the NIV) will mean

---

[16]Cf. *GELNTBSD*, § 22.36.

the full disclosure of his divine authority, which has remained hidden to the world (cf. 1 Cor 2:7-8; 2 Cor 4:3-4). So his revelation will be "from heaven," not so much stressing the angle in the sky from which he will make his appearance as the fact that he has since his ascension been at the supreme place of authority. Elsewhere angels are pictured as accompanying Christ in his return (Matt 24:31; 25:31) and more generally as agents of the final judgment (Matt 13:39; Mark 8:38; 13:37; Luke 12:8; often in Revelation). Here they are "powerful" angels, literally "angels of power," agents of the Lord's own power which will be exercised in final judgment.

"Blazing fire" could be connected either to the Lord's return in v. 7 or his judgment in v. 8 (in the Greek text the corresponding phrase occurs after "angels of power"). The NIV has taken it with v. 7, which has the virtue of understanding the three prepositional phrases as parallel descriptions of the Lord's revelation.[17] Paul's phrase is literally "a fire of flame," another example of a redundant expression used for emphasis.

Fire has a rich background on which Paul draws. In the Old Testament it is closely associated with the visible manifestation of the Lord (Gen 15:17; Exod 3:2-3; 19:18; Judg 6:21; 13:20; Num 14:14; Isa 4:5; Ezek 1:27) and with his judgment (Gen 19:24; Exod 9:24; Lev 10:2; Num 11:1; 16:35; 2 Kgs 1:10; Isa 66:15-16; Ezek 38:22; 39:6; Joel 2:30; Amos 1:4, 7; Mal 4:1). In intertestamental apocalyptic literature it is associated with the heavenly world (*1 Enoch* 14:9-22) and the final judgment (*1 Enoch* 102:1; *2 Apoc. Bar.* 37:1; 48:39; 2 Esdr 13:10-11; *Jub.* 9:15; 3:10; 1QS 2:8; 4:13; 1QH 17:13). The same associations are found in the New Testament (Matt 3:10; 7:19; Luke 3:9; 9:45; John 15:6; Rev 1:15; 4:5; 2:18; 10:1; 11:5; 19:12).[18] So as Paul addresses these Christians under persecution, the combination of images here would evoke a powerful response of confidence and eager anticipation.

---

[17]Morris, p. 202.
[18]Hans Bietenhard, "Fire," *NIDNTT*, 1:653-658.

1:8 He will punish those who do not know God and do not obey the gospel of our Lord Jesus.

The judgment to be received by the persecutors is one which they share with all of God's opponents. The basis for that judgment is not just the trouble which they have caused for the Christians. The full measure of their crime must be taken by the standard of God's revelation. Not knowing God is in the language of the Old Testament especially characteristic of the Gentiles (Ps 79:6). For Paul this ignorance is not merely a result of circumstances for which one is not responsible. Because God's "eternal power and divine nature," though invisible, have been revealed in creation, all people, including Gentiles who do not have the Scriptures, are culpable for their willful rejection of knowledge of God (Rom 1:18-23, esp. v. 20; cf. Acts 14:15-17; 17:22-28; 1 Thess 4:5).

But Paul is specifically focused here on those who persecute Christians, so these can be characterized by their rejection of the distinctive Christian message, the gospel of Jesus. This turn of phrase is ironic: "gospel" signifies "good news," so to reject such a message is especially reprehensible. While it has been argued that these two phrases describe Gentiles and Jews respectively, Paul can easily say that Jews like Gentiles have rejected the knowledge of God which they have received (Rom 2:1-29; cf. Isa 1:3) or that Gentiles like Jews have disobeyed (Rom 11:30-32). Both descriptions, therefore, apply comprehensively to all of those who oppose God and his people in Christ.[19] It is also worth noting that here Paul assumes that the gospel is a message to be not only believed but also obeyed (cf. Rom 1:5). These whom the Lord will punish are those who disobey continually; the participle translated "who . . . do not obey" is in the present tense.

---

[19]Each of the two phrases is governed by its own definite article, which might suggest that they refer to different groups (cf. J. B. Lightfoot, *Notes on Epistles of St. Paul* [Grand Rapids: Baker, 1980 (reprint 1885)], p. 103). But Bruce notes that the use of synonymous parallelism in vv. 7b-10 suggests that they are complementary descriptions of the same group (p. 151).

Thus, the punishment due these people is not the egotistic retaliation of a jilted deity but the measured and just retribution for their crime as it is fully understood. "Punish" translates a participial phrase, δίδοντες ἐκδίκησιν (*didontes ekdikēsin*), literally "giving vengeance," the noun again the one found in Deut 32:35 (cf. Rom 12:19). Seen as the deliberate rejection of the Creator and violent opposition to his salvation (cf. 1 Thess 2:15-16), their sin demands the punishment which Paul will now describe.

1:9 They will be punished with everlasting destruction and shut out from the presence of the Lord and from the majesty of his power

Again Paul's language is retributive: "they will be punished" is literally "they will pay the punishment." Eternal destruction is the fitting penalty for those who have treated the eternal God with the contempt described in v. 8. Though the phrase translated "everlasting destruction," ὄλεθρον αἰώνιον (*olethron aiōnion*; cf. 1 Thess 5:3), could refer to annihilation — the ceasing to exist for eternity, Paul amplifies the sense of this phrase with what follows, a close parallel to Isa 2:10, 19, 21. The relationship between the destruction and the exclusion is even clearer when it is noted that "shut out" has been inserted by the NIV. Literally the text reads "everlasting destruction from the presence of the Lord and the glory of his strength."

Thus, Paul apparently understands the "destruction" to refer not to an end to conscious existence, terrible as that would be, but as the eternal exclusion from God's presence. This is certainly fitting punishment for the crime of having rejected knowledge of God and his good news of salvation. "Destruction" would thus signify "ruin," the utter failure to realize the purpose of one's existence, namely the eternal fellowship with God that Paul here describes (cf. 1 Thess 4:17; Rom 8:17-18, 30; 2 Cor 4:17; Phil 3:21).[20] The reference to

---

[20]Cf. *GELNTBSD*, § 20.34; Wanamaker, p. 229.

God's power here further underlines his ability to carry out his sentence and his enemies' inability to escape it.

The "Lord" here is the Lord Jesus, as the next verse shows. Marshall notes that with the use of Isaiah's language for Yahweh here (Isa 2:10, 19, 21), Paul applies to Jesus scriptural language for God.[21] Other clear allusions to Christ's deity appear later in the chapter (v. 12).

1:10 on the day he comes to be glorified in his holy people and to be marveled at among all those who have believed.

The contrast between the response of the persecutors with their destiny and the response of the believers with theirs is sharply drawn here. Again Paul's language is probably based on the Old Testament, since it shows a striking similarity to the LXX of Ps 88:6 (89:7) and 67:36 (68:35). Those who have rejected God will be excluded from his glory (δόξα, *doxa*, v. 9); those who have believed will glorify (ἐνδοξάζω, *endoxazō*), that is, they will acknowledge and extol God's glory. His "holy" people are literally "holy ones," which could refer, as in 1 Thess 3:13, to angels (see comments above). However, as in that text, Paul more likely uses the term to refer to Christians as those who belong to God.

This sense contrasts well with the preceding discussion of those who are excluded from God's presence and parallels the next one, "all those who have believed." This phrase again contrasts with the description in v. 8. With "all" it emphasizes that Christ's coming will have its effect on more than just the first readers of this letter; they belong to a great fellowship of God's people. "Marvel" translates θαυμάζω (*thaumazō*), a word often used for the reverence of those who witness a manifestation of God or his work (e.g., Matt 8:27; 9:33; 15:31; 21:10; Mark 5:20; Luke 8:25; 11:14; Rev. 13:3).[22] With both verbs Paul uses the preposition ἐν (*en*), translated first as "in" and then as "among." Among the prepositions which Paul could

---

[21]Marshall, pp. 179-180.
[22]Franz Annen, "θαυμάζω," *EDNT*, 2:134-135.

have used, this one suggests the presence of Christ among or in the midst of the people who praise him.[23]

"On the day" refers to "the day of the Lord" (cf. 1 Thess 5:2 and comments above). The possibility that this day was past is the issue that troubles the Thessalonians (cf. 2:2). Paul's use of the phrase here is redundant: the Greek sentence reads, "when he comes . . . in that day." But the redundancy points to the teaching which Paul will spell out in 2:1-12, namely that "the day of the Lord" (2:2) cannot have arrived unless the vindication of his people and defeat of his enemies is complete.

This includes you, because you believed our testimony to you.

This sentence is an expansion of a much shorter remark which Paul has somewhat awkwardly inserted into the sentence, perhaps as a result of dictating it orally. Literally the text simply reads, "Because our testimony to you was believed." However, the awkwardness makes Paul's emphasis clearer. By repeating "believed," he has explicitly identified the readers with those who will marvel at the Lord. The implication, made explicit by the NIV's expanded translation, is that the Thessalonians can look forward to participating in the great worship celebration that will issue from the Lord's return. Just as their persecutors actually belong to a much larger group under judgment (vv. 6, 9), so they belong to a great host who will receive blessing.[24] For a small group of persecuted believers, the expectation of belonging to a vast, eternal gathering of God's people would give strong encouragement.

---

[23]Other senses for these prepositions are possible: instrumental ("by his saints"), causal ("because of his saints") or locative and distributive ("in the lives of the saints"). The locative sense without distribution, "among his saints," is consistent with the allusion to Ps 88:6 LXX. and contrasts well with the exclusion of the opponents in v. 9, as Wanamaker notes (pp. 230-231).

[24]Wanamaker, p. 231.

C. THE CONTENT OF PAUL'S PRAYER (1:11-12)

¹¹With this in mind, we constantly pray for you, that our God may count you worthy of his calling, and that by his power he may fulfill every good purpose of yours and every act prompted by your faith. ¹²We pray this so that the name of our Lord Jesus may be glorified in you, and you in him, according to the grace of our God and the Lord Jesus Christ.[a]

[a]*12 Or God and Lord, Jesus Christ*

The sentence begun in v. 3 continues here, but the content has distinctly shifted from a statement of thanksgiving to a description of Paul's prayers for the readers' future.[25] The prayer focuses generally on the their ongoing steadfastness in light of the larger purpose of God which Paul has just discussed. The prayer, in other words, is that the readers would remain faithful during the present persecution, knowing that God will be faithful to fulfill his purpose to bring them safely to full fellowship with him (cf. 1 Thess 5:23).

1:11 With this in mind, we constantly pray for you, that our God may count your worthy of his calling,

As elsewhere, Paul stresses that his prayers for the church are constant: the verb is in the Greek present tense and modified by πάντοτε (*pantote*, "constantly"), which reinforces the continuing aspect of the tense. These prayers are based on the believer's confidence in God's final deliverance and judgment at Christ's return (see above); therefore, they have as their object the fulfillment of God's saving objective. His call was extended to them for their salvation (1 Thess 2:12), which will be theirs not by being "worthy" but being counted "worthy" through God's grace (v. 12 below).

---

[25]UBSGNT places a full stop at the end of v. 10, but the εἰς ὅ (*eis ho*, "with this in mind") which begins v. 11 shows that it is still subordinated to the preceding and so a part of that complex sentence.

and that by his power he may fulfill every good purpose of yours and every act prompted by your faith.

But God's grace compels a fitting response. The recipients of the call must maintain the faith by which they first received the call, putting that faith into action (cf. Eph 2:10; 4:1) despite the opposition which they presently experience. To do otherwise is to number oneself with those described in vv. 6, 8. But this is accomplished ultimately not by the believer's own efforts. The "act prompted by your faith" is certainly the believers act, but Paul calls on God to "fulfill" it. Likewise "by his power" translates a Greek phrase placed at the end of the clause, a point of emphasis putting further stress on God's work in the lives of the suffering faithful. "Every good purpose of yours" is an ambiguous phrase: it could refer either to God's good purpose of salvation for the believers or their purpose to do good. If it connects more closely with the calling, God's purpose is emphasized (cf. Eph 1:5, 9: Phil 2:13); if it is taken as a parallel to "act prompted by your faith," the believers' purpose is intended (Rom 10:1; Phil 1:15). The link to the following phrase is a close one and so more likely determines the sense.

1:12 We pray this so that the name of our Lord Jesus may be glorified in you, and you in him, according to the grace of our God and the Lord Jesus Christ.

Paul has already stated that the Lord's glory among his people will be the outcome of his return (v. 10). Now he reiterates that point, but without specifying whether the glorification is present or future. No doubt Paul understands it as both. As Christ will be glorified among his saints at his return, so now he is glorified by them — and they by him — as, united with him, they live out their calling faithfully by his power.

To glorify the "name" is a common way in the Old Testament of expressing the exaltation of God; Paul's application of it to Jesus is consistent with his belief in Jesus' deity.[26] But

---

[26]Lars Hartman, "ὄνομα," *EDNT*, 2:520.

potentially clearer in this regard is the last phrase of this verse. "Our God and the Lord Jesus Christ" represents a Greek phrase in which one definite article governs two nouns, which is normally used to indicate that the two nouns constitute a single unit in some respect.[27] Though it is possible that Paul simply followed his habits in including the article in the phrase "the grace of [the] God" and omitting it with "Lord Jesus Christ," the possibility that the structure is deliberate cannot be dismissed. This unity could be in the giving of grace rather than in absolute identity, but even then Paul could hardly name Jesus as the source of grace with God if he did not conceive of Jesus as divine.[28] The NIV's footnote reflects the stronger interpretation of this structure.

Paul again focuses on grace as the principle undergirding the entire relationship between the Lord and his people. The readers' faithful putting into practice of their calling and the consequent glorification of Jesus is finally a working out of his grace. By the demonstration of his grace in the lives of those who have received it, the Lord's true majesty is made clear.

---

[27]Cf. MHT, 3:181.

[28]Commentators are reluctant to see this construction as deliberately identifying God and Christ because it appears to be uncharacteristic of Paul (Bruce, pp. 156-157; Wanamaker, pp. 236-237). Whether it is so very uncharacteristic depends, among other things, on the force of Rom 9:5 and the authenticity of Titus 2:13, both hotly debated points.

2 THESSALONIANS 2

III. INSTRUCTION ON THE LORD'S RETURN (2:1-12)

This section, which is central to the entire second Thessalonian letter, presents one of the most difficult interpretive problems in the New Testament. The problem can be summarized around four specific questions: (1) what is the "rebellion" (v. 3); (2) who is the "man of lawlessness" (v. 3) or "the secret power of lawlessness" (v. 7); (3) what is it that "is holding him back" (v. 6) or "now holds it back" (v. 7); (4) how does all this answer the question which Paul addresses, namely, whether "the day of the Lord" has already come (v. 2)?

The most common answers to these questions have shared an assumption about the passage: Paul speaks primarily of events which are to occur in the future as preliminaries to the return of Jesus. On this basis, conclusions, though widely diverse in particulars, have been confined to a fairly narrow scope. The "rebellion" is generally taken as the period of widespread apostasy from true devotion to God expected in Jewish apocalyptic literature just before God's final act of salvation and judgment at the end of this age. It is further assumed that Paul believes that this period lies in the future, though that may be his own immediate future.

The "man of lawlessness" is generally taken as a future political figure who will lead the climax of opposition to God. The expression is taken as referring to the same figure as the "antichrist" in 1 John 2:18, 22; 4:7, 15; 2 John 7 or the "beast" in Rev 11:7-20:10, a figure based on the Old Testament and intertestamental expectation of a great end-time opponent of

God (Dan 7:8, 25; 11:36, 40-41, 45; *As. Moses* 8:1; *Pss. Sol.* 2:29; *Mart. Isa.* 4:2-3; *4 Ezra* 5:6; *T. Isaac* 6:1; *T. Jud.* 25:3; *T. Dan.* 5:4; *Sib. Or.* 2:63, 75).[1] He will be "revealed" (v. 3) when he appears on the world stage and becomes active, a future event, though again one which may lie in Paul's immediate future. In the meantime, he is restrained (vv. 6-7) by some means, but that restraining power will at some point be removed so that he will become fully active. If this general line of interpretation accurately represents Paul's answer, then the "day of the Lord" in v. 2 probably refers not to the actual event of the Lord's return for salvation and judgment but the period immediately preceding that event. The NIV, even more so than most other English versions, strongly reflects this approach to the text; at several points, noted in comments below, where the Greek text is at best ambiguous, the translators have rendered the text in English in such a way as to point clearly toward this interpretation.

While most interpretation of this text has adhered to these established general boundaries, the specifics have varied widely. In particular, the identity of the restrainer, apparently clearly known to the readers (v. 6), has remained mysterious. Suggestions have included the preaching of the gospel, the church, Paul himself, the Holy Spirit, the Roman Empire, the Jewish nation, angels or a particular angel, and the principle of order, among others. Similar confusion reigns in regard to the identity of the man of lawlessness. Does Paul identify this figure with a person or institution of his own period of history, such as the emperor or the Roman government? Does he regard the statement, "he sets himself up in God's temple," as a literal or a metaphorical expression?[2] The answers to these questions are many and the arguments supporting them are cogent at points; consequently, absolutely no consensus among interpreters has arisen.

---

[1] Bruce provides a thorough discussion of the background and history of interpretation of the antichrist (pp. 177-188).

[2] A summary of major positions is supplied by Leon Morris, "Man of Lawlessness and Restraining Power," *DPL*, pp. 592-594.

In addition to the interpretive chaos which this approach to this text has created, it raises another problem. In 1 Thess 4:13-5:11 Paul stresses the imminence of Jesus' return. The Thessalonians' comfort in grief and their motivation to be watchful and ready for Christ's return are based on the hope that his return is imminent, that it could occur at any moment. If this text refers to events which on God's timetable must precede Christ's return, that imminence is sharply qualified, if not contradicted. This tension has led some to deny that Paul wrote 2 Thessalonians or that his view of the Lord's return had changed between the writing of the two letters.[3]

Others, however, insist that in Jewish literature the idea that the final act of judgment and salvation is imminent regularly stands together with the idea that it will be preceded by various preliminary events or signs. In particular it has been argued that in 1 Thess 5:1-11 the Lord's return is unexpected by unbelievers, while the sign provided here is only understood by believers.[4] Against this it must be said that in 1 Thess 5:1-11 the time of the Lord's coming is unknown to all; what distinguishes believers is not their knowledge of the time but their expectation of Christ's return and their consequent watchfulness. Whatever the merits of these explanations, it is admitted by all that if 2 Thess 2:1-12 refers to future events which precede Christ's return, it does create at least a difficult tension with the imminent expectation of the parousia.

Another general weakness with this approach is its lack of congruence with the question which Paul addresses. If in this text Paul is discussing events which precede Christ's return, at best he answers indirectly the question which begins the discussion, namely, whether the day of the Lord has already come (v. 2). Rather than pointing out directly that this event has not occurred, he in effect says that the day of the Lord has not come because the events necessarily prior to the day

---

[3]Cf. the discussion of this issue in C. Marvin Pate, *The End of the Age Has Come* (Grand Rapids: Zondervan, 1995), p. 222.

[4]Marshall, pp. 192-193.

have not come. While this problem is ameliorated somewhat by taking "day of the Lord" to refer to events just preceding Christ's return, the argument remains less than straightforward. One might have expected the apostle instead to point out what the day of the Lord would bring in itself, noting how those things have not yet been fully realized.

In such a situation of exegetical confusion, established patterns of interpretation deserve reexamination. If the prevailing approach to the text yields so wide a range of possible interpretations and so many problems, it may be that the prevailing approach is not in harmony with the author's intended meaning. To be sure, the traditional understanding of this text may be correct, and the particulars of Paul's meaning may be too remote for us ever to recover them. However, if another approach yields a clear interpretation in harmony with the details of the text and with Paul's teaching elsewhere, it at least deserves a hearing.

One alternative is that the appearance of the man of lawlessness refers to the Roman destruction of Jerusalem in A.D. 70.[5] This interpretation has several merits. One is that Jesus clearly refers to the destruction of the temple in the Olivet Discourse (Matt 24:15-22; Mark 13:14-20; Luke 21:20-24). Since Paul seems to allude to this teaching of Jesus both in this passage (vv. 9-10; cf. Matt 24:23-38; Mark 13:21-23) and in others in these letters (cf. 1 Thess 4:13-5:11; 2 Thess 1:7-10 and comments above), he may do so here as well. The text does refer directly to the temple (v. 4), and "lawless" is used in some other texts to refer to Romans (Acts 2:23; *Pss. Sol.* 17:11-22). Furthermore, this ameliorates somewhat the tension

---

[5]This approach seems to have been first put forth by B. B. Warfield, "The Prophecies of St. Paul," *Biblical and Theological Studies* (Samuel G. Craig, ed.; Philadelphia: Presbyterian & Reformed, 1952 [reprint 1886]), pp. 463-475; it has recently been suggested for somewhat different reasons by N. T. Wright, "Putting Paul Together Again: Toward a Synthesis of Pauline Theology (1 and 2 Thessalonians, Philippians, and Philemon)," *Pauline Theology, Volume I: Thessalonians, Philippians, Galatians, Philemon* (Jouette M. Bassler, ed.; Minneapolis: Fortress, 1991), pp. 208-209.

between the prediction of preliminary events and the imminent expectation of the Lord's return in 1 Thess 4:13-5:11.

There are, however, some serious weaknesses with this approach. One is the lack of substantial verbal parallels between this passage and the specific discussion of the fall of Jerusalem in the Olivet Discourse. Only the statement about sitting in the temple (v. 4) can be offered as a specific allusion to anything in Matt 24:15-22 and its parallels, and then only as an interpretive allusion to "abomination of desolation." If Paul is referring specifically to the Olivet Discourse, he is doing so obliquely at best.

Secondly, in order to see a reference to the destruction of the temple in v. 4, "sets himself up" must be taken figuratively while "temple" is interpreted literally. The comments on this verse below will note that the rest of the verse suggests a consistently figurative meaning for the entire expression.

Thirdly, Jesus' teaching about Jerusalem in the Olivet Discourse presents the fall of Jerusalem less as a preliminary sign of his coming than as an event not to be confused with his coming. It has the impact of a specific warning to Christians living in Palestine to flee the approaching Roman armies, to depend on God's provision for them during a time of great distress, and not to confuse this event and the false messianic claims that will accompany it with the actual return of Jesus. Paul's approach here is significantly different if he refers to that event. Most important is the observation, noted in detail in the comments below, that Paul's language in this text emphasizes not so much the future activity of the lawless one as his present activity. Though obscured at nearly every point by the NIV's interpretive translation, this observation is probably the decisive one in indicating the possibility of a different interpretation.

Recognizing that Paul emphasizes the present activity of the lawless one throughout this passage prompts us to put forward another possibility for consideration.[6] We begin with

---

[6]This line of interpretation was first suggested to me by Tom Friskney

the recognition that for Paul the "end time" has already begun with the appearance of Jesus in history and especially with his death and resurrection. In a variety of other texts, many of them already noted in previous comments, Paul points out that the promised blessings of the end time are already a reality for the Christian because in Christ God has inaugurated the fulfillment of his promises.

Likewise, the suffering of the faithful which in the Old Testament and intertestamental Jewish apocalyptic literature precedes the final act of salvation (Isa 24:17-23; Dan 12:1; Joel 2:1-11; Amos 5:16-20; Zeph 1:14-16; *Jub.* 23:11; 24:3; *2 Bar.* 22:6; 55:6; *4 Ezra* 7:37; *1 Enoch* 80:4-5), is also for Paul a present reality (cf. Rom 8:22; 1 Cor 2:6-8; 15:55-57; Eph 6:10-16; Col 2:14), one which begins with Christ's own sufferings and continues in the lives of believers as they are united with Christ and suffer as he did.[7]

The very structure of Paul's thought, then, is that the end-time events have already been manifested in Christ and are being manifested in the lives of believers. What remains to occur, as Paul has stressed in 2 Thess 1:6-10, is for Christ's return to bring an end to the suffering of his people, vindicating them before their enemies — who are also his enemies — and bringing to full realization the glory which already belongs to the people of God and the judgment that already belongs to the others.

Could this be the very point which Paul makes in this text? If the following conclusions, presented in detail in the comments below, have merit, then the answer appears to be affirmative: (1) the "rebellion" refers to Jewish rejection of the gospel, already a reality in Paul's ministry; (2) the "appearance" (or "revelation") of the man of lawlessness refers not to his activity in history, which is already a reality, but the final,

---

and is reflected in his book, *Thirteen Lessons on First and Second Thessalonians* (Joplin, MO: College Press, 1982), pp. 92-99. Here I work out this suggestion in greater detail and with a few variations.

[7]Cf. Pate, *End of the Age*, pp. 64, 106-108, 227-228.

definitive revealing that all opposition to God and Christ is ultimately the activity of the great opponent, Satan; (3) "what is holding him back" (v. 6) and "the one who now holds it back" are better rendered as "the one who now prevails" and do not refer to someone or something that restrains the man of lawlessness but instead refer to the man of lawlessness himself as one who appears to prevail in this age. If so, for Paul the "man of lawlessness" was as much a present manifestation of the end-time opponent of God as was the "antichrist" in the epistles of John (1 John 2:18, 22; 4:7, 15; 2 John 7).[8] In this case Paul in this text stresses that the Lord's work will not be complete until the opposition which the Thessalonians and other Christians already experience is revealed for what it is and is fully and finally eliminated at the Lord's return. In effect he assures the readers that the day of the Lord has not yet come because they continue to see the prevalence of evil all around them.

It might be argued that the structure of Paul's thought, with its balance between the present realization of God's end-time promises and the future completion of them, demands that the present manifestation of end-time evil climax in the appearance near the end of history of a great opponent of God. While this assumption does lend a certain symmetry to Paul's eschatology, it remains an assumption only. If the conclusions summarized above and argued below are correct, this text gives no explicit reason to expect an intensification of trouble at some point in the future. If the revelation of the man of lawlessness refers to the revealing of his activity throughout history for what it is and if "what is holding him back" is in fact "the one who prevails," then nothing in the

---

[8]The interpretation of the beast of Revelation is probably more difficult than the interpretation of the man of lawlessness and lies beyond the scope of this commentary. But it should be noted that the points of contact between John's depiction of this figure and the oppression of Christians in Asia Minor by the imperial government in the first century might suggest that the beast represented for John a similar figure of eschatological opposition already active in the present experience of his readers.

text indicates that in the future the activity of the lawless one will be any worse than it is already. This conclusion does not, however, minimize the intensity or significance of the suffering of Christians in any way. Throughout these letters Paul has shown the readers that their tribulations belong to the context of God's salvation-historical plan (1 Thess 2:14-16; 3:4-5); they are part of the end-time sufferings inaugurated by Christ, not unlike the experience of God's people in the past. These troubles, because they are part of the opposition to God's final act of salvation in Jesus, already represent the climax of evil in the world. Thus, all that remains for the future is the judgment due the opponents (2 Thess 1:6-7). The present sufferings of Christians do not require an intensification in order to fulfill the predicted sufferings of the end. Modern American Christians who have difficulty believing that opposition to the Lord and his people has already reached such a pitch have perhaps focused too much on their relative security and too little on the suffering of their brothers and sisters in other places.

If this interpretation is correct, several difficulties with this text are addressed in a single stroke. The mysterious identities of the man of lawlessness and the one who restrains are immediately resolved. If both expressions refer to Satan as he is at work in this age, then the text speaks less cryptically than is regularly assumed. Secondly, the tension between the imminence of Christ's return and the prediction of preliminary events is eliminated. If what Paul addresses here is the present activity of evil, which at once will be revealed for what it is and destroyed when Christ returns, then Christ's return remains imminent. Furthermore, the resulting emphasis of the text is that his return will mean deliverance and vindication for the believers, who in the meantime must remain alert and steadfast as they resist the deceptive activity of the Evil One and look forward to his final defeat at Christ's return, precisely the emphasis of the rest of Paul's eschatological teaching in these letters. Finally, the impact of the argument for the question which begins the discussion is direct and cogent. Paul's point is to reassure the Thessalonians that the day of the Lord has not yet occurred because when it does, the opposition which they now endure will be eliminated entirely. It offers them the reassurance that God's work in history is not finished until his people experience the fullness of fellowship with him, no longer restricted or hindered by the activity of Satan and those who belong to him.

Such are the general merits of the interpretation which this commentary sets forth; the specifics are spelled out in the verse-by-verse comments below. Recognizing, however, that this interpretation represents a departure from the approach to this text which has prevailed for some time, the comments will also note the way in which this text has traditionally been interpreted.

A. THE DAY OF THE LORD NOT YET PRESENT (2:1-2)

¹Concerning the coming of our Lord Jesus Christ and our being gathered to him, we ask you, brothers, ²not to become easily unsettled or alarmed by some prophecy, report or letter supposed to have come from us, saying that the day of the Lord has already come.

This section begins with the question which prompts Paul's discussion. As in other cases where Paul addresses a specific problem in a church, we can only speculate about the circumstances which led to the problem. The prevailing opinion is that the expectation of the Lord's return, fueled in part by 1 Thessalonians 4:13-5:11, has reached a fever pitch in the Thessalonian church, so that the Christians there believed themselves to be living in the period immediately before Christ's return. To lessen the intensity of this expectation, Paul wrote the section that follows, correcting their imminent hope for Christ's return with the reminder that certain events, namely the rebellion and the appearance of the man of lawlessness, must occur first.

This explanation has the virtue of seeing in Paul's answer a direct address of the problem. If the Thessalonian church includes a large contingent of former pagans (cf. 1 Thess 1:9 and comments above), Paul's use of language and images from Jewish apocalyptic literature might be surprising. However, if the problems in the church were prompted by a message which employed such language, we would not by surprised that Paul would correct the problem using similar language.

There are, however, other ways in which the problem may have arisen. Later in Corinth it appears that a species of teaching arose which asserted that all of God's promises, including the promise of the resurrection, had already been fulfilled in their entirety in what Christians had already received in Jesus and through the Holy Spirit. Paul appears to address this problem in its many manifestations throughout 1 Corinthians, but especially in 1 Corinthians 15. To the idea that all of God's work is complete in what the Christian has already received, Paul there asserts emphatically that God has a work yet to come, the resurrection of the dead at Christ's return. Later Paul reflects a similar idea in 2 Tim 2:18, where he refers to those who teach that the resurrection had already occurred. The problem may be similar in Thessalonica. The possibility that some had taught the Thessalonians, with alleged apostolic authority, that the Lord's work was finished, in effect that the promise of a coming "day of the Lord" had been fulfilled, is all the more likely because Paul addresses a church not far removed geographically, culturally or chronologically from the Corinthian church.[9] As noted below, this

---

[9]This possibility is ignored by Wanamaker, who writes, "It is difficult to know in what sense the Thessalonians may have thought that the day of the Lord had come, since clearly the coming of Jesus at the end of the age could not have happened" (p. 237). A position similar to the one taken here was argued by Walter Schmithals, who linked the teaching to Gnosticism (*Paul and the Gnostics*, [J. E. Steely, trans.; Nashville: Abingdon, 1972], pp. 166-167, 202-208). This hypothesis has been rightly criticized as anachronistic, since Gnosticism as such cannot be shown to have existed in this

scenario allows the phrase "day of the Lord" to have its usual meaning for Paul: it refers not to the period just preceding the end but to the end itself, which will bring the final victory of God's purposes in the world (cf. 1 Thess 5:2 and comments above).

The value of this text for the modern reader lies in precisely this area. Ultimately the New Testament's expectation of the Lord's return promises the ultimate fulfillment of God's eternal good purposes for creation and humanity. As long as evil is active in the world, even more when it appears that evil prevails, God's purpose remains incomplete. So in addressing the question of the Lord's coming, Paul is not simply settling the matter of the eschatological calendar. He is asserting the utter goodness and power of God, which will finally prevail completely over every manifestation of evil. When his people are persecuted, they can be assured that God's power and goodness will one day triumph fully.

2:1 Concerning the coming of our Lord Jesus Christ and our being gathered to him,

Paul announces here the general subject which he will address. "Coming" is παρουσία (*parousia*), a term which Paul uses later in this section (vv. 8-9) and often in the first letter (1 Thess 2:19 [see comments]; 3:13; 4:15; 5:23) to refer to the Lord's return as his visitation or presence as an important

---

period. However, Schmithals notes sufficient parallels between the problems in Thessalonica and Corinth to establish the probability that they had similar sources which at points resembled the full-blown Gnosticism of the second century. Bruce objects, "But if the Thessalonians had really given up the futurist eschatology of 1 Thess 4:13-5:11 for such a radical spiritualization, it would not have helped the situation for them to be given further futurist eschatology such as is presented in vv 3-8" (p. 166). But this seems to be precisely what Paul does in 1 Cor 15:50-58, and it must be asked whether presenting again a futurist eschatology is not precisely what such a radical spiritualization would demand, particularly if the spiritualization had been presented to the churches as a reinterpretation of apocalyptic language which exaggerated Paul's own emphasis on the present fulfillment of God's end-time promises.

official. This visitation also signifies the gathering of his people to be with him, as Paul has stated specifically in 1 Thess 4:17. If, as both internal evidence and tradition would indicate, 1 Thessalonians was written before this letter, Paul is in effect reminding the readers of the content of that first letter and offering a clarification or expansion on its teaching. The word translated "being gathered, ἐπισυναγωγή (*episynagōgē*) occurs only here and at Heb 10:25, but the cognate verb appears in Matt 24:31; Mark 13:27. So the unusual expression here may echo the teaching of Jesus about his return. This gathering fulfills the expectation of the Old Testament that the scattered people of God would be gathered again (Isa 43:4-7; 52:12; 56:8; Jer 31:8; Ezek 28:9; Ps 106:47) and for Christians signified the gathering of believers from all parts of the earth as well as the reuniting of the living and the dead.

The fact that Paul here equates the "coming" of the Lord, implying his abiding presence, with the "gathering" of his people again leaves us with little reason to see the gathering as an secret event years prior to a second, open return of Christ when he will remain on earth.[10] When it is observed that this coming also will mean the final defeat of the great opponent (v. 8), that conclusion is even more secure. Whatever the specific interpretation of this section, it is at least clear that the Lord's coming and the gathering of his people are a single event which signal the end, not the beginning, of the troubles described in the following verses.

we ask you, brothers, 2:2 not to become easily unsettled or alarmed by some prophecy, report or letter supposed to have come from us,

Apparently the Thessalonian church had received some communication asserting what Paul indicates here and purporting to have come from him or his associates. Paul's difficulties with others who claimed apostolic authority equal to or greater than his own are very much in evidence in the

---

[10]Bruce, p. 163.

Corinthian letters and Galatians; here the problem seems to be some who represent themselves as actually speaking for Paul. The string of terms which Paul uses here — prophecy (literally "spirit," πνεῦμα, *pneuma*), report (literally "word," λόγος, *logos*) or letter — probably indicates that Paul knows that the Thessalonians have been disturbed by a message but is uncertain as to how it came precisely. It is possible that the "letter" to which Paul refers to 1 Thessalonians, since the problem may have arisen from a misunderstanding of it. Since "supposed" is a likely inference from the Greek text but is not strictly necessary, Paul could refer to an authentic letter. But the combination of terms more likely indicates some imitation of the inspired messages delivered through a prophet or apostle and falsely claiming to have come from Paul or his associates. In effect Paul is calling for a specific application of his instructions in 1 Thess 5:21: the Thessalonians are to test this alleged apostolic message by what they know to be true about the gospel, as Paul will remind them of it in vv. 3-12. He further addresses the problem of messages falsely claiming to come from him in 3:17.

Paul urges them not to be "easily" shaken, literally "quickly" (ταχέως, *tacheōs*). As in Gal 1:6, any departure from confident faith in the gospel is quick, since the right response is to hold faithfully to the message until Christ returns (1 Thess 5:4-11). Two verbs describe the effect of the false message on the Thessalonians: σαλεύω (*saleuō*), which indicates a shaking from a position of confidence, and θροέω (*throeō*), which implies a mental arousal or disturbance.[11] Both are used here in a negative sense, indicating not excitement but distress. They demonstrate that the problem addressed is not merely a matter of abstract theology; it seriously affects the readers' entire Christian outlook.

saying that the day of the Lord has already come.
The specific problem concerns whether the "day of the

---

[11] BAGD, pp. 364, 740.

Lord" has already come. As noted above, a key interpretive question in this section is whether this phrase refers to the Lord's coming itself or includes the period immediately preceding the Lord's coming. In favor of the latter is the sense it makes of Paul's argument if he is discussing events which occur prior to the Lord's return. If "day" includes the period just before Christ comes back, then the Thessalonians have received a report that those days have come and so they are living in a state of great excitement and anticipation, indicated with "unsettled or alarmed" in this verse. Paul in turn tones down their agitation by stating in what follows that Christ will not return until the man of lawlessness makes his appearance on the world stage, that in effect his appearance is what will signal the period just before the end.

There are, however, several specific difficulties with this interpretation. One is the fact that Paul represents the situation of the Thessalonians not merely as over-excitement but actual disturbance. The verbs in v. 2 are more consistently understood if Paul sees the Thessalonians' situation not simply as too much of a good thing, that is, anticipating Christ's return, but as a threat to their confident hope. More significant is the fact that in the other eight uses of "day of the Lord" or the equivalent in Paul's letters (1 Cor 1:8; 2 Cor 1:14; Phil 1:6, 10; 2:16; 1 Thess 5:2, 4; 2 Thess 1:10; N.B. that Paul uses the expression much more frequently than any other New Testament writer), it never refers to anything other than the actual climax of God's work in salvation and judgment. This meaning is confirmed for this passage in the way that Paul begins the discussion in v. 1, referring to "the coming of our Lord Jesus Christ and our being gathered to him." Therefore, though in other literature it is at best conceivable that the phrase could be used for the period preceding this climax, there is little in this text or in Paul's letters generally to indicate that meaning here.[12]

---

[12]G. B. Caird notes that in the Old Testament, though the phrase "day of the Lord" can be used as a metaphor to refer to some act of God in history

Alternately the verb ἐνίστημι (*enistēmi*) may mean "be imminent" instead of "has come."[13] However, such a meaning is not clearly attested for this word, since in the examples in which it may be implied the sense of "be present" is equally consistent.[14] Furthermore, the verb here is in the perfect indicative, indicating a past action and so allowing at best only the awkward sense, not attested in any other use, of "has become imminent."[15] The NIV's rendering of the verb is highly preferable.

If in this sense "the day of the Lord" had already come, then God's work in history is finished. For the Thessalonian Christians — small in number, persecuted by their neighbors, and suffering the grief of separation from dead brothers and sisters — that prospect would be disturbing and depressing indeed. Their hope of final vindication and glorification, of which Paul wrote in 1:5-10, would vanish. They would have no prospect that God would finish the work begun in them (Phil 1:6). They would indeed "be pitied more than all men" (1 Cor 15:19). Reassuring them that this is in fact not the case is Paul's task in the following verses.

B. THE APOSTASY AND THE MAN OF LAWLESSNESS (2:3-12)

Following the tradition of most English versions, the NIV translators have made a number of interpretive decisions that

---

not temporally connected to the end of history, it always views that event as "an anticipation and embodiment of the universal judgment to come" but not as a predictive sign of the end (*The Language and Imagery of the Bible* [Philadelphia: Westminster, 1980], pp. 237-260).

[13]Hippolytus of Rome indicates that a Christian leader in third-century Rome, described as "a pious and humble man, but not hold[ing] strictly to the Scriptures," apparently took the verb in this sense as a reference to his own time (*Commentary on Daniel 4*, 19; cf. HCNT § 824).

[14]BAGD, p. 266.

[15]Cf. Wanamaker, p. 240.

sharply affect the impression which this text makes on the reader. In particular, the Greek present tense has been rendered with the English future in vv. 4, 9, and an object for the verb translated "is holding"/"holds" has been supplied in vv. 6-7. While none of these renderings is impossible, the fact that so many unusual translations are necessary to support the traditional interpretation of this passage suggests that another interpretation may more closely reflect Paul's meaning. In the comments below, the specifics of Paul's Greek text will be examined closely and alternative translations suggested. These will converge on a single point, that Paul sees the activity of the man of lawlessness not as something which lies in the future but as something already present, something which already dominates this age but which will come to its outright end when Christ returns.

If this interpretation is correct, then the impact of this text for the Thessalonians is as clear as it is for the Christian of any period who doubts the future return of Christ. Paul's reminder is that as long as evil is active in the world — claiming God's place, appearing to prevail in everyday life, deceiving the spiritually gullible and so denying them salvation — God's work in Christ is not complete. But because God's promise is faithful and his power supreme, Christ will indeed return to destroy all evil and the one who stands behind it, establishing the fullness of his righteous kingdom for which his people yearn.

1. The Apostasy and the Revelation of the Man of Lawlessness (2:3)

³Don't let anyone deceive you in any way, for that day will not come until the rebellion occurs and the man of lawlessness[a] is revealed, the man doomed to destruction.

[a]3 Some manuscripts *sin*

2:3 Don't let anyone deceive you in any way, for that day will not come until the rebellion occurs

In response to the false report which the Thessalonians have received, Paul first urges a healthy and holy skepticism. The message that the day of the Lord has come is deception, like that of the serpent with Eve (2 Cor 11:3; 1 Tim 2:14), because of what Paul is about to explain. Paul warns against this deception emphatically; "anyone . . . in any way" is literally "not anyone . . . in no way," a double-negative expression that stresses the prohibition.

Following the warning about deception, the rest of the verse in the Greek text is an anacoluthon, a subordinate clause with no clause to complete it. Literally the text reads, "Because unless the rebellion comes first and the man of lawlessness is revealed." Translators must supply the clause introduced with "because" (ὅτι, *hoti*), which can be clearly inferred from v. 2. Since the question concerns the coming of the day of the Lord, Paul obviously expects the reader to infer that the day is preceded by the rebellion and revelation of the man of lawlessness.

Interpreters of this passage have generally taken the "rebellion" to refer to something in the future, a widespread departure from the church, a civil rebellion or a combination of the two which will be an immediate prelude to the Lord's return. Though the language of this text could be consistent with that idea, elsewhere Paul gives reasons to believe that he saw this rebellion as something already at work during his lifetime. "Rebellion" translates ἀποστασία (*apostasia*), sometimes rendered "apostasy"; in the LXX this word and its cognates are especially used to refer to sinful departure from the worship of God.[16] Especially in light of v. 11, this is clearly its sense here. In intertestamental Jewish apocalyptic literature, this word group was used sometimes to refer to a great period of religious unfaithfulness just before the age to come (*Jub.* 23:14-23; *4 Ezra* 5:1-13; *2 Apoc. Bar.* 70:1-10; *1 Enoch* 5:4;

---

[16]Wolfgang Bauder, "Fall, Fall Away," *NIDNTT*, 1:606-608.

91:3-10; 93:9; 1QpHab 2:1), but in some cases it clearly referred to the present departure of members of a Jewish sect (1QS 7:18-22).

Grammatically the sentence allows this rebellion to be an event in either the future or the present for Paul: the verb ἔλθῃ (*elthē*) is in the subjunctive mood, which has no time value, and the rest of the clause requires only that this event occur before the day of the Lord. Clearly elsewhere Paul indicates that such rebellion is already a reality (1 Tim 4:1; 2 Tim 3:1). But what is most significant for understanding this word as Paul intended it is the concern which he expresses elsewhere for the rebellion against God of those Jews who have rejected the gospel (1 Thess 2:14-16; Rom 9-11). This point is difficult to appreciate for modern Christians who take for granted the division between Christians and non-Christian Jews, but for Paul and his contemporaries this was a crucial problem.[17] For early Christians who proclaimed that through Jesus they had received the fulfillment of God's promises to Israel, the unbelief of so many in Israel demanded an explanation. Part of that explanation is probably implied here: Jewish refusal of the gospel is a manifestation of the expected end-time rebellion. So here Paul uses "rebellion" as it is used in the Old Testament, to refer to the falling away of those who are ostensibly God's people. If the Thessalonians had undergone persecution prompted by Jewish opponents of the gospel (Acts 17:5-9), Paul's meaning would be entirely clear and relevant to them.

and the man of lawlessness is revealed, the man doomed to destruction.

The revelation of the man of lawlessness is similarly regarded by most interpreters as a future event, specifically as

---

[17]Cf. Pate, *End of the Age*, pp. 228-229. I have argued at length that Luke-Acts is largely concerned with explaining that the gospel may be the message of the fulfillment of Israel's promises despite the fact that Israel's response to the gospel is divided in *Jewish Responsibility, passim*.

the appearance at the end of this age of an archenemy of the Lord, one who is presently restrained from appearing by some being or force. Certainly some Jewish groups of this period expected such a figure to appear in the future, though some of the intertestamental literature which has been interpreted as referring to such a figure may in fact have been intended to refer to some specific opponent of God's people at the time of writing. The question here, though, is whether Paul uses "is revealed" to refer to the appearance of this figure in history or to something else.

While the traditional meaning is not impossible, Paul elsewhere uses this verb, ἀποκαλύπτω (*apokaluptō*) and its cognate noun ἀποκάλυψις (*apokalypsis*) to indicate not that something formerly inactive becomes active but that something formerly hidden to the world but nevertheless real becomes visible to all. Hence in 1:7 the revelation of Christ is the making visible to all of his supreme authority as judge, authority which has been his since his resurrection but has not been perceived by any but his followers. Likewise, as Bruce notes, in Rom 8:19 the revealing of the sons of God is the final disclosure that the Christians are indeed God's sons, the unveiling of the identity which has always been theirs but has been hidden to unbelievers.[18] If the word has similar impact here, then Paul refers not to a point when the man of lawlessness becomes fully active in history but the point when he is revealed for who he is. This interpretation is corroborated when we observe that the rest of the text stresses not the future activity of this figure but his present activity. Hence, Paul's point is to say that the readers can be sure that the day of the Lord has not yet come because God's purpose will not be complete until this man of lawlessness, already at work in the world, is revealed for who he is, the archenemy of God and deceiver of humanity.

Exactly who is this "man of lawlessness"? He is generally assumed to be a figure of history, what might be termed a

---

[18]Bruce, p. 74.

political figure, who will bring to a climax all human rebellion against God. Beyond that general identification, interpreters have found no unity whatever in understanding this expression. Noting especially stress on the present activity of this lawless one, some have understood the writer to be referring to the Roman government or emperor. Some therefore see this prophecy as a failed one, since Rome has fallen and the expected "day" has not come.[19] Others have attempted to reclaim this line of interpretation, offering that the rebellion and the revelation of the man of lawlessness refers to the destruction of Jerusalem, which Paul merely presented as a necessary preliminary to the Lord's return, not necessarily as an event which point to Christ's return immediately afterward.[20] Luther identified the man of lawlessness with the pope, a conclusion clearly based on his own polemical needs and now almost universally abandoned. The predominant view remains that this "man" is an uncertain figure of the future, whose appearance is the immediate harbinger of the Lord's return.

As already indicated, this traditional interpretation runs afoul of the stress in the text on the present activity of this evil one. Moreover, the fact that his evil activity is expressed as comprehensively as it is in the text that follows and the focus elsewhere in the New Testament on Christ's final destruction of Satan and his minions suggest that the "man of lawlessness" is here a way of referring to Satan as the one who stands behind every act of rebellion against God's work. If, as noted above, "revealed" has its expected sense here, then Paul's point would be that Christ's work, to be completed on his "day," is not finished until Satan, the Evil One, is revealed to all as the one who stands behind all human rejection of God's will.

"Man of lawlessness" is an apt description of such a figure. For Paul God's law was, among other things, that which

---

[19]Cf. Wanamaker, p. 248.
[20]N. T. Wright, "Putting Paul Together Again," pp. 208-209.

defined God's people as those who genuinely belong to him.[21] Lawlessness can therefore be used as a comprehensive description for the one who opposes all of God's work for his people and inspires rebellion against him (cf. Rom 6:19; 2 Cor 6:14; Titus 2:14; 1 John 3:4). "Man" translates ἄνθρωπος (*anthrōpos*), which normally refers to a human being. However, the word was commonly used with a weakened sense, almost as an indefinite pronoun, when the emphasis was not on the word "man" but on the words which qualify it.[22] That would be the case here, where the emphasis lies on "lawlessness" as the characteristic of this figure (cf. Rev 13:18). This is confirmed by the next expression: the second occurrence of "man" in the NIV translates υἱός (*huios*), literally "son," which is used in a similar indefinite fashion to put the emphasis on the descriptive noun "destruction" (cf. Matt 8:12; 13:38; Luke 16:8; 20:34; John 17:12; Acts 3:25; Eph 2:2; 5:6; Col 3:6). That the terms do not necessarily stress humanity in this context is indicated later in the text, where Paul will refer more indefinitely to "the mystery of lawlessness" (v. 7) and "the lawless one" (v. 8; cf. Matt 6:13).

As the NIV footnote indicates, many Greek manuscripts read "man of sin" instead of "man of lawlessness," substituting ἁμαρτία (*hamartia*, "sin") for ἀνομία (*anomia*, "lawlessness"). This variant is widely attested, but since "lawlessness" occurs twice later in this passage, it appears to be the more likely original reading. A later copyist may have substituted "sin" since it is a more common word in Paul's letters.

"The one doomed to destruction," as indicated above, is literally "the son of destruction." The same term is used of Judas Iscariot in John 17:12. Like the first expression, this one suggests the activity of this opponent, but it points also to his destiny. "Destruction" is ἀπώλεια (*apōleia*), signifying complete loss or ruin, often used of the final destruction of

---

[21]Frank Thielman, "Law," *DPL*, pp. 534-535.
[22]BAGD, p. 69.

judgment.[23] Paul will later speak generally of those who "perish" (v. 10), a cognate of this word. The implication as the section develops is that the one here described brings destruction on those whom he deceives as all who follow him will share in the destruction which will finally be his (v. 8). The combination of terms at the beginning of the section thus serves not only to identify the subject of Paul's discussion but also to warn against following him and sharing his fate.

2. A Description of the Man of Lawlessness (2:4)

⁴He will oppose and will exalt himself over everything that is called God or is worshiped, so that he sets himself up in God's temple, proclaiming himself to be God.

2:4 He will oppose and will exalt himself over everything that is called God or is worshiped,
Assuming a future point of reference to the entire context, the NIV inserts "will" twice in this text. On this reading the activity of the man of lawlessness lies in the future from Paul's perspective. Literally, however, Paul's words have no explicit reference to the future. "Will oppose" and "will exalt" represent two Greek present participles which have no particular time value but stress that the action named is continuing. Literally this part of the text could be translated, "the one opposing and exalting himself over everything that is called 'God' or an object of worship." The NRSV captures the literal sense clearly: "He opposes and exalts himself above every so-called god or object of worship." At this point, therefore, it is at least uncertain whether the man of lawlessness is a present or future figure. The language later in this section will resolve this question.

The description given here is one of comprehensive opposition to God and utter arrogance and presumptuousness.

---

[23]Armin Kretzer, "ἀπόλλυμι, ἀπώλεια," *EDNT*, 1:135-136.

Paul is no doubt echoing earlier biblical expressions of great opponents of God, like Isaiah's prophetic description of Babylon (Isa 14:12-15), Ezekiel's of Tyre (Ezek 28:2, 11-19) or Daniel's of Antiochus IV Epiphanes (Dan 8:11, 23-26; 9:26-27; 11:31, 36; 12:11; cf. 1 Macc 1:54).[24] These figures have several features in common: they oppress the people of God, assume the supreme place of God and demand worship, and finally meet a decisive judgment which puts an end to their presumption.

For each prophet these descriptions have a significance wider than their immediate reference to specific historical figures. Babylon in Isaiah stands at the head of a catalogue of nations, all of which will be judged by the universal God for their rebellion against him (Isa 13-26). It is, in effect, the archetype of all sinfulness in this section of Isaiah. Likewise, in Daniel the Abomination of Desolation is the most horrid of the opponents of Daniel's visions, but all such opponents and their human kingdoms will be destroyed with the coming of God's kingdom (Dan 7:13-14, 23-28; 9:27; 11:31; 12:11).[25] In Ezekiel Tyre is pictured as the great opponent in Eden, the serpent (Ezek 28:12-17).

It can be argued with some cogency, then, that these prophets saw the particular manifestations of evil to which they were referring as part of a larger pattern of human sinfulness which stands under the comprehensive judgment of God. This pattern continues in later Jewish literature: in *Sib.*

---

[24]Roger D. Aus has suggested a specific allusion to Isa 66:6 LXX in this verse because both texts use ἀντικεῖμαι (*antikeimai*, "oppose") and refer to the temple ("God's Plan and God's Power: Isaiah 66 and the Restraining Factors of 2 Thess 2:6-7" *JBL* 96 [1977] 539). The similarities are too slim, however, to argue for a specific allusion.

[25]Daniel's "abomination of desolation" is, of course, employed by Jesus in the Olivet Discourse as an image for the coming Roman destruction of Jerusalem (Matt 24:15-22; Mark 13:14-20; cf. Luke 21:20-24). Unlike the passages under consideration here, however, Jesus' "abomination" is not viewed as an embodiment of rebellion against God or a special object of judgment. It is therefore unlikely that Paul uses this part of the Olivet Discourse at this point.

Or. 5:33, for example, Nero is described as declaring himself as God's equal, though he proves not to be.

These prophetic descriptions of supreme pride and sinfulness suggest intriguing comparisons to the description of the first sin of Genesis 3 (cf. Ezek 28:12-17). There the temptation is to become "like God" (Gen 3:5) through a deliberate act of rebellion against God. Likewise, the sin of Babel in Genesis 11, motivated by the desire "to make a name for ourselves," has as its objective to be able, like God, to do whatever the people of Babel desire (Gen 11:4, 6). Against this background it is not surprising that Paul would use similar language to describe the one who stands behind every act of sinfulness as supremely arrogant and presumptuous, to the point of usurping the very place of God himself. The idea that Paul refers not to a specific person who will appear in history to manifest these evil qualities but to the archenemy of God who provokes all such manifestations is consistent with the what follows this initial description. It is also consistent with his usage elsewhere, as he focuses the struggle between the people of God and God's enemies as the final spiritual battle between the people of God and Satan (Rom 16:20; 2 Cor 2:11; 11:13-15; Eph 2:1-10; 6:10-17; 1 Thess 3:5).[26] If the end of the age has truly begun with the cross, it should be no surprise that for Paul the end-time struggle with evil should already be actualized.

The specifics of Paul's description here are consistent with this interpretation. "Oppose" translates ἀντίκειμαι (*antikeimai*), which is used elsewhere for opposition to Jesus, his disciples or the gospel (Luke 13:17; 21:51; 1 Cor 16:9; Phil 1:28). In 1 Tim 5:14 Paul uses the same expression found in this text to refer to the devil, and similar examples can be found in the Apostolic Fathers (*1 Clem.* 51:1; *Mart. Pol.* 17:1).[27] "Exalt" is ὑπεραίρω (*huperairō*), used to refer to an

---

[26]Pate expresses this idea well: "For Paul, the historical enemies of God as specified in Judaism are spiritualized and transformed into the Devil and his host" (*End of the Age*, p. 121).

[27]BAGD, p. 74.

inappropriate or exaggerated exaltation of the self (cf. 2 Cor 11:7). The first object of this opposition and exaltation is "everything that is called God." Such a comprehensive description is necessary to point out that Paul speaks not merely of paganism, which might make claims for deities other than the God of Israel, but to that which falsely claims superiority to anything regarded as deity. Paul may have in mind a perspective like the one found in Deut 32:16-17: the pagan gods are but representatives of demons. The one who ultimately claims priority over all such "gods" is the prince of demons. That point is reiterated with "object of worship," σέβασμα (*sebasma*), which broadens the point to include anything that might receive human reverence and so be a rival to the lawless one.[28]

so that he sets himself up in God's temple, proclaiming himself to be God.

The arrogation of divine status which Paul describes is pictured in concrete terms here. "Temple" here is ναός (*naos*), which normally is used to refer specifically to the central "house" of the temple, the Holy Place and Most Holy Place, representative of the dwelling of God.[29] The image of an opponent of God who desecrates his temple has a long history in Jewish history and literature. The Philistines (1 Sam 4:10-11) and the Egyptians (1 Kgs 14:25-26) both put the tabernacle or temple to the sack, but it is the Babylonians who bring destruction to Solomon's temple and so stand as the archetypical temple violators.

Even closer to the image here, though, was the action of Antiochus IV Epiphanes, the Seleucid king who in 167 B.C. erected a statue of Zeus in the Jerusalem temple. Also similar were the actions of the Roman general Pompey, who when he captured Jerusalem in 63 B.C. entered into the Most Holy Place, and Caligula, who in A.D. 41 unsuccessfully planned to

---

[28]Werner Foerster, "σέβομαι, κτλ," *TDNT*, 7:173-174.
[29]Udo Borse, "ναός," *EDNT*, 2:457.

have his own image erected in the temple.³⁰ After Paul wrote, of course, the temple was again destroyed by the Romans in A.D. 70.

While all of these events closely parallel Paul's description, none literally matches it: the Babylonians' destruction of the temple and Pompey's entry into it are not the same as receiving worship in the temple, Antiochus did not demand worship of himself (though Daniel nearly describes him so [Dan 11:36], and the title "Epiphanes" did imply a divine claim) but of a pagan god and erected the image at the altar rather than in the temple building (1 Macc 1:54), and Caligula's image was never actually put in place. So if Paul's expression is intended to remind the reader of these events, as it appears to be, he would seem not to be uttering a prophecy which he expects to be fulfilled with absolute literalness but supplying a vivid, evocative image for the broader kind of hubris which he describes throughout this verse.³¹ That understanding is confirmed by the phrase which follows, "proclaiming himself to be God," which serves to specify the meaning of the previous expression. All in all the text drives home the emphatic point that the man of lawlessness seizes for himself divine authority which is in no way his, thereby assuring his utter defeat.

3. Reminder of Oral Instruction on the Subject (2:5)

⁵Don't you remember that when I was with you I used to tell you these things?

---

³⁰Josephus, *Jewish War* 2.124-186, 192-197; Philo, *Embassy to Gaius*, 186-189, 263-268; cf. *HCNT*, § 826.

³¹Wanamaker argues that the phrase must for Paul refer to a literal event, ignoring the language that surrounds the text. His statement that a metaphorical interpretation of this phrase "confuses the symbolic meaning of the act of usurpation in the temple at Jerusalem with the language used to describe it, seeing a metaphor in the language instead of referring to the symbolic nature of the deed committed by the person of lawlessness" (p. 247) merely begs the question.

Paul's instruction in this passage is no innovation for the readers but is based on the oral teaching which they had first received while he was establishing the Thessalonian church (cf. 1 Thess 2:13; 3:4; 4:1). His language here indicates that the readers should know this point very well: οὐ (*ou*, "don't") indicates that the question anticipates a positive answer. This teaching had been a point of continued instruction: "used to tell" translates the imperfect-tense verb ἔλεγον (*elegon*) which implies a continuing action.

If this teaching was a matter of repeated instruction for the Thessalonians, we might expect to see it reflected elsewhere in these letters. Paul may well have in mind the kind of instruction found in 1 Thess 3:4, that persecution is inevitable for believers, 1 Thess 1:10 and 2:16, that God's wrath is coming on unbelievers, and 2 Thess 1:6-10, that God will bring a final judgment on all who oppose him and his people. The difference in this passage as opposed to those is that Paul expresses these ideas with apocalyptic language, probably because the false report (v. 2) had employed similar images for different ends.

4. The One Who Restrains/Prevails (2:6-10)

⁶And now you know what is holding him back, so that he may be revealed at the proper time. ⁷For the secret power of lawlessness is already at work; but the one who now holds it back will continue to do so till he is taken out of the way. ⁸And then the lawless one will be revealed, whom the Lord Jesus will overthrow with the breath of his mouth and destroy by the splendor of his coming. ⁹The coming of the lawless one will be in accordance with the work of Satan displayed in all kinds of counterfeit miracles, signs and wonders, ¹⁰and in every sort of evil that deceives those who are perishing. They perish because they refused to love the truth and so be saved.

2:6 And now you know what is holding him back, so that he may be revealed at the proper time.

The concept that the "man of lawlessness" is a figure who has yet to appear in history largely hinges on the interpretation of this verse and v. 7. "What is holding him back" translates a Greek substantive participle, τὸ κατέχον (*to katechon*), from the verb κατέχω (*katechō*). There is considerable reason, however, to question the accuracy of the translation "holding . . . back" in this context. While κατέχω often does mean to restrain or hold back, it has this meaning only when it occurs with an object. Though an object has been supplied for this verb in the NIV and most English versions, there is no object in either occurrence of the verb in the Greek text of vv. 6-7. It is therefore more likely that it carries the intransitive sense, normal when it has no object, of "prevail."[32] In this case, the text can be translated, "And you know what prevails now." If this is Paul's sense here, this expression probably does not refer to one opposed to the man of lawlessness but serves as another way of referring to the man of lawlessness or his activity. He is, indeed, the one who now prevails, who works pervasively through the world system in opposition to God's purposes (cf. Eph 2:2).

Paul says that the readers already know the identity of this restraining/prevailing one, presumably from the instruction which they have already received (v. 5). Traditionally it has been assumed that while he was in Thessalonica Paul had identified orally for the Thessalonians the identity of the one who restrains the man of lawlessness, information now lost to us. But if the interpretation set forth here is correct, Paul is merely reminding the readers, as he has elsewhere, of the application of the core of the gospel which they have already received, namely, that evil and the Evil One will appear to prevail in this age until Christ returns.

---

[32]Cf. LSJ, p. 926; Wanamaker, p. 253. This meaning was noted as a possibility by Frame (pp. 258, 262) and acknowledged as the best of many possibilities by Best (pp. 298-299, 301).

"Now" clearly contrasts with "at the proper time," literally "at his/its own time." But is it the prevailing or the Thessalonians' knowing that Paul stresses is "now"? Though the effect is largely the same, the Greek word order suggests that "now" is connected to "the one who prevails," providing a contrast to his future revelation and defeat. However, the text also contrasts the Christians' present knowledge of the prevailing one with the future revelation to all of his true identity, so the difference is slight at best.

In v. 6 Paul's expression for the restraining/prevailing one is neuter, suggesting an abstraction or principle ("*what* is holding him back"; better, "what is prevailing"), whereas in v. 7 the expression is masculine, ὁ κατέχων (*ho katechōn*), indicating a person ("the one who now holds him back"; better, "*the one who* now prevails"). This difference is relatively inconsequential, however, since a similar alternation between masculine and neuter expression also occurs with "lawless one" (vv. 3-4, 8, masculine; v. 7, "secret power of lawlessness," neuter). If Paul is indeed discussing the pervasive power of evil in the world which ultimately derives from Satan himself, such an alternation between masculine and neuter is quite consistent with his point.[33] The masculine pronoun "him" in the latter part of the verse (αὐτόν, *auton*) can therefore easily have the same referent as "what prevails" in the first part of the verse, its gender assigned by its larger sense.[34]

The second part of the verse makes a statement of contrast: the readers know the one who restrains/prevails "so that he may be revealed at the proper time." Again, if "revealed" has

---

[33]Cf. the discussion of the shift in gender in Glenn S. Holland, *The Tradition that You Received from Us: 2 Thessalonians in the Pauline Tradition* (HUT 24; Tübingen: Mohr, 1988), p. 124.

[34]A similar alternation between masculine and neuter with the same participial lemma and the same referent can be found in Matt 13:19, where the neuter τὸ ἐσπαρμένον (*to esparmenon*, "what was sown") and the masculine ὁ . . . σπαρείς (*ho . . . spareis*, "the [seed] sown") alternate. The use of masculine pronouns with neuter antecedents which have personal referents is one species of the *constructio ad sensum*; cf. BDF, § 134.

the sense it carries elsewhere for Paul (cf. v. 3 and comments above), this revelation signifies not the beginning of the activity of the man of lawlessness but the final disclosure that all opposition to God and his people has been inspired by the great Evil One. In this case "his time" is not the time when he will be more powerful, since he prevails "now"; rather, it refers to the time of his destruction, the emphasis in vv. 7-8. Emphasizing that even the present dominance of the man of lawlessness is under the supervision of God's final authority, Paul expresses the final revelation and destruction of the man of lawlessness as the purpose of his present activity. Though the dominance of evil might make it appear that God has lost control, his purpose will be fully and finally realized in the future. Thus, Paul can even present the final revelation of this opponent as the purpose of his present dominance: "so that" translates a Greek articular infinitive which almost certainly expresses the purpose of the "prevailing," not of what the Thessalonians "know."[35]

2:7 For the secret power of lawlessness is already at work;

Paul's language is compressed and difficult, but the point emerges clearly when this verse is connected to the verses that precede and follow. "Secret power of lawlessness" translates τὸ μυστήριον . . . τῆς ἀνομίας (*to mystērion . . . tēs anomias*), literally "the mystery of lawlessness." Even those who assume that in this text Paul predicts the future appearance in history of an "antichrist" note that he asserts the present activity of the principle of lawlessness here. But the reason that Paul refers to this activity as a "mystery" is clearer when we understand that the future revelation of the man of lawlessness points not to his becoming more active but his being revealed for what he is. In this case, the present lawlessness activity of the lawless one is a "mystery" precisely because the world does not yet recognize it for what it is, as they also fail to recognize the "mystery" of God's purpose in

---

[35]Wanamaker summarizes the reasons for this conclusion (pp. 253-254).

history declared in the gospel (1 Cor 2:1, 7; 4:1; 15:51; Eph 1:9; 3:3-4, 9; 5:32; 6:19; Col 1:26-27; 2:2; 4:3; 1 Tim 3:9, 16), though it is clearly known by the Christians (v. 6). The warning about the deceptive power of evil in vv. 9-12 is entirely consistent with this understanding: the world, under the deceptive power of Satan, does not yet realize the nature of "the god of this age" (2 Cor 4:4).

The verb translated "is . . . at work," ἐνεργεῖται (*energeitai*) is grammatically ambiguous. It could either be in the middle voice, in which case it merely indicates that lawlessness is at work, or in the passive voice, in which it would mean "has been put at work" and implies that someone has taken that action. It appears that Paul probably uses this verb with impersonal subjects like "mystery" with the simpler middle sense.[36] However, if Paul does in fact use the verb as a passive here, he could be implying either that the mystery is put in place by Satan (v. 9) or more broadly through the providence and judgment of God (vv. 11-12).

but the one who now holds it back will continue to do so till he is taken out of the way.

As in v. 6, "the one who now holds it back" is better rendered as "the one who now prevails." This phrase constitutes the subject of the clause, but Paul has given no predicate. The NIV supplies "will continue to do so," which probably reflects Paul's general implication. The NIV also translates Paul's μόνον (*monon*) as the conjunction "but"; however, this conjunctive use of the word is not clearly attested in Paul's letters elsewhere. The usual meaning for μόνον is "only," which fits the text well here, yielding the result, "The one who prevails now [will continue to do so] only until he is taken out of the way."[37] However, it is also possible that the Greek conjunction ἕως (*heōs*,

---

[36]Cf. BAGD, p. 265. For a contrasting view see Wanamaker, p. 255.

[37]Aus has argued that "taken out of the way," a Greek phrase unattested elsewhere (ἐκ μέσου γένηται, *ek mesou genētai*) is Paul's translation of a Hebrew verb found in Dan 11:31 and 12:11 ("God's Plan," 542-543). The evidence for this hypothesis falls short of establishing probability.

"till") is out of its usual position, in which case the sentence could be taken with good sense as, "The mystery of lawlessness is already at work only until the one who prevails is taken out of the way."[38] In this case, what Paul supplies here is the additional assurance that the dominance of the man of lawlessness, already experienced by the readers, will last not forever but only until he is removed by the Lord at his coming, as the next verse will further explain. If the traditional interpretation is followed and "the one who holds it back" is the opponent of the man of lawlessness, then the text is ambiguous as to whether it is the restrainer or the man of lawlessness who is taken away. If the view put forward here is correct, no such ambiguity arises because the two are identical.[39]

2:8 And then the lawless one will be revealed, whom the Lord Jesus will overthrow with the breath of his mouth and destroy by the splendor of his coming.

The close connection between the revelation of the man of lawlessness and his final judgment, implied in the earlier discussion, is explicit here. It must be carefully noted that if this "revelation" signifies intensified activity, nothing at all in this text expresses it. If Paul is referring to a future appearance of an antichrist and a period of greater evil, that period of evil must be assumed between the revelation and the Lord's coming mentioned here.

Paul has shifted from the neuter back to the masculine for the lawless one, focusing on the unveiling of the evil personality who is ultimately responsible for the work of lawlessness in

---

[38]BDF, § 475.1, argues for the postpositive use of ἕως here, noting other examples of similar Pauline transpositions of conjunctions to emphasize the preceding word or phrase (Rom 12:3; 1 Cor 3:5; 6:4; 7:17; 9:15; 11:14; 2 Cor 2:4; Gal 2:10; Col 4:16).

[39]Aus objects that the man of lawlessness cannot be the one taken out of the way because his destruction in the next verse would then be out of place ("God's Plan," p. 551). This objection, however, hinges on an overly literalistic approach to the apocalyptic language here, where revelation, removal and destruction can easily be viewed as parts of the same act.

this age. "Then" (τότε, *tote*) connects this unveiling with the removal of the prevailing one in the previous verse; "whom" (ὅν, *hon*) connects it to his destruction. The resulting sequence signifies the comprehensive elimination of every aspect of his activity: (a) he will no longer be present to prevail in the world; (b) he will be revealed to all for who he is; (c) he will be utterly ruined for any further activity.

The description of Jesus' decisive activity against the lawless one emphasizes his supreme power in contrast to the opponent's pretensions (v. 4). As the great enemy of Dan 8:23-25 could not be defeated by any human hand, this greatest enemy will be defeated instantly by the Lord himself.[40] Jesus is first of all "Lord," implying his divine authority (cf. 1 Thess 1:1 and comments above). His power is so superior that he is able to bring immediate and effortless destruction on his opponent "by the breath of his mouth." Paul has probably borrowed this expression from the description of the coming king in Isa 11:4; the apocryphal 2 Esdr 13:9-11, 38 uses a similar image to indicate the messiah's total triumph over his enemies.

Likewise, the "splendor of his coming" will be such that all who have opposed him will be thoroughly overwhelmed. This phrase combines two significant words. "Splendor" translates ἐπιφάνεια (*epiphaneia*), often used as a technical term for the visible manifestation of a deity, especially a sudden appearance in a hostile situation.[41] In the New Testament it is used only of the appearance of Christ, usually of his return (1 Tim 6:14; 2 Tim 4:1, 8; Titus 2:13), though once of his first appearance on earth (2 Tim 1:10). Here it especially implies that the one who is truly divine but is hidden in this age will by his appearance utterly shatter all the pretensions of his opponent. This event is identified as his "coming," or παρουσία (*parousia*), used elsewhere in 1-2 Thessalonians for Christ's return as the visitation of a great dignitary (1 Thess 2:19; 3:13;

---

[40]Cf. Aus, "God's Plan," pp. 543-544.
[41]BAGD, p. 304; Wanamaker, p. 258.

4:15; 5:23; 2 Thess 2:1; see comments above). This expression is apt for the point that Paul makes here, but it also supplies the basis for further comparison with the lawless one in the verses that follow.

2:9 The coming of the lawless one will be in accordance with the work of Satan displayed in all kinds of counterfeit miracles, signs and wonders,

In this verse the NIV translators have made their most significant interpretive move, rendering a present, indicative verb, ἐστιν (*estin*), as a future, "will be." While such futuristic uses of the present tense are possible, there is little to support such a translation here except for the assumption that the entire text discusses the future appearance of the man of lawlessness.[42] Elsewhere Paul indicates that he regards the Satanic activity described here as already at work in the world (2 Cor 11:14; 1 Tim 3:1-9; cf. Rom 1:18-32; 1 Cor 2:8), so in light of the unequivocal statement of v. 7, this present-tense verb should be taken in its ordinary sense, as it is rendered in the NRSV: "The coming of the lawless one is apparent in the working of Satan . . . ."

The idea of false miracles has a long history in Scripture. Pharaoh's priests were able to duplicate in part the works of Moses (Exod 7:11-12, 22; 8:7, 18; 9:11) and later the Pentateuch warned of false prophets who could deceive with similar signs and induce Israel to worship false gods (Deut 13:1-3). In the Olivet Discourse Jesus picks up the pentateuchal language and applies it to the false prophets who will be characteristic of the age in which his disciples await his return (Matt 24:11, 24; Mark 13:22). These lure the people of God to follow a false messiah, just as the false prophets of old encouraged the worship of false gods. The same concept is

---

[42]Cf. BDF, § 323: "Ordinarily a temporal indication of the future is included." One example of a futuristic present may be ἐφίσταται (*ephistatai*) in 1 Thess 5:3, though the emphasis there may still be that destruction always comes suddenly on those not prepared for judgment (see comments above).

found in Rev 13:13-14, where the beast from the earth performs false miracles. As a corollary, the Gospels indicate that Jesus is accused of performing his own miracles by demonic power (Matt 12:24; Mark 3:22; Luke 11:15). Paul is probably picking up on the language of the Olivet Discourse but is doubtlessly aware of the larger biblical context of Jesus' statement also. For Paul such deceptive activity is entirely in accord with the character of Satan, who "masquerades as an angel of light" (2 Cor 11:14) and "has blinded the minds of unbelievers, so that they cannot see the light of the gospel and the glory of Christ" (2 Cor 4:4). Hence, these signs represent his "work" or activity in the world, the visible manifestation of one who remains invisible until he is revealed at the Lord's return.

The terms used here for these false miracles are commonly found in combination in the New Testament referring to the miracles of Jesus or the apostles (John 4:48; Acts 2:22, 43; 4:30; 5:12; 6:8; 14:3; 15:12; Rom 15:19; 2 Cor 12:12; Heb 2:4; cf. Acts 7:36). Here these are literally "power and signs and wonders of a lie," the last term identifying them unequivocally as false because of their power to entice people away from the truth of Jesus. Hence, Paul makes a play on words at the beginning of the verse, speaking of the "coming" of the lawless one, his παρουσία (*parousia*), a counterfeit of the coming of Jesus which the readers anticipate (v. 8). Though "coming" is certainly an adequate translation of this expression in this context, the English reader must not misunderstand it as having a future orientation. As noted above, the verb in this verse stresses the present reality of this activity, and *parousia* indicates less a future coming than the visitation of a dignitary or his presence with a people. Thus, the expression here suggests that the Christians must endure this false visitation, recognizing it for the lie that it is, until the genuine visitation reveals its genuine nature.

It may be argued that the phrase "in accordance with the work of Satan" indicates that Satan is distinct from the man of lawlessness. This may not be the case, however, if Paul's point is that the Christians can already perceive this work of lawlessness, even supported by false signs, to be the work of Satan himself, since they have been taught to expect such counterfeiting by him. Throughout the text "man of lawlessness" then indicates the clandestine activity of Satan in this age, whereas the name "Satan" here reveals the full identity of the one who is secretly responsible for that work.

2:10 and in every sort of evil that deceives those who are perishing.

The description of the current activity of the man of lawlessness continues here, now with an emphasis on its consequences and the responsibility of those who follow it. "Every sort of evil that deceives" is literally "all deceit of unrighteousness," pointing comprehensively to every aspect of evil which would seduce people away from salvation and toward destruction. By this expression Paul indicates that this seductive influence is to be found in more than what could narrowly be described as miracles. Those who fall prey to this deceit are already under judgment for their choice; hence, Paul uses a present participle, ἀπολλυμένοις (*apollumenois*, "those who are perishing") to stress that their ruin is a continuing reality (cf. 1 Cor 1:18; 2 Cor 2:15; 4:3).

They perish because they refused to love the truth and so be saved.

Though these have fallen prey to the deception of the Evil One, they are not helpless victims. Their fate is a result of their willful decision to reject the message of salvation. Literally Paul's statement is "they did not receive the love of the truth so that they would be saved." By naming "the *love* of the truth" as the object of their refusal, he stresses that in rejecting the gospel, the heart of God's truth, these have repudiated any commitment to truth of any kind, devoting themselves instead to the deception of the Evil One. They have in effect "exchanged the truth of God for a lie" (Rom 1:25). Having rejected salvation, they are therefore already perishing. Paul's language here is sharply dualistic, drawing a strict division of humanity into two camps, the saved and the perishing. As far as this text is concerned, there is no middle ground of uncertainty.

5. God's Consequent Actions (2:11-12)

[11]For this reason God sends them a powerful delusion so that they will believe the lie [12]and so that all will be condemned who have not believed the truth but have delighted in wickedness.

2:11 For this reason God sends them a powerful delusion so that they will believe the lie

In the previous verse Paul has noted that the deceptive activity of Satan in no way compromises human responsibility. Here he indicates that Satan's activity in no way compromises God's sovereignty. This same interplay between the deceit of the Evil One, human refusal of God's will, and God's control of the universe is also seen in such episodes as the hardening of Pharaoh's heart, which is both Pharaoh's own action (Exod 8:15, 32; 9:34; cf. 1 Sam 6:6) and the action of God (Exod 4:21; 7:3; 9:12; 10:1, 20, 27; 11:10; 14:4, 8); the evil spirit which troubles Saul, sent by God as a judgment on Saul's stubborn disobedience (1 Sam 16:14; 18:10; 19:9; cf. 15:11, 16:1); and, most directly, in Paul's statement that in response to human rejection of knowledge of God, God "gave over" humanity to idolatry and degeneracy (Rom 1:18-32).

In all these cases God's rule over the world is preserved along with human responsibility. In each case God sends that which leads to hardening, deception and sin, but in each case he sends it only in response to the rejection of his message which the human subject has already chosen. In effect God gives to those who reject him a greater measure of that which they have chosen for themselves, demonstrating to those with the will to see the consequences of the choice which was made.⁴³ Here the concept is much the same. Satan's deceptive activity should not be seen as a failure of God's rule over the world. Rather, God's larger purpose of judgment and redemption, in which his free creatures experience the full consequences of their choices, is achieved as the full force of rejecting God's truth is felt in Satan's deceptive power. In this sense, even though the adversary appears to prevail now, he is still subject to the rule of God (cf. Job 1:6-12; 2:1-6), ironically bringing to bear the consequences of judgment on sinful humanity in this age even as he will himself be fully judged in the age to come.

The language of these verses closely connects them to the statement about Satan's deception in vv. 9-10. "For this reason" translates διὰ τοῦτο (*dia touto*), used also by Paul in the similar discussion in Rom 1:26, indicating that the acceptance of Satan's deception is the reason God acts as he does here. "Powerful delusion" is literally "a working of error"; ἐνέργεια (*energeia*, "working") is the same term used for the "work" of Satan in v. 9 and is the cognate of the verb rendered "is . . . at work" in v. 7. Likewise, "lie" (ψεῦδος, *pseudos*) is repeated from v. 9, where the NIV translates the same Greek word as "counterfeit." "So that they will believe the lie" is also syntactically parallel to "and so be saved" in v. 10 (both are articular infinitives introduced by εἰς (*eis*), indicating purpose), sharply contrasting the consequences of acceptance or rejection of the truth.

2:12 and so that all will be condemned who have not believed the truth but have delighted in wickedness.

Rejection of the truth is again underlined in v. 12, where Paul reiterates the point of v. 10 that these are judged for their refusal to believe the truth. In place of believing truth these have "delighted in wickedness," literally "approved of

---

⁴³On the larger theological issues involved in this activity of God, see Cottrell, *God the Ruler*, pp. 164-168, 209-212.

unrighteousness." This last expression, ἀδικία (*adikia*, "wickedness, unrighteousness") probably stands as a reminder of the lawlessness (ἀνομία, *anomia*) of the one who inspires it (v. 7). Paul's aim throughout is to make the readers see that this work of Satan is ultimately used by God in his providence to achieve his own purpose of judgment in the world. We should certainly understand that it is not God but Satan who deceives, but that he does so by the permission of God, who thereby accomplishes his objective to bring to bear on sinners the full consequences of their rejection of his salvation.

The effect of these last four verses on the readers is to do more than correct their understanding of the Lord's coming. By attributing unbelief to the deceptive work of Satan and its consequences to God's judgment, Paul has provided a partial answer to a question which must have troubled the small, persecuted Thessalonian church, namely, why did the truth of the gospel not persuade everyone who heard it? Likewise, this instruction would reinforce their own loyalty to the gospel, since it stated in unequivocal terms the nature of the division between believers and unbelievers.

The complexity of the interpretive issues surrounding vv. 1-12 are such as to require a concluding summary of the interpretation argued above. In short: Paul regards the promised end-time to be already present because of the work of Christ. The prevalence of evil, variously manifested, is ultimately the work of Satan. That fact is already recognized by the Christians, but the world is unaware of it, having fallen prey to Satan's deceptive powers. But when Christ returns, he will reveal Satan and his activity for what it truly is, ending his rule over this age and consigning him to eternal punishment. Therefore, as long as evil still prevails in the world, the Christians can know that God's work is not yet complete. They can therefore be confident in the faithfulness and power of God, remaining true to the gospel despite the difficulties they face and looking forward to their vindication at the final judgment.

IV. RENEWED THANKSGIVING, ENCOURAGEMENT AND PRAYER (2:13-17)

As in 1 Thess 2:13, Paul renews the letter's initial thanksgiving (cf. 1:3). Here the repetition of the thanksgiving allows Paul to remind the readers again of their standing with God as those who have responded in faith to the gospel. This reminder has special impact because of the preceding discussion. The readers need to remember this status as they continue to resist the deceptive power of evil (vv. 9-12). Furthermore, after the emphasis in the preceding section on the work of God which still lies in the future, this section will remind the readers again of what they have already received. If the problem of 2:2 stemmed from seeing all of the promises of God as already fulfilled, the Thessalonians should not conclude from Paul's counter-argument that all of the fulfillment still lies in the future. Remembering what they have already received holds the key for steadfastness in awaiting the fulfillment yet to come.

Such steadfastness is exactly what Paul seeks to stimulate in this section, and so he ends it, as in 1 Thess 3:11-13, with a prayer for the readers' future, focusing on God's work in enabling the readers to remain firm against the pressures of this age. This in turn becomes the transition point for the final section of the letter in ch. 3.

A. THANKSGIVING FOR THE SALVATION OF THE THESSALONIANS (2:13-14)

¹³But we ought always to thank God for you, brothers loved by the Lord, because from the beginning God chose you[a] to be saved through the sanctifying work of the Spirit and through belief in the truth. ¹⁴He called you to this through our gospel, that you might share in the glory of our Lord Jesus Christ.

[a]*13* Some manuscripts *because God chose you as his firstfruits*

2:13 But we ought always to thank God for you, brothers loved by the Lord,

Paul begins this section with the emphatic personal pronoun ἡμεῖς (*hēmeis*), perhaps to shift the focus of attention after the long discussion of the lawless one (cf. 1 Thess 2:17 and comments above). As in 1:3 (see comments above), Paul expresses the thanksgiving indirectly as that which he "ought to do." Again the term expresses obligation or necessity. That obligation is based on the readers' standing with God. Paul points to this status first with "brothers," his habitual form of address in both letters (1 Thess 1:4; 2:1, 9, 14, 17; 3:7; 4:1, 10, 13; 5:1, 4, 12, 14, 25; 2 Thess 1:3; 2:1, 15; 3:1, 6, 13), which suggests their shared membership in God's family. The point is reinforced by "beloved by the Lord," which, like the similar phrase in 1 Thess 1:4 (see comments above) stresses that the readers are the unworthy objects of divine favor. There the reference is to the love of God the Father; here "Lord" refers to Jesus, again assuming his divine status equal to the Father. Paul may focus particularly on Jesus' love here because of the earlier focus on Jesus' return or because of the assurance it gives as he returns for judgment.[44]

because from the beginning God chose you

Paul's explicit reason for the thanksgiving is God's choosing of the readers to be his people, again echoing 1 Thess 1:4. As in that passage, this combination of expressions stresses that through their response to the gospel the readers have been incorporated into the people of God, what might be termed the Israel of fulfillment. Such an identity would be too precious to lose through a lack of diligence in resisting the evil power that prevails in this age.

A rather difficult textual problem occurs in this verse, as indicated in the NIV's footnote. The expression ἀπ' ἀρχῆς (*ap'*

---

[44]Marshall, p. 206. Wanamaker notes that Paul stresses Christ's love especially in passages dealing with certainty of salvation (Rom 8:35; 2 Cor 5:14; Gal 2:20).

archēs, "from the beginning") followed in the NIV, appears as ἀπαρχήν (*aparchēn*, "firstfruits") in several manuscripts. Either expression is coherent in the context, both have wide attestation in the manuscripts, and the difference between the two, since no spaces appeared between words in Greek uncial manuscripts, is only one letter.

There are, however, several reasons to conclude that "firstfruits" is Paul's original expression here: (1) *ap' archēs* is not used elsewhere in Paul's letters, but πρὸ/ἀπὸ τῶν αἰώνων (*pro/apo tōn aiōnōn*, "from eternity") appears with a similar meaning in 1 Cor 2:7 and Col 1:26 and πρὸ καταβολῆς κόσμου (*pro katabolēs kosmou*, "from the foundation of the world") does the same duty in Eph 1:4; (2) Paul uses ἀρχή (*archē*) to mean "power" everywhere but Phil 4:15; (3) Paul uses ἀπαρχή six other times; (4) in two other texts copyists altered ἀπαρχήν to ἀπ' ἀρχῆς (Rom 16:5; Rev 14:4), even though the latter expression did not fit those contexts.[45] On balance then, the reading in the NIV footnote is probably to be preferred.[46] "Firstfruits" suggests the Old Testament offering of the first part of the harvest to the Lord, a pledge that the remainder of the harvest, though not yet received, would be dedicated to him as well (Deut 26:1-11). As a small group facing an enormous struggle for their faith, the Thessalonian Christians needed the reminder that as "firstfruits" they too were pledged to God as his possession and were the vanguard of a greater people of God to be harvested in the future (cf. 3:1).[47]

to be saved through the sanctifying work of the Spirit and through belief in the truth.

The purpose of God's choosing of the readers is their salvation, the very thing refused by those under the deception of

---

[45]Cf. Metzger, *Textual Commentary*, pp. 636-637.
[46]For the contrary view see Marshall, p. 207.
[47]Wanamaker argues that there is no specific sense for "firstfruits" which coheres with the context but does not consider this possibility (p. 266). For other alternatives see Bruce, p. 190.

evil in v. 10. This salvation comes by two means. "Sanctifying work" or "sanctification" (ἁγιασμός, *hagiasmos*; cf. 1 Thess 4:3 and comments above) indicates a making holy, the particular work of the Spirit both in identifying the Christian as one who belongs to God (Eph 1:13; 4:30; cf. 2 Cor 1:22) and in producing in the believer a life that imitates God's holiness (Gal 5:22-25; 1 Thess 4:7-8). It is possible that πνεῦμα (*pneuma*) refers to the human spirit here, in which case it gives the object of sanctification: "through sanctifying the human spirit." But Paul's repeated statements elsewhere about the Spirit's work in sanctification suggest that the NIV's rendering is correct. "Belief in the truth" certainly contrasts with the false belief of vv. 10-12, again underlining that those who have believed the gospel are resisting the trend and pressure of this age. Maintaining such belief and growing in the sanctification that accompanies it are the obvious, fundamental responses of anyone who values his standing as one of God's saved people.

While it has been argued that the order of these two phrases, first the work of the Spirit and then faith, indicates that the work of the Spirit is the cause of that faith, nothing in this text indicates that connection explicitly. More likely is the connection which each idea makes to the concepts of the surrounding context than a cause-and-effect connection between them. And as Marshall notes, if the Spirit's work guarantees the result of faith, then the command of v. 15 to remain firm in the faith has little cogency.[48] In fact, the statement that God chose his people "through" or "by" (ἐν, *en* used instrumentally) their faith in the truth is more consistent with the concept of conditional election than the Calvinistic view.

2:14 He called you to this through our gospel, that you might share in the glory of our Lord Jesus Christ.

The new sentence here in the NIV is in fact a continuation of the previous sentence. "To this" refers loosely to the entire

---

[48]Marshall, "Election and Calling," pp. 273-274.

preceding discussion, including membership in God's people, salvation, the sanctifying work of the Spirit, and belief in the truth; a Greek neuter pronoun ὅ (*ho*) refers not to any one word in the preceding clause but to the entire preceding idea. Here Paul stresses that God's choice of the readers is actualized through their response to the gospel (cf. 1 Thess 1:5 and comments above). As noted in the discussion of 1 Thess 1:4 above, Paul's larger concept is not that God first chooses unconditionally those who will be his and then causes them to believe in Jesus; rather, as Rom 8:29 implies, he chooses them conditionally, on the basis of their faith which he foreknows. It is probably significant here that Paul stresses that the call is issued through the gospel: one becomes a member of God's family through heeding the message of salvation (Rom 10:17; cf. Rom 10:10-11), not by a direct operation of God on the heart which then causes belief.

The purpose of this call is to obtain (περιποίησις, *peripoiēsis*, "share"; cf. 1 Thess 5:9) the Lord's own glory (cf. 1 Thess 2:12 and comments above; Rom 8:17, 29-30; 1 Cor 15:43; 2 Cor 3:18; Phil 3:21). In light of Paul's earlier discussion, this glory is primarily what the believers will share with him when they are gathered (v. 1) at his triumphant return (v. 8; cf. 1 Cor 15:43; Phil 3:21), though Paul also understands glory to be a present possession through God's call (Rom 8:30). Again, in light of what Christ's return will mean both for believers and opponents, the need to stand firm in the faith which brought them this salvation is entirely clear to the readers.

B. ENCOURAGEMENT TO REMAIN FAITHFUL TO THE TRADITIONS DELIVERED BY PAUL (2:15)

¹⁵So then, brothers, stand firm and hold to the teachings[a] we passed on to you, whether by word of mouth or by letter.

[a]Or *traditions*

2:15 So then, brothers, stand firm and hold to the teachings we passed on to you,

The implication of vv. 13-14 is now made explicit; Paul uses two Greek particles ἄρα οὖν (*ara oun*, "so then") to stress that this command is a direct inference from the previous discussion. Paul uses two verbs to express this command, both in the Greek present tense to emphasize continuing action. The Thessalonians must first of all "stand," as Paul urged in 1 Thess 3:8 (Cf. 1 Cor 16:13), remaining firm in their faith so that the result of their faith, the fullness of salvation, will be theirs. In effect, they are told not to be affected as Paul had described in v. 2. This standing firm is specified with the second verb and its object. Holding a genuine faith means not holding to the gospel teaching which they have received (cf. 1 Cor 11:2). Paul uses παράδοσις (*paradosis*) here, which, as reflected in the NIV's footnote, commonly referred to traditions delivered by word of mouth (cf. 1 Thess 2:13; 4:1; 2 Thess 3:6). This term underscores that the Thessalonian church must remain true to the original gospel deposit, including what Paul has just clarified about the day of the Lord, not accepting any of the innovations or misunderstandings with which they have been confronted. This original deposit is theirs through Paul's own teaching. As Paul noted in the first letter, they can have confidence in this teaching both because of the way Paul brought it to them (1 Thess 2:1-12) and because of what it produced in their lives (1 Thess 1:4-10).

whether by word of mouth or by letter.

That teaching, first delivered orally, is now supplemented by the letters which they have received. Whether Paul is referring to 1 or 2 Thessalonians or both is a moot point, since his expression here implies any letter that he might write. Linking letters to oral teaching reflects Paul's perspective that his letters served as substitutes for his own presence and direct teaching activity with the church. Both now are to serve as the touchstones by which they will measure the content of their faith and evaluate other teaching which they will encounter. That Paul was conscious of the authority of his teaching is abundantly clear here. Though he does not seek to "canonize" his letters with this statement, the authority which he expresses here is the basis for the later formal recognition of his letters as Scripture (cf. 1 Thess 5:27 and comments above).

C. PRAYER FOR THE LORD'S ENCOURAGEMENT AND STRENGTH (2:16-17)

¹⁶May our Lord Jesus Christ himself and God our Father, who loved us and by his grace gave us eternal encouragement and good hope, ¹⁷encourage your hearts and strengthen you in every good deed and word.

Like the prayer of 1 Thess 3:11-13 (see comments above), this one is expressed as a wish. Paul begins with an emphatic reference to Christ: "himself" translates the Greek pronoun αὐτός (*autos*), which puts particular emphasis on the subject. Paul also mentions Christ before the Father, an unusual position for Paul which may reflect further emphasis, though Paul may have mentioned Christ first to avoid awkwardness with the long phrase describing God at the end of the verse. Having just referred twice to the Lord's glory (vv. 8, 14), Paul now calls on this glorious one to bring his power to bear on the readers' lives. Likewise, God is the one "who loved us," as in v. 13, and who has acted "by grace," a concept clearly integral to the point in vv. 13-14. Through his gracious love he has already given "eternal encouragement," enabling them to face with assurance the persecutions of the present and the judgment of the future (2 Thess 1:5-10). Likewise they have "good hope," a phrase commonly in use in the first century to refer to life after death,[49] enabling them to face the kind of difficulties described in vv. 3-12 with confidence.

---

[49]Marshall, p. 211; Wanamaker, p. 271.

Because he has already given "eternal encouragement," God can be counted on to encourage the readers in every situation. So just as before (1 Thess 3:11-13), Paul prays that God would give to the Thessalonians more of what he has already given them, especially under their pressurized circumstances. "Encourage" is coupled with "strengthen," the Greek verb στηρίζω (*stērizō*), which indicates especially causing the object to be "more firm and unchanging in attitude or belief,"[50] again an appropriate prayer when the problems addressed in vv. 1-13 are in view. Paul sees this strengthening of attitude and mind to have a comprehensive effect on behavior, as he prays that it may take place both in "deed and word." The inclusion of this last term may suggest that the Thessalonians' own right proclamation of the gospel, threatened by the false teaching of v. 2, will be reinforced by God's encouragement.

---

[50]*GELNTBSD*, § 74.19.

2 THESSALONIANS 3

V. EXHORTATIONS (3:1-16)

As in most of his letters, Paul ends 2 Thessalonians with a series of instructions and exhortations as to how the gospel is to be lived. Here Paul focuses most of his attention on one subject, the treatment of those who refuse to work (vv. 6-13). But his concern is broader, and so are the instructions of vv. 1-5 and 14-15.

A. GENERAL EXHORTATIONS (3:1-5)

¹Finally, brothers, pray for us that the message of the Lord may spread rapidly and be honored, just as it was with you. ²And pray that we may be delivered from wicked and evil men, for not everyone has faith. ³But the Lord is faithful, and he will strengthen and protect you from the evil one. ⁴We have confidence in the Lord that you are doing and will continue to do the things we command. ⁵May the Lord direct your hearts into God's love and Christ's perseverance.

This section is loosely composed, focusing largely on the faithfulness of God and the readers' response to it. The theme of God's faithfulness has in fact been the focus of much of ch. 1-2, since confidence in the face of prevailing opposition and in the time of judgment depends on confidence in God's faithfulness. So here that aspect of the earlier discussion becomes a particular subject of direct exhortation.

Because God is faithful, the readers should pray for Paul (vv. 1-2), and continue in their Christian lifestyle (v. 4), looking to the Lord to enable their perseverance (v. 5).

3:1 Finally, brothers, pray for us that the message of the Lord may spread rapidly and be honored, just as it was with you.

"Finally," translating τὸ λοιπόν (*to loipon*), marks sometimes the last section of a letter (2 Cor 13:11; Phil 4:8) and other times a section distinct from the one before (1 Cor 4:2; Phil 3:1; 1 Thess 4:1). Those two functions are largely the same here. Paul asks for prayer as he does in Rom 15:30-32; Eph 6:10-20; Col 4:3. In each case the focus of Paul's request for prayer is the work and outcome of his ministry, and so it is here. The verb "pray" is in the present tense, stressing continuing action. "May spread rapidly" is literally "run" (τρέχω, *trechō*), a vivid metaphor expressing Paul's desire for the swift spread of the gospel in light of the imminent return of the Lord. The use of this verb with a nonhuman subject is unusual, so Paul may be alluding to Ps 147:15, which pictures the word of God as running swiftly.[1]

"Be honored" is literally "be glorified" (δοξάζω, *doxazō*), perhaps in part a reminder of the glory of Christ (2:14) which will be acknowledged by those who believe the gospel and which those who believe will share. Both of these verbs are also in the Greek present tense, indicating that Paul wants the gospel, the universal message of salvation, to spread continually and be honored continually. Paul's earlier stress on the model response of the Thessalonian Christians (1:3; 2:13; 1 Thess 1:3, 5-10; 2:13) probably provides the basis for the remark "just as it was with you." Paul wants this same response from others, so that all would have the results of salvation which Paul has described at length through this letter. Alternately this last phrase may be understood as a present,

---

[1]Wanamaker, p. 274.

"just as it also is with you," in which case Paul is giving encouragement to the church to work to spread God's word in their own region, though the earlier stress on the Thessalonians' reception of the word favors the NIV's interpretation.

3:2 And pray that we may be delivered from wicked and evil men, for not everyone has faith.

This verse actually continues the sentence begun in v. 1, expressing another specific petition which Paul asks the readers to make. The spread of the gospel in his ministry will require his personal safety. No less than the readers (2 Thess 1:5-7), Paul is subject to the opposition that characterizes this age (2:1-13). He therefore asks for prayers for his deliverance from such opposition. "May be delivered" translates ῥύομαι (*rhyomai*), which in the New Testament always is used of rescue caused by God, sometimes from sin (Rom 7:24; Col 1:13) but sometimes from the perils of life in the sinful world (Rom 15:31; 2 Cor 1:8-11; 2 Tim 3:11; 4:17; cf. 2 Tim 4:18). In effect what Paul calls for is that the final deliverance of God from persecutors (1:5-10) would be realized in a preliminary way in his preaching ministry. But Paul was, of course, very much aware that though God does deliver his people from persecution, they should still expect to suffer (1 Thess 3:3-4; see v. 3 and comments below). The prayer is similar enough to Matt 6:13 to offer the possibility that Paul is alluding to Jesus' model prayer.

Two terms describe the persecutors. They are "wicked," ἄτοπος (*atopos*), which suggests something which is not fitting or appropriate.[2] Some have seen this as a substitute for ἄνομος (*anomos*), or "lawless," which is commonly linked with "evil" in the LXX, assuming Paul to refer to Jewish opponents for whom "lawless" would be inappropriate.[3] But the idea that Paul is preoccupied with Jewish opponents stems in part from

---

[2]*GELNTBSD*, § 88.111.
[3]Marshall, p. 214.

a misreading of 1 Thess 2:13-16 (see comments above) and so this conjecture must be rejected. But there may be a certain irony in the use of ἄτοπος. Christians would commonly be accused of advocating or practicing things not in keeping with the established social order (Acts 25:5; cf. Acts 16:20-21; 18:13; 19:26; 21:28; 24:5-6). But for Paul, who understands that the true order is established by God, those who oppose the gospel are truly out of line with what is fitting. The second term, "evil," πονηρός (*ponēros*) is a more common term for anything wicked or evil. Its use in v. 3 to refer to the "evil one" links the gospel's human opponents to the supreme opponent of God. Instead of merely letting the adjectives alone identify the opponents, Paul includes the noun ἄνθρωπος (*anthrōpos*, "men"), here referring to human beings of either gender and perhaps distinguishing Paul's opponents as mere humans as compared to the sovereign God whom they oppose.

At the core of this evil is the rejection of the gospel. "Not everyone has faith" is a simple reminder of what Paul has assumed throughout the letter, that many reject the gospel and so oppose the purpose of God in history. This rejection of faith establishes the essential difference between Christians (1:3-4, 10-11; 2:13) and their opponents (2:11-12). This understanding of the force of this phrase is more likely than the idea that Paul here gives the reason for his ongoing mission of evangelistic preaching: not all have faith, and so Paul must continue to preach to bring them to faith. In either case, the NIV translators here have rightly understood πίστις (*pistis*, "faith") to mean the response of belief and trust rather than "the faith" as a system of belief.

3:3 But the Lord is faithful, and he will strengthen and protect you from the evil one.

Paul shifts his focus here from a request for prayer on his behalf to a reminder of the character of the Lord to whom the prayers are addressed. This in turn leads to a shift from concern for his own protection to that of the readers. In contrast to the opponents' lack of faith (πίστις, *pistis*, v. 2), the Lord is always faithful (πιστός, *pistos*). He can therefore be depended upon under all circumstances, including the antagonism of mere humans to his people and will. The readers can therefore depend on his deliverance, for which they pray on Paul's behalf (v. 2), as they face that antagonism. Such deliverance, however, may not take the precise form which we might expect. The word will indeed spread rapidly and Christ be glorified, but not necessarily as his opponents are prevented from persecuting his people. The deliverance which Paul seeks is first of all strengthening (cf. 2:17; 1 Thess 3:2, 13) to resist the pressure. Secondly it is protection from the Evil One who stands behind all such opposition to God and his people (2:9). To succumb to the Evil One is ultimately to turn back from the faith which has brought the Christians into harmony with God and his purpose; it is to fall prey to his deceptive activity as described in 2:3-12. Against this ultimate threat God is faithful to provide the needed protection (cf. Rom 8:31-39). By this provision he is glorified, for the message of the cross is demonstrated through his people's faithful endurance of suffering (cf. Col 1:24).

It has been widely noted that Paul here refers to the faithfulness of the Lord, probably referring to Christ, instead of God, as is his habit elsewhere (1 Cor 1:9; 10:13; 2 Cor 1:18; 1 Thess 5:24). The shift may stem from the focus on Christ's return, the final act of divine faithfulness, which underlies the entire letter.

The NIV translators have opted to translate τοῦ πονηροῦ (*tou ponērou*), which could be either masculine or neuter (cf. Matt 5:37; 6:13), as a masculine. If it is masculine, it refers to the Evil One, Satan. If it is neuter, then it refers to evil as an abstraction. While it is true, as Wanamaker observes, that only in Eph 6:16 among the letters attributed to Paul do we find another reference to Satan as "the Evil One,"[4] it is also true that only in Rom 12:9 does he use this term to refer to

---

[4]Wanamaker, p. 277.

evil in the abstract. The verb "protect" probably favors a personal object, so some probability favors the NIV's rendering. Again Paul may allude to the model prayer of Matt 6:13.

3:4 We have confidence in the Lord that you are doing and will continue to do the things we command.

The faithfulness of God to protect his people cannot be excluded from his people's faithful response, though even here Paul expresses a confidence "in the Lord," based on union that exists between the Lord and his people through which they receive the strength to remain faithful. Paul has confidence (cf. Rom 8:38; 2 Cor 2:3; Phil 1:6) in the Thessalonians because of what he has already observed of their growth and steadfastness in their faith as they have been enabled by the Lord (1 Thess 1:6-10; 2:13-14; 3:6-8; 2 Thess 1:3-5). The knowledge of their past faithfulness gives Paul confidence in their continued practice of the gospel both for the present as he is away from the church and for the future with all of its contingencies. Such practice consists of doing "the things we command," which includes not only the behavioral instruction, as contained in the next section of this chapter and in 1 Thess 4:1-12; 5:12-22, but also the eschatological teaching, which directly affects their hope and perseverance. Faithfulness to the "traditions," which Paul has enjoined elsewhere (1 Thess 2:13; 4:1; 2 Thess 2:15; 3:6), is the concept still expressed here.

3:5 May the Lord direct your hearts into God's love and Christ's perseverance.

The request for prayer and statements of God's faithfulness and of confidence the readers' faithful response leads Paul again to express his own wish-prayer (2:16-17; 1 Thess 3:11-13), reflecting his reliance on the faithful God to supply the resources for the Thessalonians faithful practice of the gospel. The prayer is indirectly addressed to "the Lord," probably meaning Christ, though for Paul such a prayer can as easily be addressed to God the Father. In 1 Thess 3:11 Paul prayed that God would "direct" (κατευθύνω, *kateuthunō*) him to be reunited with the Thessalonian church; here he looks for their hearts (cf. 1 Chr 29:18; Prov 21:2), signifying their entire inner being, to be directed to an increasing experience of what they have already received. Again the prayer is that deliverance should take the form not of an absence of difficulty but of the resources to endure the difficulty for the Lord's glory.

Though "God's love" could conceivably refer to the person's love for God, Paul normally uses this phrase for God's love for humanity. That love is a fitting subject here, since it provides the basis for confidence in the coming judgment as well as in the persecutions of the present. "Perseverance" here translates ὑπομονή (*hypomonē*, cf. 1:4; 1 Thess 1:3), which indicates particularly endurance in difficulty. As with God's love, Christ's perseverance may mean either the perseverance which he had or that which he gives. But these two may be so closely identified for Paul as to be indistinguishable in this context. This perseverance is especially Christ's because his obedience in accepting the cross (Phil 2:8) provides the archetype by which the Christian's endurance of suffering is defined (2 Cor 4:11).[5] It is therefore both the endurance which he had and which he gives to his people. We might paraphrase this as "Christ's kind of perseverance."

B. EXHORTATIONS REGARDING CHURCH DISCIPLINE (3:6-15)

In the section that follows Paul concentrates on certain members of the church whose behavior urgently requires correction. Most of the attention is given to those who had given up working and were living by the charity of their brothers and sisters (vv. 6-13), but Paul also discusses those who are willfully disobedient of his instructions in broader terms (vv. 14-

---

[5]Cf. Scott J. Hafemann, "Suffering," *DPL*, pp. 919-921.

15). For both Paul requires specific discipline. These are to be treated as outsiders, no longer a part of the community of God's people, cut off from fellowship with the church and the benefits which such fellowship entailed. This pattern of exclusion as a means of discipline had its roots in the synagogues, where unrepentant offenders were cut off from all connections to the Jewish community and, by that token, from the people of Israel as a whole. As the church believed itself to be the people of God of fulfillment, its method of discipline was much the same. So in 1 Cor 5:1-13 Paul orders that the Corinthian church expel an immoral member and others like him who refuse to repent of their sin when confronted with it (cf. Rom 16:17; 1 Tim 1:20; James 5:19-20; 1 John 5:16-17; 2 John 10-11; 3 John 10; Jude 22-23). But the purpose of such discipline was not to inflict punishment but to induce the sinner's repentance (see v. 15 below). So Jesus instructs his disciples in Matt 18:15-17, the foundation for all disciplinary practice in the New Testament, and so apparently Paul recommends that the one excluded in 1 Cor 5:1-13 be restored because of his repentance in 2 Cor 2:5-11 (cf. 1 Cor 5:5).[6]

The difficulties of following similar disciplinary practices in the modern church are well known.[7] Persons cut off from a church's fellowship for some repeated and notorious sin may go to another church, deflecting the impact of the discipline, or may sue the church and its leaders for defamation of character. And when many churches lack the face-to-face accountability of the house churches of the first century, the discipline may be difficult to enforce for some and may go unnoticed by others. But the alternative is even less acceptable: a fellowship in which sin is ignored and repentance is optional, essentially indistinguishable from the surrounding society. Without the thoughtful and deliberate application of such disciplinary practice as a part of the renewal of the genuine, intimate fellowship that existed among the earliest Christians,

---

[6]Cf. Thomas E. Schmidt, "Discipline," *DPL*, pp. 214-218.
[7]Cf. the remarks of Marshall, pp. 229-230.

modern Christians can make little claim to have restored the life of the New Testament church.

1. Exclusion of the Willfully Idle (3:6-13)

⁶In the name of the Lord Jesus Christ, we command you, brothers, to keep away from every brother who is idle and does not live according to the teaching[a] you received from us. ⁷For you yourselves know how you ought to follow our example. We were not idle when we were with you, ⁸nor did we eat anyone's food without paying for it. On the contrary, we worked night and day, laboring and toiling so that we would not be a burden to any of you. ⁹We did this, not because we do not have the right to such help, but in order to make ourselves a model for you to follow. ¹⁰For even when we were with you, we gave you this rule: "If a man will not work, he shall not eat."

¹¹We hear that some among you are idle. They are not busy; they are busybodies. ¹²Such people we command and urge in the Lord Jesus Christ to settle down and earn the bread they eat. ¹³And as for you, brothers, never tire of doing what is right.

[a]6 Or *tradition*

Most of Paul's concern for discipline in the Thessalonian church is taken up with a single problem, those in the church who have abandoned work and are depending on the generosity of other Christians for their support. This problem was addressed more briefly in 1 Thess 4:11-12 and 5:14, while Paul had laid the foundation for those exhortations by emphasizing his own self-support in 2:9. Apparently, though, Paul's first reminder on this subject did not correct the problem, so here he addresses it at length, using some of the harshest language in the Thessalonian letters.

It has been widely assumed that some in the Thessalonian

church abandoned work because of their vivid expectation of the Lord's return in the very near future. Several considerations argue against that conclusion, however. Most obvious is the fact that in neither epistle does Paul connect the instructions about work to any specific eschatological theme. That is especially obvious here, where the subject is treated at length without any reference to the discussion of 2:1-12. Secondly, as noted above the Thessalonians' problem regarding eschatology seems to have been not too vivid an expectation of the Lord's return in the near future but the belief that the return was somehow already accomplished (see discussion of 2:1-12 above). Thirdly, even if 2 Thess 2:1-12 indicates such an overly-imminent expectation, 1 Thessalonians shows no evidence of such a belief and yet reflects the same problem with idleness. More likely, then, is the hypothesis that some in the church stopped working simply because they found it possible to do so because of the generous sharing practiced among early Christians. R. Russell has noted that in a port city like Thessalonica, unemployment and underemployment among the working classes would have been common.[8] In the context of the church, Christians of means would have shared with those in need. Some who began with genuine needs apparently took advantage of such sharing and deliberately avoided supporting themselves even when they had the opportunity.

The idlers were able to give up working because of the radical generosity practiced among early Christians.[9] Acts asserts that Christians from the earliest days of the church were abundantly generous with each other (Acts 2:44-46; 4:34-37), though such generosity was not without its problems (5:1-11), and that Christian sharing even transcended the bounds of

---

[8] R. Russell, "The Idle in 2 Thess 3.6-12: An Eschatological or a Social Problem," *NTS* 34 (1988) 105-119.

[9] The evidence for widespread sharing among early Christians obviates the need for a more elaborate hypothesis like that of Jewett, who suggests that the "disorderly" were claiming something like the apostolic right to be supported (*Thessalonian Correspondence*, pp. 104-105).

ethnicity as Gentile Christians shared with their Jewish Christian brothers and sisters (11:27-30). Paul's collection on behalf of the Jerusalem church reflects this practice of generosity as well (Rom 15:25-27; 1 Cor 16:1-3; 2 Cor 8-9). Though the motivation for such sharing was multifaceted, at its core was the conviction that the church constituted the people of God in the age of fulfillment, defined by Christ's own self-sacrificial love. Believers therefore had a stronger commitment to the welfare of fellow Christians than they had even to themselves (Phil 2:1-11). Furthermore, if a part of God's intention for his people was the ideal, "There shall be no poor among you" (Deut 15:4), the church had an obligation to share generously to bring that ideal closer to reality. But not all motives in the early church were pure, and so abuses, like the one Paul addresses here, did indeed arise (cf. 1 Tim 5:3-16).

Paul's response shows that he views this issue not merely as an economic problem but as a problem of Christian fellowship. Those who fail to work, he says, are placing undue burdens on others, violating the bonds of fellowship of which they take advantage. They also use their free time to interject themselves into others' affairs, causing further disruption of the fellowship. But he also reminds those who are in a position to share that the irresponsibility of some does not remove from them the obligation to help those with genuine needs. Throughout the text Paul assumes economic ideas such as the right to personal property and the need for productive work, but he instructs the church on the basis of their obligations in Christ, not economic rights or requirements (cf. Eph 4:28).

Because Paul addressed this issue in the context of Christian fellowship, modern Christians must be careful in trying to derive from this passage direct guidance for social policy in government. The Roman government had in place an elaborate program of "bread and circuses" to support laborers who were displaced by the widespread use of slaves, and a larger social system of patronage functioned in the Greco-Roman world, through which the wealthy often supported some who were idle among the laboring classes.[10] Neither Paul nor any other New Testament writer addresses this larger political and social reality of their time. Paul's concern here is entirely for the church and its fellowship, where he sees a level of mutual commitment which demands that those with means support those without but that those who can support themselves should cause no unnecessary burdens to others.

3:6 In the name of the Lord Jesus Christ, we command you, brothers, to keep away from every brother who is idle and does not live according to the teaching you received from us.

The seriousness with which Paul addresses this problem is evident from the very beginning. "Command" translates παραγγέλλω (*parangellō*), indicating the strong obligation which comes with these instructions. The same word was used in 1 Thess 4:11 (rendered "told" in the NIV), where Paul indicated that he had this command previously, apparently during his stay in Thessalonica. Underlining the obligation even more is the phrase "in the name of the Lord Jesus Christ," pointing to the final source of authority for the command. As in 1 Cor 1:10 and 5:4, it is used as a part of an instruction regarding life in the church, in the latter case also dealing specifically with a matter of church discipline (cf. Col 3:17; 2 Thess 1:12).

"Is idle" here represents the verb περιπατέω (*peripateō*, literally "walk") and indicating a general manner of life, modified by the adverb ἀτάκτως (*ataktōs*), a cognate of the word found in 1 Thess 5:14 (see comments above). As in that case, the broadest sense of this adverb is "disorderly," though it is often used, as this context indicates, to refer to willful and rebellious irresponsibility.[11] The NIV's translation is clearly correct in rendering the term as it does, but the English-

---

[10]For a brief introduction to these topics and references to further sources see Russell, "The Idle," pp. 110-119; Ferguson, *Backgrounds*, pp. 55-56.

[11]A useful summary of uses of the word in this sense is provided in MM, p. 89.

speaking reader should understand that Paul speaks not generally of all idleness but specifically of the idleness which a person chooses in deliberate rebellion against the obligations of the Christian fellowship. Paul clearly does not criticize those who have no ability or opportunity to support themselves; in such cases he urges the Christians to continue to share (v. 13). Rather, he has in mind those who take advantage of others' generosity when they could do otherwise (cf. 1 Tim 5:2-8).

This idleness would be self-condemning in light of what Paul is about to discuss. However, because regular instruction on Christian conduct apparently included injunctions on the obligation to work, Paul appeals to that instruction. The "teaching" here is the Greek παράδοσις (*paradosis*), literally "tradition" (so the NIV footnote) which had been delivered both orally (v. 10; 2:15; cf. 1 Thess 2:13; 4:1) and by means of Paul's example (vv. 7-9) when he was present with them. "Received" (παραλαμβάνω, *paralambanō*) is also a technical term of oral teaching. These traditions have authority not simply because they are traditional but because they come from an authoritative source, Paul the apostle, and are grounded in the message of Christ, the final authority.

Having already received this teaching, and having been reminded of it again in 1 Thess 4:11-12; 5:14, the willfully idle will now stand under a stricter form of discipline. Paul orders, as he does for others whose sin is blatant and unrepented, that the church withdraw from such people. While a part of the reason for such a withdrawal is to avoid the disrepute which would come on the church (1 Thess 4:12), to relieve Christians of means from any obligation to share with those who refuse to work, and to protect the church from further corruption, the primary motivation is to correct the sinful behavior that has not yielded to less severe measures. Exclusion from the fellowship signifies not just lost contact with Christian friends or even the loss of financial support; it indicates an exclusion, which will become eternal if no repentance is forthcoming, from the very people of God and a consequent return to the domain of the Evil One (cf. 1 Tim 1:20; Matt 18:18-20).

3:7 For you yourselves know how you ought to follow our example.

The idea that "tradition" in the world of Paul could include personal example is well attested. Later rabbinic teaching, probably reflecting the practices under which Paul was instructed, often involved the students' observation of the example of the teacher (*m. Sukk.* 3.9; *b. Ber.* 241, 27b). Paul has previously indicated that the Thessalonian Christians eagerly imitated his lifestyle in submission to Jesus (1 Thess 1:6; 2:14; see comments above; cf. 1 Cor 4:16; 11:1; Eph 5:1). Here he indicates that they should do so consistently.

We were not idle when we were with you, 3:8 nor did we eat anyone's food without paying for it. On the contrary we worked night and day, laboring and toiling so that we would not be a burden to any of you.

Paul had carefully reminded the Thessalonians of his self-support when he was with them (1 Thess 2:6b-9; see comments above). His motive for supporting himself, as he expressed it in 1 Thess 2:9, was "not to be a burden to anyone" so that nothing would stand in the way of the gospel. Here Paul's example serves to illustrate that same motive. For Paul self-support was not a matter of rugged individualism or personal pride but a means of ensuring that the gospel was heard and that genuine Christian fellowship was not hindered. As he indicated in the earlier letter, Paul had worked "night and day," probably spending days in the workshop and preaching and teaching at night. Also as in 1 Thess 2:9 (cf. 2 Cor 11:27), Paul describes this work as "laboring" (κόπος, *kopos*), implying work to the point of weariness, and "toiling" (μόχθος, *mochthos*), indicating an exceptional exertion of energy.[12] This Paul did instead of being "idle" as are the offenders

---

[12]*GELNTBSD*, § 42.47-48.

addressed here, or even accepting food (ἄρτος, *artos*, literally "bread," the staple food of Paul's time) from anyone literally "as a gift." The expression "eat bread" probably reflects a Semitic idiom for receiving sustenance (cf. Gen 3:19) and so refers to all of Paul's necessities.

3:9 We did this, not because we do not have the right to such help, but in order to make ourselves a model for you to follow.

The "right" which Paul asserts here is ἐξουσία (*exousia*), probably referring to the authority which he could exercise as an apostle to receive support for his work (cf. 1 Cor 9:4-18; Matt 10:9-10; Luke 10:7-8), or more broadly, the authority regularly granted in Paul's time to religious teachers by their disciples which obligated the disciples to support their teacher. Paul reminds the Thessalonians of his unexercised authority in this area not because some in the church were challenging Paul's authority but because the fact of his authority is necessary to bring to bear the force of his example. Paul's argument is from the greater to the lesser.

The Thessalonian Christians had an obligation to support Paul because of his labor in preaching and teaching on their behalf. Yet Paul willingly yielded that benefit for the sake of the gospel. In effect he "moonlighted" to ensure that he created no financial burden for his converts and no impression that he was motivated by greed (1 Thess 2:4-5, 9-10). This is the greater case. The lesser case is that of the idle in the Thessalonian church. The obligation of the church to support the idle is in fact nonexistent, as Paul will argue. The church has an obligation to subsidize only those who cannot support themselves, as Paul will remind them (vv. 10, 13), so these idlers have no claim on others' generosity. Moreover, they are called on merely to fulfill their ordinary social responsibility of labor and self-support, not to double their labors as did Paul. Even if the idle are hardened to other appeals, this example of Paul should serve to bring shame on any continued, unwarranted dependance on others' generosity. If they are to respond properly, the Pauline "model" must be followed continually: the infinitive "to follow" is in the Greek present tense, indicating continuing action.

3:10 For even when we were with you, we gave you this rule: "If a man will not work, he shall not eat."

This command should have been familiar to the idlers from the beginning, as it constituted a memorable part of Paul's oral instruction. "Rule" paraphrases the Greek verb παραγγέλλω (*parangellō*), repeated from v. 6 and indicating again the giving of a command. The content of the command is deliberately terse and parallel, probably to make it easier for the Christian converts to remember. "Will" here does not indicate the future tense but translates θέλω (*thelō*), indicating a willingness to do the action mentioned. So Paul's original oral instruction specifically censured the refusal to work, not the inability to work. The sanction placed on such people is that they "shall not eat," a phrase translating an imperative verb which might be translated "must not eat." Clearly the church could not stop the idle from obtaining bread from other sources, so the point is that the church should not subsidize those in their fellowship who refuse to support themselves when they have the means and opportunity. All the verbs in this command are in the present tense and emphasize continuing action, so the instruction might be translated, "If anyone continually does not want to keep working, he must not keep eating."

3:11 We hear that some among you are idle. They are not busy; they are busybodies.

Presumably Paul has received the report about the Thessalonians' continuing idleness from the associate who delivered the first letter to the church, perhaps Timothy. The idleness is again expressed as it was in v. 6, with the Greek verb meaning "to walk" and signifying a manner of life combined with an adverb indicating willful idleness. The second sentence of this verse renders well Paul's play on words (cf. Rom 12:3; 1 Cor

7:31; 2 Cor 1:13; 3:2; 6:10; Phil 3:2-3). Literally these people do not work (ἐργάζομαι, *ergazomai*) but meddle in others' affairs (περιεργάζομαι, *periergazomai*).[13] Elsewhere Paul connects the idleness of those supported by the church with the temptation to intrude into others' business (1 Tim 5:13). Such activity compounds the offense to the Christian fellowship.

3:12 Such people we command and urge in the Lord Jesus Christ to settle down and earn the bread they eat.

The command here is given solemnly, similar to v. 6: "in the Lord Jesus" suggests either by his authority or, if Paul is using his "in Christ" formula, to refer to the basis of this command in the common fellowship that Christians share through their relationship with Christ (cf. 1 Thess 4:1 and comments above; Rom 9:1; Eph 4:17). In either case "Lord" underlines Christ's divine authority. "Command" is used again as in vv. 6 and 10, coupled with "urge," παρακαλέω (*parakaleō*, cf. 1 Thess 2:3, 12; 3:2, 7: 4:1, 10, 18; 5:11; 14; 2 Thess 2:16-17), lending additional force to the instruction. The NIV's rendering of the command itself is a dynamic equivalent of Paul's words. He uses ἡσυχία (*hēsuchia*), roughly corresponding to "settle down" but literally meaning "quietness" (cf. 1 Thess 4:11 and comments above; 1 Tim 2:2), to indicate the manner in which these idlers should support themselves. Here this quietness clearly contrasts with the activity of busybodies just described, not, as some have argued, with too much excitement about Christ's imminent return. With such quiet labor these people will be able to pay for what they eat as did Paul (cf. vv. 8, 10), removing undue burdens from their brothers and sisters.

3:13 And as for you, brothers, never tire of doing what is right.

This command could be a general reminder to continue doing good. But in this context it appears to deal in some way

---

[13]Cf. *GELNTBSD*, § 88.243.

with the problem of the indolent (the parallel in Gal 6:9 presents a similar ambiguity). Paul may be urging the responsible members of the church to continue their present self-support. But he may also be underlining the ongoing need for Christians to share of their substance with genuinely needy brothers and sisters.[14] The temptation would be to stop sharing altogether because some had abused their generosity. Paul warns against taking such an attitude. So here, with an emphatic pronoun, ὑμεῖς (*humeis*, "as for you"), he shifts the focus from those who have been willfully idle to the rest of the church. Though Paul habitually addresses the Thessalonian Christians as "brothers," the term here may serve to remind them again of the relationship out of which their obligation to share arises. "Tire" here translates ἐγκακέω (*enkakeō*), indicating discouragement, despair or lost motivation,[15] the very attitudes that could arise from others' taking advantage of one's generosity, as had been the case. "Doing what is right" translates a Greek present participle; the good which the responsible Christian does for his brothers and sisters is a continuing duty.

2. Exclusion of the Disobedient (3:14-15)

[14]If anyone does not obey our instruction in this letter, take special note of him. Do not associate with him, in order that he may feel ashamed. [15]Yet do not regard him as an enemy, but warn him as a brother.

This section closes with a repetition of the command to discipline by exclusion from the Christian fellowship those

---

[14]Marshall argues that Paul included here the continuing support of the willfully indolent because of the gracious nature of Christian love, though this did have a final limit expressed in v. 14 (p. 226). If this is Paul's point, however, little sense can be made of the injunction to keep away from these in v. 6 or "he shall not eat" in v. 10.

[15]Cf. BAGD, p. 215; *GELNTBSD*, § 25.288.

who disobey (cf. v. 6). Undoubtedly this has particular reference to the idle of vv. 6-12. However, it appears that Paul has deliberately stated this instruction as a general command so that the church will understand that others who might deliberately disobey the apostle's instruction should be similarly excluded. If the church has been troubled by ideas such as the ones which Paul addresses in 2:1-12, those responsible may ultimately require similar exclusion (cf. 2 Tim 2:17-18).

3:14 If anyone does not obey our instruction in this letter, take special note of him. Do not associate with him, in order that he may feel ashamed.

The disobedience which Paul refers to here is clearly not the occasional episode of sin into which Christians fall but the repeated, blatant, unrepented sin of the kind described above. This point is made clear by Paul's use of the present tense for the verb "obey"; the statement could be translated, "If anyone continually does not obey . . . ." Such people are to be noted by the church. The verb used here, σημειόω (*sēmeioō*) is normally used for the marking down of records;[16] Paul could use it here to refer to written records or charges to be kept by the church in cases of discipline.[17] However, the word is also used figuratively to mean giving attention to something for the purpose of remembering it in the future,[18] and that is sufficient to explain its use here.

Such people are to be excluded from fellowship, as in v. 6, again visibly demonstrating the threat of exclusion from the commonwealth of God's people. Paul's verb here is the same one found in the similar context of 1 Cor 5:9, 11: συναναμείγνυμι (*sunanameignumi*), literally meaning "to mix up together," but often used of the association of persons.[19] The implication is a complete cutting off of any social contact with such a person.

---

[16]BAGD, p. 748; MM, p. 573.
[17]Schmidt, "Discipline," p. 216.
[18]*GELNTBSD*, § 29.3.
[19]BAGD, p. 784.

The object of this discipline is indicated at the end of the verse: to produce shame in the offender. Those who refuse to heed lesser warnings may be impressed with their guilt through the cutting off of contact and even see the potential eternal consequences.

3:15 Yet do not regard him as an enemy, but warn him as a brother.

The implication that the purpose of discipline is redemptive is made explicit here. The shame of v. 14 is intended less as a punishment against the sinner and more as a stimulus to repentance. Exclusion from fellowship does not imply hostility between the church and the offender. It should not lead to insults, gossip, or violence of any kind. The offender is to be regarded as a brother or sister; final judgment ultimately belongs to God alone. So the purpose of the exclusion is correction: "warn" translates νουθετέω (*noutheteō*), which indicates correction of behavior or belief, as in 1 Thess 5:12, 14 (see comments above). Paul probably refers to the corrective power of the exclusion itself, preceded as it would have been by repeated verbal exhortations. Scrupulously maintaining this outlook will protect the church from vindictiveness and judgmentalism.

VI. CONCLUSION (3:16-18)

¹⁶**Now may the Lord of peace himself give you peace at all times and in every way. The Lord be with all of you.**
¹⁷**I, Paul, write this greeting in my own hand, which is the distinguishing mark in all my letters. This is how I write.**
¹⁸**The grace of our Lord Jesus Christ be with you all.**

Paul's concluding remarks are brief but pointed. Here he includes a wish-prayer for the readers (v. 16; cf. 1 Thess 5:23-24), an authentication of the epistle as genuinely Paul's (v. 17; cf. 2:2), and a final prayer for blessing (v. 18; cf. 1 Thess 5:28).

3:16 Now may the Lord of peace himself give you peace at all times and in every way. The Lord be with all of you.

This prayer is similar to the one in 1 Thess 5:23-24, though here "Lord" probably refers to Christ rather than God the Father as in the earlier passage, perhaps because of the central focus on Christ's work in destroying evil in 2:8 (cf. Eph 2:14; Col 1:20). The association of God with peace is also found in concluding statements or prayers in Rom 15:33; 16:20; 2 Cor 13:11; Phil 4:9; peace is more broadly Paul's concluding wish in Eph 6:23. As in the salutations and earlier concluding prayer, peace signifies the whole of the Christian's harmonious relationship with God which in turn creates harmony among fellow Christians who share that relationship. Paul explicitly stresses that this peace is comprehensive, to be experienced through all times, in every way, and among all of the Christians to whom the Lord's presence is promised. It will come to the Thessalonians despite — and even in the midst of — the persecutions which they now experience (1:5-6) and will be fully realized when Christ returns as savior and judge (1:6-10; 2:8).

3:17 I, Paul, write this greeting in my own hand, which is the distinguishing mark in all my letters. This is how I write.

This seemingly innocuous remark is the subject of some controversy. Some who argue that 2 Thessalonians is a post-Pauline pseudepigraph insist that this remark is out of place in an authentic letter, especially since Paul's signature is lacking in the other canonical letters. It is therefore seen either as the pseudepigrapher's too-eager attempt to make the letter appear to be authentic or an attempt by a later writer to discredit 1 Thessalonians, which lacked the signature. However, it must be questioned whether someone attempting to make a post-Pauline letter appear authentic would risk such a statement, since the pseudepigrapher would presumably know Paul's authentic letters well enough to realize that Paul did not habitually sign his letters exactly in this way. This statement, therefore, is still powerful evidence in favor of the authenticity of this letter, despite the fact that we no longer have access to Paul's actual signature.

But if Paul did not sign all his letters as he did here, in what sense did he intend this statement? It should be observed, first of all, some other letters do include handwritten greetings from Paul. The nearest parallels are 1 Cor 16:21 and Col 4:18, but handwritten greetings are also explicit in Gal 6:11 and Phlm 19. Furthermore, it may well be that Paul wrote a portion of the ending of his letters, perhaps the final wish for blessing, in his own hand (cf. 1 Thess 5:27-28 and comments above). Surviving papyrus letters from this period often show a change of handwriting at the end.[20] At any rate, Paul's statement here is clearly a generalization rather than an absolute.

Apparently in light of the false messages which the Thessalonian church had received in Paul's name (2:2), Paul found it necessarily to explicitly authenticate this letter. His handwriting would have been easily distinguishable from the hand of the amanuensis who wrote out the rest of the letter, since professional scribes could be expected to have neater (and smaller, cf. Gal 6:11) handwriting than others. Though some have insisted that this statement is less a matter of authenticating the letter than of asserting Paul's authority, it is difficult to see no authenticating purpose in light of 2:2.

3:18 The grace of our Lord Jesus Christ be with you all.

With the exception of "all," which Paul may have inserted here to include even the idle Christians of 3:6-12, this greeting is identical to the one in 1 Thess 5:28 (cf. 2 Cor 13:13; Gal 6:18; Eph 6:24; Phil 4:23; Col 4:18; 1 Tim 6:21b; 2 Tim 4:22; Titus 3:15; Phlm 25). Paul again takes the usual formal element of a closing greeting and uses it for his distinct purposes. For the apostle of grace, a wish for God's grace was always a fitting note on which to end an epistle.

---

[20]Bruce, p. 216.